SCIENCE AnyTime™

Harcourt Brace & Company

Orlando   Atlanta   Austin   Boston   San Francisco   Chicago   Dallas   New York
Toronto   London

Authors

Napoleon A. Bryant, Jr.
Professor Emeritus of Education
Xavier University
Cincinnati, Ohio

Marjorie Slavick Frank
Specialist in Literacy and Language Development
Adjunct Faculty, Hunter, Brooklyn, and
Manhattan Colleges
Brooklyn, New York

Gerald Krockover
Professor of Science Education
School of Mathematics and Science Center
Purdue University
West Lafayette, Indiana

Mozell Lang
Science Specialist
Michigan Department of Education
Lansing, Michigan

Carol J. Valenta
Director of Education
California Museum of Science and Industry
Los Angeles, California

Barry A. Van Deman
Director
International Museum of Surgical Science
Chicago, Illinois

Advisors

Betsy Balzano
Professor
State University of New York
Brockport, New York

Anne R. Biggins
Speech-Language Pathologist
Fairfax County Public Schools
Fairfax, Virginia

Walter Brautigan
State University of New York
Brockport, New York

Gerard F. Consuegra
Director of Curriculum Coordination and
Implementation
Montgomery County Public Schools
Rockville, Maryland

Robert H. Fronk
Head, Science Education Department
Florida Institute of Technology
Melbourne, Florida

Carolyn Gambrel
Learning Disabilities Teacher
Fairfax County Public Schools
Fairfax, Virginia

Joyce E. Haines
Instructor of Humanities
Haskell Indian Nations University
Lawrence, Kansas

Chris Hasegawa
Associate Professor of Teacher Education
California State University
Sacramento, California

Asa Hilliard III
Fuller E. Calloway Professor of Urban Education
Georgia State University
Atlanta, Georgia

V. Daniel Ochs
Professor of Science Education
University of Louisville
Louisville, Kentucky

Donna M. Ogle
Chair, Reading & Language Arts Department
National-Louis University
Evanston, Illinois

Young Pai
Interim Dean, School of Education
University of Missouri
Kansas City, Missouri

Susan Cashman Paterniti
School Board Member
Port Charlotte, Florida

Barbara S. Pettegrew
Associate Professor
Otterbein College
Westerville, Ohio

Stearns W. Rogers
Professor of Chemistry
McNeese State University
Lake Charles, Louisiana

CONTENTS

Unit A

Growing Up Green

How People Use Plants

CORN
SEEDS

Unit B

Currents and Coastlines

Exploring Ocean Ecosystems

GULF STREAM

ATLANTIC OCEAN

Pass the Word

Using Energy and Technology

Mountains and Molehills

Rocks, Minerals, and Landforms

Unit E

A Walk in the Forest

Comparing Ecosystems

SCIENCE ANYTIME

Calvin and Hobbes are setting out on an expedition to find answers to questions they have. What do you suppose they want to know? What do you want to know about in science? How did Hobbes use what he learned? Sometimes the search for answers leads you through some interesting experiences.

The following pages show an exciting process you will use this year as you study science.

Wonder.

Many science discoveries
begin when someone says,
"I wonder . . ." What do *you*
wonder about?

Plan.

Scientists wonder and then plan how they will find answers to their questions. You too can be a scientist by planning ways to answer questions you wonder about. You may do some things with your class. Other things you may do in a small group or by yourself. However you work, your plan will guide you.

....Investigate:....

Finding answers to your **I Wonder** questions will lead you to do investigations. Investigations can be activities, research, reading, talking to experts, using a computer, or watching videos.

Your investigations may answer some of your questions, but they may also lead to new questions.

I

INVESTIGATE

Reflect.

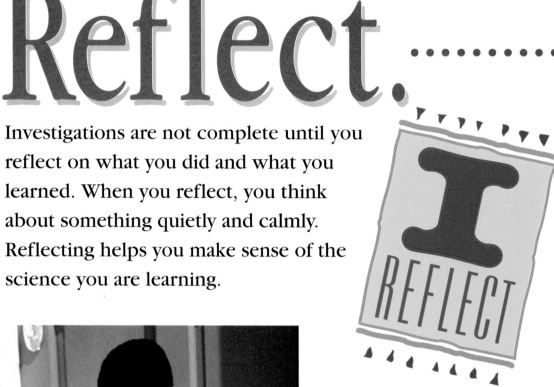

Investigations are not complete until you reflect on what you did and what you learned. When you reflect, you think about something quietly and calmly. Reflecting helps you make sense of the science you are learning.

You will have many opportunities to share your science discoveries with others. By sharing, you will continue to learn about your topic and about communicating to others what you have discovered. As you listen to others share, you will also continue to learn.

I SHARE

Share

Act.

People who make discoveries often try to use what they have discovered. You may take action this year by growing herbs for use in cooking, by making a rock collection, by finding fossils, by setting up an aluminum recycling center at school, or by helping to clean up a nearby stream.

I ACT

As you **wonder, plan, investigate, reflect, share,** and **act,** you will be a scientist at work. What an exciting year of science discoveries lies ahead!

GROWING UP GREEN

Growing Up Green

How People Use Plants

I WONDER

Science begins with wondering. What do you wonder about when you see plants like the ones shown?

Work with a partner to make a list of questions you may have about plants. Be ready to share your list with the rest of the class.

◁ **Arizona desert with rainbow**
▽ **Artichoke plant**

I PLAN

You may have asked several questions such as these as you wondered about plants. Scientists also ask questions. Then they plan ways to help them find answers to their questions. Now you and your classmates can plan how you will investigate plants.

My Science Log

- Why do plants need sunlight?

- How do plants help people?

- What is the difference between a fruit and a vegetable?

- What things are plants used for?

With Your Class

Plan how your class will use the activities and readings from the **I Investigate** part of this unit.

On Your Own

There are many ways to learn about plants and how they are used. Following are some things you can do to explore plants by yourself or with some classmates. Some explorations may take longer to do than others. Look over the suggestions and choose . . .

- **Projects to Do**
- **People to Contact**
- **Books to Read**

PROJECTS TO DO

SEED PLANTING

Most plants grow from seeds, which you can find right in your kitchen. After you have eaten an apple, an orange, or a grapefruit, save the seeds. Plant them in potting soil. You can use cut-down milk cartons or yogurt cups with a small hole in the bottom for pots. Keep the pots in a warm place, and water the soil. When the seeds sprout, make sure they get plenty of sunlight. Which seeds sprout? What do the plants look like? If you care for your plants well, they will grow into little trees.

PAPER RECYCLING

Trees are the world's largest plants. Paper is made from trees—millions of them each year.

You can save trees by recycling paper. If your school does not recycle, start recycling in your class. First, set up a box in the classroom. Throw all clean waste paper into that box for one week. At the end of the week, weigh the paper in the box. How much paper did your class throw away in a week? Sort the paper by types (computer paper, construction paper, notebook paper). Find out which of these types of paper your school can recycle. Ask other classes to join you in a recycling project.

PEOPLE TO CONTACT

IN PERSON

Farmers know a lot about plants, especially the ones they raise as crops. Call a farmer. Ask the farmer to visit your class and talk about food plants.

Another way to learn about plants is to talk to a horticulturist. Horticulturists study the growth and care of plants. You can find them at botanical gardens, greenhouses, or local colleges and universities.

Use what you learn about plants to make a bulletin board for your classroom. Include information about how the plants are used.

BY MAIL

There are many government agencies and private groups that work with plants. They study the growth of plants as well as how we use the plants. Some of these groups help protect endangered plants. You can write to these agencies and groups for information. Here is a list of places you might try.

- Sierra Club
- Tree People
- American Forestry Association
- National Park Service
- U.S. Department of Agriculture
- your state agriculture department or extension service
- your state department of environmental protection

BOOKS TO READ

Retold by Celia Barker Lottridge (Macmillan, 1989). Only the lion knows the name of the tree—*ungalli.* The hungry animals must say the name before the tree will give up its fruit. Two foolish animals, the gazelle and the elephant, learn the name from the lion but then forget it. The animals are still hungry. Read this book to find out how the small, slow tortoise remembers. Close your eyes. Can you remember?

The Life and Times of the Apple

by Charles Micucci (Orchard Books, 1992), Outstanding Science Trade Book. You know that apples taste delicious and that we can eat them both raw and cooked. This book will show you how much more there is to know about apples. They have been known since prehistoric times. There are songs, sayings, stories, and poems about the apple. Sit down with an apple and read this book. You will enjoy them both.

More Books to Read

The Big Tree

by Bruce Hiscock (Atheneum, 1991), Outstanding Science Trade Book. This book begins two hundred years ago or more when a seed fell to the ground. It landed in fertile soil and received the air, water, and sun it needed to grow. Read to find out what happens to the tree when most of the forest is cut down. Will it be a home for animals for years to come?

Corn Belt Harvest

by Raymond Bial (Houghton Mifflin, 1991), Outstanding Science Trade Book. How is corn grown and harvested? In this book, you will see a machine called a *corn picker* that picks, shucks, and shells the corn. Then the corn kernels are dumped into a truck to be taken away. What happens next? Machines and people handle the corn many different ways before it comes to our tables.

Cranberries

by William Jaspersohn (Houghton Mifflin, 1991), Outstanding Science Trade Book. Native Americans picked wild cranberries to use for food, for medicine, and for dye for their blankets. Now cranberry growers use machinery and helicopters to harvest them. Read this book to learn interesting facts about cranberries and how they are grown and harvested.

I INVESTIGATE

To find answers to their questions, scientists read, think, talk to others, and do experiments. Their investigations often lead to new questions. In this unit, you will have many chances to think and work like a scientist. How will you find answers to questions you asked?

► COMPARING When you compare objects or events, you look for what they have in common. You also look for differences between them.

► MEASURING Measuring is a way to observe and compare things accurately. When you measure, you often use an instrument, such as a ruler or a balance.

► HYPOTHESIZING You form a hypothesis when you want to explain how or why something happens. Your hypothesis is an explanation based on what you already know. A hypothesis should be tested in an experiment.

Are you ready to begin?

SECTIONS

Growing Our Food

Do you eat cereal? How about corn on the cob? Green peas? Apples? Spaghetti? All of these foods come from plants.

In this section, you will find out how food plants grow. You will start a garden in a plastic bag and see how plants grow in different soils.

You'll also get a look at farms of many kinds. You'll discover that farms in different parts of the world grow different foods. Then, since looking at all this food might make you hungry, you'll make a tasty treat yourself.

1 ENERGY FROM THE SUN

Why do some people eat plant parts like potatoes, tomatoes, bananas, and grapes? They taste good, but plants also have something in them that your body needs. It's something your body can't make for itself.

A Plant Book for Carlitos

Keep reading to find out what plants can do that you can't and why that makes plants important.

 Mia was looking out the window of her house one day. She saw the flowers she and her family had planted in the spring. She also saw the vegetable garden with its tomatoes, carrots, beans, and corn.

Mia decided she wanted to make a book about plants for her little brother, Carlitos. She would use the garden flowers and plants as part of her book.

Mia found some paper, a pencil, and some colored markers. Now she was ready to begin. First she drew the outline of the garden. Then she was ready to put in the plants. But she wanted to be very sure that she showed all of the important parts.

She decided to draw the garden and then add extra pictures to show Carlitos the parts most plants have.

Mia drew a picture of a tomato plant. She even showed what it looked like under the ground. She drew and labeled the roots, stem, and leaves. Then she drew in little yellow flowers.

Next, she thought about what to tell Carlitos about the plant. She wanted to be sure he knew something about why its leaves are green. Mia knew that the leaves contain tiny particles called *chlorophyll* and that the chlorophyll is important. She decided it would be best to show Carlitos what the chlorophyll does for the plant by drawing a diagram to explain it.

The most important part of this food-making process is the sun. Chlorophyll needs the energy from the sun to make food. So, without the sun, there would be no food.

Flowers

The plant takes in carbon dioxide from the air.

Leaves

The green stuff in the leaves is called *chlorophyll*. Without it, plants couldn't make their own food.

The plant only uses part of the carbon dioxide it takes in. It puts the leftovers back into the air. The leftover gas is oxygen.

Stem

Roots

A14

Mia finished making the book for Carlitos and called him to come and see what she had made. Carlitos came running because he liked books and reading. He snuggled down beside Mia on the window seat.

Mia read the book to him and showed him the diagram of how plants make food. "Do I make food in my body the way a plant does?" asked Carlitos.

Mia replied, "No, Carlitos. Your body can only use energy that you get from eating plants or from eating animals that have eaten plants. Then your body uses this energy from food to help you grow, play, work, think, and sleep.

"Here's a question for you. You know you get oxygen from the air you breathe. When you breathe out, you give off carbon dioxide. How does that help plants?"

Carlitos piped up, "Carbon dioxide? What I breathe out, the plants need to make food! And I can breathe in the oxygen they don't need!

"Thanks, Mia, for making me this neat book. I can't wait to take it to school with me on Monday."

THINK ABOUT IT

Write in your own words how chlorophyll helps plants.

Photosynthesis

In her book, Mia shows Carlitos how plants make food. Look at the diagram that shows more about how plants make food.

Carbon dioxide is taken into the leaf from the air.

The process by which plants make food is called **photosynthesis** (foht uh SIN thuh sis). *Photo* means "light," and *synthesis* means "putting together."

Plants make food mainly in their leaves. In her book, Mia talks about the green substance **chlorophyll** (KLAWR uh fil), which is found inside tiny structures called *chloroplasts* (KLAWR uh plasts).

A chloroplast is like a little food factory. Its chlorophyll takes in energy from the sun. Then the leaf uses the energy to make sugar from carbon dioxide and water.

Where does a plant get the materials it uses in photosynthesis? The leaves take in carbon dioxide from the air, and the roots take in water from the soil.

Water from the soil goes into the roots.

Study the diagram to learn more about photosynthesis.

Light from the sun shines on a leaf.

Oxygen is given off into the air.

THINK ABOUT IT

Why is photosynthesis important to you?

A17

Is This Plant Making Food?

The process of photosynthesis can't be observed easily. But in this activity, you'll discover evidence of what happens in the process.

DO THIS

❶ Cut off a piece of elodea that will fit into the test tube. Put the piece into the tube so that the tip of the plant is near the tube's closed end. Fill the test tube with water.

❷ Fill the large container $\frac{2}{3}$ full with water.

❸ Put your thumb over the opening of the test tube. Turn it upside down in the container of water. Draw what you see in the test tube.

❹ Put the container in bright sunlight. Wait for 10 minutes. Draw what you see now.

❺ After another 10 minutes, draw the contents of the tube once more.

MATERIALS
- elodea plant
- scissors
- test tube
- large plastic container
- water
- watch or clock
- Science Log data sheet

THINK AND WRITE

1. You observed the contents of the test tube three times, in steps 3, 4, and 5. How did the contents look different each time you observed them?

2. An elodea plant is in bright sunlight. How can you tell that the plant is making food? (Hint: Think about what plants give off when they make food.)

3. **HYPOTHESIZING** You form a hypothesis when you want to explain how or why something happens. Your hypothesis is an explanation based on what you already know. Use what you learned in this experiment to write a hypothesis about why plants are important to a healthy planet. Compare your hypothesis to those of your classmates.

LESSON 1 REVIEW

❶ How do green plants make food?

❷ Suppose you put a test tube containing elodea and water into a dark closet. What do you think you would observe after 20 minutes?

2 HOW FOOD GROWS

Potato plants, apple trees, and grapevines are very different from one another. Although the foods we get from these plants taste different, amazingly the plants all use the same things to grow.

As you do this lesson, try to discover what plants need. Think about where they grow and what they use.

WATERMELON SEEDS

ACTIVITY

Sprouting Seeds

In this activity, you'll watch some vegetable seeds sprout. What do these seeds need as they begin to grow into new plants?

MATERIALS

- spoon
- mixed seeds
- paper towel
- scissors
- ruler
- tape that sticks on both sides
- water
- self-sealing plastic bag
- hand lens
- Science Log data sheet

DO THIS

❶ Start with a spoonful of mixed seeds. Sort them. How many kinds do you have? Record your observations.

❷ Fold the paper towel so it will fit into the plastic bag.

❸ Cut one piece of tape for each type of seed. Make each piece about 10 cm long. Stick the pieces of tape onto the towel in rows.

❹ Stick a few seeds onto each piece of tape. Put only one type of seed on each piece.

❺ Put the towel into the bag. Wet the towel with water. Seal the bag. Tape it to the inside of a window.

❻ Observe the seeds every day for 10 to 14 days. Record your observations.

THINK AND WRITE

1. Compare how quickly you saw changes in the different types of seeds.

2. After 10 days, use the hand lens to look at the rows of seeds. Draw and describe the differences you see.

3. Water, light, warmth, and air were around the seeds in the plastic bag. Do you think the seeds needed all of these things to sprout? Design an experiment to find out.

A21

What Do Plants Need?

You have learned some of the things animals need to stay alive. Now you'll find out that plants need some things, too.

Carbon Dioxide

Carbon dioxide gas from the air enters plants through tiny holes in the leaves called *stomata*. Plants need carbon dioxide for photosynthesis.

Water

Soil contains water, which plants need in order to live. Plants take in water through their roots. One way they use water is to carry out photosynthesis.

Soil

Plants need materials called *nutrients* (NOO tree uhnts) in order to grow. You get nutrients from the food you eat. Plants absorb the nutrients they need from soil.

Sunlight

Plants need sunlight to carry out the process of photosynthesis. Photosynthesis starts when sunlight shines on the green leaves of plants.

Chlorophyll

The leaves of plants have green structures called *chloroplasts,* which contain chlorophyll. Chlorophyll absorbs energy from the sun. It uses that energy to make food. The food-making process is called *photosynthesis.*

THINK ABOUT IT

What would happen to plants if there were no carbon dioxide?

ACTIVITY

Which Soil Is Best?

Now you know that plants need soil. Think about the following question. Does the type of soil a plant grows in make a difference?

DO THIS

1 Take four of the plants out of their store pots. Dump the soil out of the pots. Gently rinse the roots to remove the soil.

2 Put three of the plants into empty pots each with a different material—sand, potting soil, vermiculite. Put water with fertilizer into the plastic cup and place a plant in it.

3 Remove the fifth plant from its pot. Rinse its roots. Replant it in the same pot and soil.

4 Put the plants in a place where they will all get the same amounts of heat and light. Water the plants as needed, but remember to give all the plants exactly the same amount of water.

5 Observe the plants each day for 14 to 21 days. Measure their height, and count the number of leaves on each plant. Make one bar graph for the height of the plants. Make another bar graph for the number of leaves.

THINK AND WRITE

1. Why did you replant one plant in the original pot with the original soil?

2. Which plant grew the most? Which plant grew the least? Which plant seemed the most healthy? Which plant seemed the least healthy?

3. Compare the two graphs you made. How are they the same? How are they different?

4. What do your results tell you about the things plants need from soil?

5. **MEASURING** In scientific experiments, measuring is done to gather information. Think about what you measured in the activity. How could you have gathered the information without measuring?

QUICK CHECK

LESSON 2 REVIEW

❶ What do plants need in order to grow and make food?

❷ When you buy plant "food" for house plants, what you're really getting is fertilizer. Why is the name *plant food* incorrect?

3 FARMING

Farming in Europe during the Middle Ages ▶

You're walking through the supermarket with your dad. He wants you to help out. He gives you a list of items to find.

While you're hunting for the things on your list, you take a good look around. There must be thousands of boxes, jars, bags, and cans on those shelves. Nearly all of them contain food that came from a farm.

In this lesson, you'll read about farms of today and long ago. You'll also find out why people in Los Angeles, Atlanta, and Chicago often don't eat reindeer and lingonberries—and why people in northern Sweden do.

Bringing in hay in the 1800s was still mostly done by hand. ▼

The History of Farming

Farming has changed over time, but some type of farming has been done for thousands of years.

Suppose you had lived 15,000 years ago. How would you have gotten food? You would have spent a lot of time wandering around, looking for something to eat. You would have gathered wild plants. You would have hunted animals. It would have taken most of your time just to get your meals each day.

◀ Farmer of ancient Egypt plowing with oxen

A26

You don't have to do all that today, because food is grown for you on farms. It's hard to believe that this wasn't always so.

Farming started about 10,000 years ago. The first farmers lived in fertile river valleys in Egypt, India, China, Mesopotamia, and North America.

Farming changed the way people lived. Farmers had to stay in one area to tend their fields. So wandering tribes began to settle in one place. They built villages near their fields.

▲ Plowing with oxen is still practical in very wet areas.

The earliest farmers had to work hard to raise food. They had simple tools to dig holes for planting. They also used knives made of stone and metal to harvest their crops. But they did everything by hand.

As time passed, people invented better tools. They made plows to break up the soil for planting.

Animals shared the work. At first ancient farmers pulled their own plows. Then they learned to use oxen to pull plows. By the tenth century, farmers began to use horses.

Horses could plow four times as fast as oxen. So horses helped farmers do much more work in less time.

▲ Plowing fields by hand and horse is still done today in some places.

In the 1700s and 1800s, machines were invented to plant and harvest crops. This saved time and work.

In the late 1800s, steam and gasoline engines were improved. They gave more power to farm machines and helped farmers do even more work.

At the same time, scientists were improving plants. They began to combine natural plants in the laboratory to create new types. The new types of plants grew faster and produced more food.

In the 1800s, farmers began to use chemical fertilizers to supply soil with nutrients. By the 1940s, **pesticides** (PES tuh sydz) became widely used in North America and Europe. Pesticides are chemicals that kill crop-eating insects.

All these changes meant that farmers could feed many more people. The first farmers raised just enough food for themselves. By 1850 each farmer raised enough food for five people. Today each farmer raises enough to feed about 80 people.

Although chemicals have helped farmers grow more food, there are problems. Chemical fertilizers that are sprayed on fields can sink into the soil. And they can run off the soil and pollute water. Pesticides can also poison the soil and water. The fertilizers and pesticides used for growing foods can harm people who eat the foods.

▲ Today, machines can be used to harvest crops.

Some farmers are trying to solve these problems by farming without chemicals. These farmers are called *organic farmers*. They use manure and decayed food and plants, called **compost** (KAHM pohst), to give plants nutrients. Organic farmers often get rid of insect pests with other insects. For example, an organic farmer might put ladybugs in a bean field to eat pesky black flies. 📖

THINK ABOUT IT

Organic farms produce less food than huge farms that use chemicals. Food from organic farms usually costs more, too. Some people think that more-healthful food and less-polluted land are worth these costs. What do you think? Explain your answer.

ACTIVITY

Plowing

Plowing soil gets it ready for planting. In this activity, you will try to plow different types of soil.

MATERIALS

- 4 large aluminum pans
- sand
- piece of sod (large enough to fit pan)
- potting soil
- claylike soil
- wooden building block
- Science Log data sheet

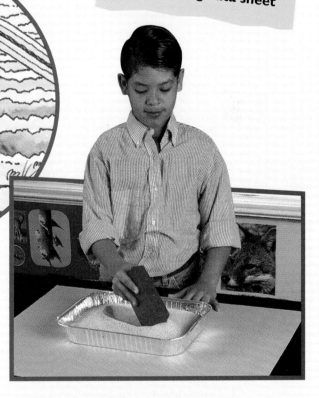

DO THIS

1. Put the sand, sod, potting soil, and claylike soil in separate pans.

2. Use the block as a model plow. Press a corner of the block into the pan of sand. Push the block's corner about 3 cm below the surface of the sand. Then push the block across the pan.

3. Use the block in the same way to plow through the material in each of the other pans.

4. Record your observations.

THINK AND WRITE

1. Of the materials you tested, which would be easiest to plow and which would be hardest? Explain your choices.

2. Design a new type of plow that can cut through soil easily. Draw your design and explain how it works.

Peanuts—Their Story

Do you ever eat peanuts? How do you like them—in shells, roasted, dry, or maybe made into peanut butter? Read on to find out some interesting things that Mary and Tom learned about peanuts.

The Peanut Patch

by **Eileen Van Kirk**
from *Highlights*

LITERATURE Mary and Tom waved as their uncle pulled into the driveway of their new house.

"How do you like living down here in Georgia?" asked Uncle Jed, climbing out of his pickup truck.

"It's nice," said Mary. "But it's different."

"It's not like being back in Vermont," agreed Tom.

"Why don't you plant a garden?" suggested Uncle Jed. "Nothing like a garden to help you get the feel of a new place."

"What should we plant?" asked Mary.

"How about peanuts?" suggested Uncle Jed. "They're different from anything you can grow in Vermont."

"That's a great idea," said Tom.

So Tom and Mary staked out a sunny patch in the garden and began to dig. When they had the soil nice and crumbly, they planted five rows of peanuts. They raked the soil smooth and put up a sign that said THE PEANUT PATCH.

They took good care of their garden. They watered it when it was dry and kept it free of weeds and bugs. Then one day bright green shoots poked their way out of the ground. Soon the shoots grew into vines with lots of yellow flowers.

"How are the peanuts coming?" asked Uncle Jed.

"Fine," said Tom. "We've seen lots of flowers, and that must mean lots of peanuts."

"But the plants do keep drooping onto the ground," said Mary.

"That's all right," said her uncle. "They all do that. When you harvest your peanuts I'll show you how to make a rack to dry them on."

But days went by and there were no peanuts to be seen. All the flowers were gone by now and the leaves were beginning to wilt, but they did not find one peanut. One day Uncle Jed asked if they were ready to build the drying rack.

"There's no need," said Tom. "We haven't got any peanuts to dry."

"Are you sure?" said Uncle Jed.

"Come and see for yourself," said Tom. The three of them trooped over to the peanut patch. Mary and Tom showed Uncle Jed the bare vines. "Well, that's too bad," said Uncle Jed. But there was a twinkle in his eye, and he seemed more amused than sorry. "I guess the only thing for you to do is dig them up."

When he'd left, Tom picked up the garden fork. "I don't see what's so funny," Tom said crossly. "But we might as well get rid of these useless things." He uprooted a large peanut plant and tossed it into the wheelbarrow.

"Hey," said Mary. "Shake the soil off first, or this wheelbarrow will be too heavy to push." She picked up the plant, and then she gasped.

"Tom, look!" exclaimed Mary. "Peanuts! Lots and lots of peanuts."

Tom looked at the plant Mary was holding. Clusters of fat peanuts clung to stems that had grown down from the vines and burrowed beneath the soil.

"You mean peanuts grow under the ground?" cried Tom.

"It sure looks like it," said Mary. They both began to laugh.

"Uncle Jed, Uncle Jed," they cried as they ran into the house. "We found the peanuts."

Uncle Jed grinned. "I told you they were different than anything that grew in Vermont!" 📖

THINK ABOUT IT

1. Where did Mary and Tom expect to see peanuts growing?

2. Why are peanuts unusual plants?

Farms Around The World

The small garden in "The Peanut Patch," is like a farm in many ways. It has soil, food plants grow there, and people are needed to care for it.

Farms are found all over the world. But the types of crops farmers grow are different. The type of soil, the amount of rain, and the weather in an area all help determine what is grown.

▲ Farmers build terraces to grow crops like rice on steep land in the Philippines.

Farmers in Kenya grow pineapples in large fields like this. ▶

▲ This flat, dry area of Australia is perfect for growing oats.

▲ Irrigation helps farmers in Israel grow fruit on very dry land.

▲ North American farmers grow cranberries in fields called *bogs*. Farmers flood their fields to harvest the floating berries.

LESSON 3 REVIEW

❶ Over the last few hundred years, how have farmers increased the amount of food they grow?

❷ How is organic farming different from other kinds of farming?

❸ Why do you think some people say that we shouldn't use organic farming?

A33

4 WHAT GROWS WHERE

What do you think of when someone says *Italian food* or *Chinese food*? Why do people in different countries eat certain types of food?

The dishes we know today as Italian or Chinese were invented long ago, when people could cook only the plants and animals that were nearby. So Italian dishes are made with plants and animals that were common in Italy. Chinese dishes are made with foods that were common in China.

In this lesson, you'll find out where common plants first grew. You'll find out how people used these plants to make many of the dishes we know today. You'll also have the chance to make and eat one of these dishes yourself.

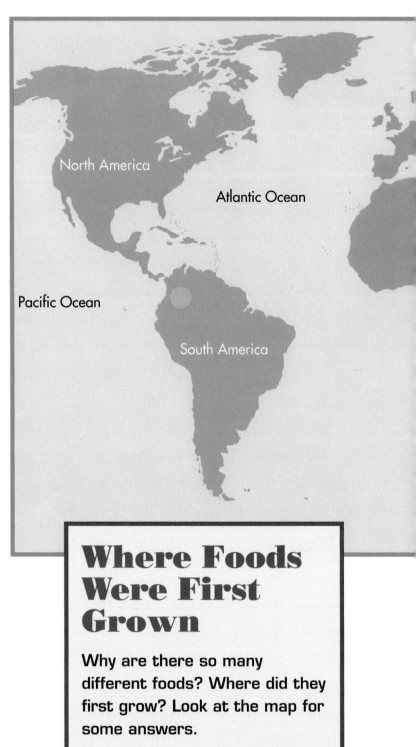

Where Foods Were First Grown

Why are there so many different foods? Where did they first grow? Look at the map for some answers.

A34

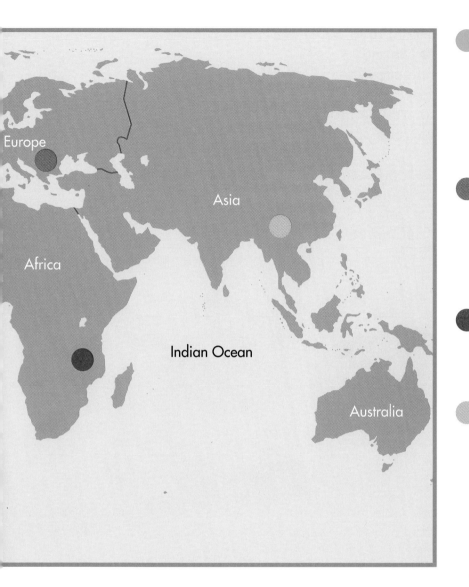

South and Central America

Corn, potatoes, bananas, beans, grapes, avocados, and strawberries

Eastern Mediterranean

Wheat, barley, oats, figs, olives, and lettuce

Eastern Africa

Coffee, millet, okra, and soybeans

Eastern Asia

Garlic, onions, oranges, peaches, soybeans, rice, ginger, almonds, and tea

When people moved from place to place, they took seeds for food plants with them. This movement of foods changed the crops people grew and the way people cooked. The tomato was taken to Europe from the Americas. Today Italian food is famous for its tomato sauces. The apple tree was brought to America from Europe. Today nothing is more American than apple pie!

THINK ABOUT IT

Sometimes people have recipes that were handed down from grandparents or other relatives. Write down one of these recipes your family uses. Share it with the class.

Making a Mexican Snack

A tortilla is a thin pancake made from crushed corn. Tortillas are an important Mexican food. They are sometimes called the bread of Mexico.

Some cooks fry tortillas and serve them flat with toppings of vegetables and meat. You can also fold a fried tortilla and fill it. That's a taco. You can fold a tortilla tightly around a filling. Then you can cover it with sauce. That's an enchilada.

Today people all over the United States prepare Mexican food. Here's a chance to make a Mexican snack with tortilla chips and your own salsa. Salsa is a Mexican sauce made from tomatoes. It can be mild or spicy.

SALSA

- 1 can crushed tomatoes
- $\frac{1}{4}$ cup chopped onions
- $\frac{1}{2}$ teaspoon vinegar
- 1 tablespoon salad oil
- 1 tablespoon oregano
- 1 tablespoon crushed parsley

Put the tomatoes in a large bowl. Add the other things one by one. Stir gently. Spoon the salsa on some tortilla chips.

THINK ABOUT IT

1. What is the main plant in a tortilla? in salsa?

2. Explain why corn and tomatoes are important in Mexican cooking.

Foods from Around the World

Now you will look at some foods from countries around the world. Think about the ones you have tried. Which do you like best?

Italy

When you think of Italian food, do you think of pasta? Pasta is made from wheat. It comes in many forms, such as spaghetti, macaroni, and flat noodles. Meat and milk products have always been scarce in southern Italy. So people there serve pasta with tomato sauces and with dishes containing lots of vegetables. Dairy cattle are common in the north. So people in northern Italy often serve pasta with butter or cream sauce. Rice dishes are common in the Po Valley of Italy, where farmers grow lots of rice.

China

There are several types of Chinese cooking. The type of food that's prepared depends on the region. Rice is used a lot in Chinese cooking because it first grew in East Asia and grows well there due to wet conditions. But in areas of northern China, wheat is an important crop. In those areas, noodles and dumplings made from wheat flour are common.

Mexico

Many Mexican dishes have been passed down from the Native Americans who were the first people to live in Mexico. Corn was their most important food because it grew in Central and South America. Other plants—such as tomatoes, several types of beans, and chili peppers—were also used in their cooking. These plants are still common in Mexican cooking today.

Nigeria

Nigerians grow foods such as sorghum, millet, yams, rice, beans, cassavas, and plantains. These are all important in Nigerian cooking. Cooks make dumplings out of sorghum and millet. Fufu is made from pounded yams. A popular stew is served over millet in the north and over cassavas and yams in the south. Nigerians cook with peanut oil and palm oil. Peanuts and palms grow on many farms.

India

Indian cooking is known for its spices—cumin, clove, ginger, cardamom, pepper. These spices grow in India. They were used at first to preserve food in the hot climate. In places where wheat is the most important grain, a flat wheat bread is served. In places where rice is the most important grain, people make rice bread. Many locally grown fruits and vegetables are used. They include eggplant, okra, potatoes, spinach, and mangoes.

United States

The dishes people eat in the United States come from all parts of the world—just as the people do. Germans brought sausages to this country. Italians brought us pasta with red and white sauces. We got stir-fried vegetable and meat dishes from the Chinese and flour and corn tortillas from the Mexicans. Foods plentiful in different parts of the United States have also shaped our eating habits. For example, Louisiana cooks often use rice and seafood because both are common there. What foods are common where you live?

QUICK CHECK

LESSON 4 REVIEW

❶ Describe some prepared dishes that are common in your part of the country. What are the main food plants used to make them?

❷ Why are the dishes you named in question 1 popular? Is it because the plants they're made from grow where you live? Or is it because the dishes are eaten in countries that people in your area came from?

DOUBLE CHECK

SECTION A REVIEW

1. Describe two ways that photosynthesis benefits people.

2. Why do farms around the world look so different?

3. Could people and animals exist without plants? Explain your answer.

Plants We Eat and Drink

How many roots, flowers, and grasses will you eat today?

When you eat carrots, you're chewing plant roots. When you eat broccoli, you're eating flowers. Some of the most popular breakfast cereals are made from a grass—called corn.

As you read this section, you'll learn about plant parts that we eat. You'll also have the chance to grow and eat some common foods. Keep notes in your Science Log.

1 CEREALS

What comes to your mind when someone says *cereal*? You probably think of the breakfast cereal you eat in the morning.

In this lesson, you'll learn that the word *cereal* means different things. You'll learn about different types of cereals. Then you'll have the chance to make something to eat from a cereal.

ACTIVITY

What's in Breakfast Cereal?

Breakfast cereal is actually made from plants called *grains*. Now take a closer look at breakfast cereals. By doing this, you can see what types of cereal grains you're eating.

DO THIS

❶ If you have one, bring a cereal box from home. If you don't, get one from the school cafeteria. Look at the list of ingredients on the box. Find the names of grains, such as wheat, corn, rice, oats, rye, and barley.

❷ When your turn comes, write the name of your breakfast cereal on the chalkboard. Then write the names of the grains that are in it.

❸ Record the information from the chalkboard.

THINK AND WRITE

1. Which cereal grain is most common in breakfast cereals? Why do you think this is so?

2. What other ingredients are common in breakfast cereals?

MATERIALS
- cereal box
- chart on the chalkboard
- Science Log data sheet

ACTIVITY

Make Your Own Cornmeal

Whole grains are usually fed to animals that are raised for food. People also eat whole grains, but sometimes these grains are ground up before people eat them. They can be ground coarsely into meal or ground finely into flour. In this activity, you'll grind some grains into meal.

DO THIS

❶ Put a spoonful of corn kernels into the mortar.

❷ Using the pestle, tap the corn in the mortar. Continue until the corn is broken into small pieces.

❸ After you have broken the corn into pieces, use the pestle to grind the corn.

❹ Pour your cornmeal into one bowl. Pour the packaged cornmeal into the other bowl.

❺ Describe the differences you see between the bowls of cornmeal.

THINK AND WRITE

Explain the differences in the look of the two bowls of cornmeal.

Pestle

Mortar

A Cornmeal Treat

Now that you've seen how whole grains of corn are made into cornmeal, try a popular cornmeal treat. Follow the directions on the recipe card.

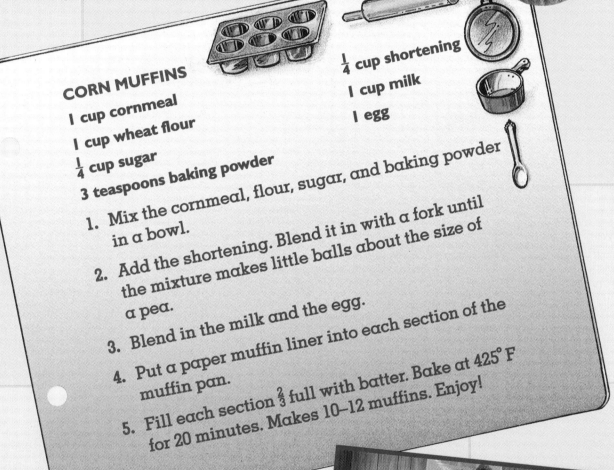

CORN MUFFINS

1 cup cornmeal

1 cup wheat flour

$\frac{1}{4}$ cup sugar

3 teaspoons baking powder

$\frac{1}{4}$ cup shortening

1 cup milk

1 egg

1. Mix the cornmeal, flour, sugar, and baking powder in a bowl.

2. Add the shortening. Blend it in with a fork until the mixture makes little balls about the size of a pea.

3. Blend in the milk and the egg.

4. Put a paper muffin liner into each section of the muffin pan.

5. Fill each section $\frac{2}{3}$ full with batter. Bake at 425° F for 20 minutes. Makes 10–12 muffins. Enjoy!

THINK ABOUT IT

1. What cereals were used to make your muffins? How can you tell?

2. Compare the texture and color of the corn muffins with the texture and color of white bread.

How Cereals Grow

Were you surprised to find out that you eat cereals that aren't breakfast cereal? It may also surprise you that cereals are grasses. But they're not the same as the grass you see in lawns and parks.

Wheat, corn, rice, oats, rye, and barley plants are all grasses. These plants are tall, with stiff stems and long, narrow leaves. They usually have small flowers. Grains are the fruits of these grasses. They usually look like seeds. Often the plants themselves are also called grains.

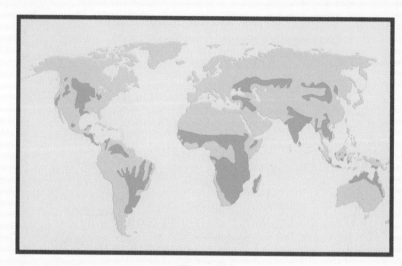

▲ Grasses grow naturally on the world's grasslands. The grasses people plant on farms also grow well on the grasslands.

Wheat

Have you eaten wheat germ or bran? These are parts of whole-wheat grains. Sometimes the wheat germ and bran are removed from the grains. The part that's left is ground into flour. This flour is white flour, not whole-wheat flour.

Wheat flour—white or whole-wheat—is in most of the bread you eat. It's also in breakfast cereals, pasta, and many other foods. Wheat grows in many places. All the wheat that farmers harvest each year would fill a train long enough to go around the world more than twice.

Corn

Do you like corn on the cob? How about popcorn? Cornmeal is made into corn bread and corn muffins. Corn also can be made into hominy, which may then be ground into hominy grits.

When corn is made into corn syrup, it becomes a sweetener for many packaged foods. Another product made from corn is cornstarch, which is used as a thickener in some recipes.

The United States grows half of the world's corn crop. Up to 90 percent of that corn is used to feed animals.

Rice

Is one of your favorite breakfast cereals made with rice? Chances are, it is. People in this country also eat a great deal of rice in other ways.

Farmers grow rice in fields on terraced hillsides. Rice fields must be flooded with water in order for the rice to grow. In eastern countries such as China, Japan, and the Philippines, rice is an important cereal grain.

Oats

Like corn, nearly all the oats grown in the world are fed to animals, such as horses. This is why people say a lively horse "feels its oats."

Most of the oats people eat are rolled oats. When cooked, rolled oats become oatmeal—or, sometimes, oatmeal cookies. Oats are also made into breakfast cereals that you don't have to cook.

The country that produces the most oats is the United States. Oats also are grown in Canada, Russia, northern Europe, and other places around the world.

Barley

Some of the soups and breakfast cereals you eat may contain barley. Barley is also fed to animals.

Barley was grown in Egypt and China thousands of years ago. It can grow on high mountains and in dry climates.

Rye

Have you ever had Swiss cheese on rye? The rye bread in the sandwich is made from a mixture of rye flour and wheat flour. The black breads of Europe are made of rye flour only. Pumpernickel is a black rye bread that is also made in the United States.

Rye can grow in soil that is too poor in nutrients for other grains. It can also grow in regions that are too cold for other grains.

Only a small amount of the rye grown in the United States is eaten by people. Like oats and corn, rye is fed to animals.

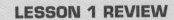

LESSON 1 REVIEW

❶ Why are cereals important foods?

❷ The United States grows large amounts of corn, wheat, oats, and rye. Why does the diet of people in the United States contain more corn and wheat than oats and rye?

A47

2 FRUITS, NUTS, AND VEGETABLES

The grains of cereal grasses are the main plant parts you eat. But they aren't the only ones. When did you last have lettuce, carrots, potatoes, or orange juice? Each of these foods comes from a plant part that's *not* a cereal grain.

In this lesson, you'll take a look inside fruits. Then you'll take a reading journey to South America to meet the people who gave us potatoes.

I'm Having Roots for Lunch

What plant part does a carrot look like to you? How about spinach? The plant parts you eat are usually cut up or mashed, so you can't always tell what plant parts they are. If you could look closely at the whole plant, you could find out.

Most foods that come from leaves look leafy. Some foods that grow underground are roots. Others are underground stems, or tubers. Foods that have seeds in them are fruits.

▲ Potatoes are vegetables.

A48

▲ Oranges are fruits.

Nuts are actually a type of fruit. The fruit has a hard shell on the outside, and the part that you eat is actually the seed. You've probably enjoyed eating walnuts, cashews, pecans, and pistachios.

▼ Which ones are vegetables?

THINK ABOUT IT

Write down the names of all the foods you ate yesterday. Write the plant part next to each fruit and vegetable you ate.

A49

ACTIVITY

Looking Inside Fruits

On a flowering plant, any part that has seeds in it is a fruit. Find the seeds inside fruit.

DO THIS

MATERIALS
- fruit
- balance
- plastic knife
- Science Log data sheet

1 Use the balance to measure the mass of the fruit. Record the mass.

2 Predict the number of seeds inside the fruit. Record your prediction.

3 Cut the fruit apart. Draw what you see.

4 Take out the seeds and count them. Find their mass. Record your observations.

THINK AND WRITE

1. Compare your prediction with the actual number of seeds in the fruit.

2. How much of the fruit's mass was not made up of the seeds? How much of the fruit's mass could you eat?

3. MEASURING What did you measure in this investigation? After measuring, you sometimes use your measurements to calculate the amount or value of something. What did you calculate in this investigation?

Looking Ahead Plants have played an important part in history. In the following selection, you'll find out how a vegetable, the potato, affected the lives of native South Americans.

A50

Potatoes
from the Andes to You

by **Paulette Bourgeois**
from ***The Amazing Potato Book***

Life and Death in the Andes

Ten thousand years ago the ice age was just coming to an end in North America. But in South America, natives were growing crops in the steamy jungles of the Amazon Basin. They could have lived there happily forever except that fierce, marauding tribes forced the local Native Americans up the Andes mountains in search of peace and safety. By 2500 B.C., the Native Americans were living on a barren, frigid Andean plateau 3.3 km (2 miles) high in the sky. It was a harsh existence. Blizzards blew even in August and there could be killing frost in the middle of summer.

▲ **Small farms high in the Andes Mountains of Ecuador**

But the Native Americans survived because they learned how to grow and store the pebble-sized purple, red, and yellow vegetables that grew underground. They called them *papas* (PAW-pus). Later, in other countries, these vegetables would be known as potatoes. The tiny rugged plants survived even when the leaves withered on frosty nights. Since it was the only thing to eat, the Native Americans learned how to cultivate and use the *papas* all year long. They

didn't know it, but their *papas* were rich in almost all the nutrients the Native Americans needed to survive.

The growing, gathering, and storing of the *papas* was an almost full-time village activity. It took three people to dig out all the tiny potatoes: two to lever the potatoes out of the ground with a tool called a *taclla* (TACK-lee-a) and another to lift away the earth and uncover the *papas*. The natives couldn't work long in the thin air before they collapsed in exhaustion.

Ancient Instant Potatoes

The Native Americans grew two kinds of potato crops. The first was called *chchoqhe* (CHOE-kay) and it was similar to a baking potato. The Native Americans baked it in hot coals, just as you would roast potatoes at a campfire.

The second type of crop, the *lukki* (LOU-key) potatoes, could grow in almost any weather, but the flesh was bitter when baked. The Native Americans turned those potatoes into

a dried food called *chuño* (CHOON-yo) that could be eaten throughout the winter. Here's how they made it: once the *lukki* potatoes were harvested, they were placed under a bed of straw and left outside. For nights on end, the potatoes froze. When the *lukkis* were shriveled and watery, the workers laid another layer of straw on top. Then the entire village stomped on the potatoes! When all the water was squished out, the potatoes were left in the sun to dry.

The potatoes could be stored in a dry place over winter. For dinner, the Native Americans mixed the *chuño* with water and other vegetables and cooked the mixture into a stew. But it wasn't an international gourmet hit. When the explorers came, they wrote home to say that they had eaten the native food and that it not only looked like cork, it tasted like it, too!

QUICK CHECK

LESSON 2 REVIEW

❶ Tomatoes, squash, and cucumbers are usually called *vegetables*. How can you tell that they are really fruits?

❷ Certain types of potatoes grow well in the Andes. In which area of North America might these plants grow well—the hot, lowland tropical rain forest of Puerto Rico or the cool mountains of Colorado? Explain.

❸ Native people in South America use potatoes as a major part of their diet. You probably eat a lot of potatoes, too. Write down all the ways you eat potatoes. How would your life change if you couldn't eat potatoes anymore? How would it change the lives of the South Americans if they couldn't eat potatoes anymore?

3 HERBS AND SPICES

What would cinnamon toast be without cinnamon? What would a dill pickle be without dill? Or ginger ale without ginger? They just wouldn't be the same without the taste that herbs and spices give them. In this lesson, you'll find out where herbs and spices come from. You'll also grow some yourself.

Herb and spice plants often have a strong flavor and smell. They give that flavor and smell to foods and make them taste better.

People used spices long ago to help preserve foods in places where the weather was hot. Today we use herbs and spices for their taste.

Peppermint ▶

▼ Basil

▼ Parsley

◀ Garlic grows below ground.

A55

ACTIVITY

Sorting Herbs and Spices

Herbs are usually plant leaves. They grow best in areas that have four seasons. Spices can be seeds, flower buds, stems, berries, or roots. They have a stronger flavor than herbs. Spices usually grow in the tropics, where it is hot most of the time. Find out more by investigating on your own.

DO THIS

❶ Draw a simple plant on the poster board. Include roots, stems, leaves, flowers, and fruits. Label your drawing.

❷ Take one herb or spice from each container.

❸ Look at each herb or spice. Which part of the plant do you think it comes from? Discuss your thoughts with your group.

❹ On your drawing, paste each herb or spice next to the matching plant part. When you're finished, compare your drawing with those of other groups. Decorate the classroom with the drawings.

MATERIALS

- boxes of whole herbs and spices
- poster board
- markers
- white glue
- Science Log data sheet

THINK AND WRITE

1. What clues did you use to decide which parts of the plant the herbs and spices came from?

2. Which plant parts are most often used for herbs and spices?

A56

Grow Your Own Herbs

People all over the world cook with herbs and spices. Some of these herbs and spices grow only in certain places. But you can grow others right in your classroom.

DO THIS

 1 Plant the seeds in the pots.

2 Water the seeds. Place the pots on a sunny windowsill.

 3 Observe the pots for several weeks. Keep the soil moist. Record your observations.

THINK AND WRITE

1. How long did it take your seeds to sprout? Compare your results with those of other groups.

2. How are the dried herbs and the herbs you grew alike? How are they different?

3. **COMPARING** When you compare objects, you observe ways in which they are alike and different. Sometimes the objects are nearly the same. Sometimes they're very different. How similar to each other were the objects you compared? Explain.

MATERIALS
- small pots
- soil
- herb seeds
- water
- dried herbs of the same type as the seeds
- Science Log data sheet

LESSON 3 REVIEW

1 What is your favorite food that has herbs and spices in it? What herbs and spices does it contain?

2 Look at cookbooks that have recipes from other countries. List some of the herbs and spices often used in foods of countries such as Italy, China, and India. Compare them to the spices used in your home.

4 DRINKS FROM PLANTS

What are your favorite plant juices? Are they fruit juices, vegetable juices, or some of both?

Some people drink plant juice often, maybe even every day. Now you're going to invent your own new juice flavor. Then you'll read about some friends who used plant juice to earn money and have fun.

MATERIALS

- several types of fruit juices and vegetable juices
- clear plastic cup
- empty juice bottle with a wide opening
- paper cups
- Science Log data sheet

ACTIVITY

Make a Plant Drink

This is where you get to make a new drink. Use fruit or vegetable juices, and be sure you write down what you used and how much.

DO THIS

❶ Combine two or more juices to make a new drink. Record how much of each type of juice you use for your new drink. Give it a name.

❷ Share your drink with your classmates. Ask them to guess what's in it.

❸ Write down your recipe.

THINK AND WRITE

1. Would it be easier to get juice from a watermelon or from a pear? Explain.

2. How do you think the water in rainfall becomes part of the juice in plants?

Sipping Plants

What's in those plant juices? Mostly water. Plant juices are the water in plants, mixed with other substances. It's the other substances that give each juice its own flavor. Luckily for us, the juice is often tasty.

Another type of drink made from plants is herbal tea. Herbal teas have become very popular in recent years, and many flavors are available. You might think that each flavor comes from a single plant. Actually, many herbal teas are mixtures of several different plants. The flavor depends on which plants are used and how much from each plant is used.

Herbal teas may be made from flowers, fruits, leaves, or roots. Hibiscus flowers and rose hips from the fruit of the rose plant are often used. A fruity taste comes from the peel of oranges and lemons. Leaves from spearmint, blackberry, camomile, and alfalfa plants add flavor. Roots from the chicory plant are also used.

THINK ABOUT IT

What are your favorite plant drinks?

Using Fruit Juice

Now read a story about some children who used a fruit drink for a school project.

Lemonade Stand

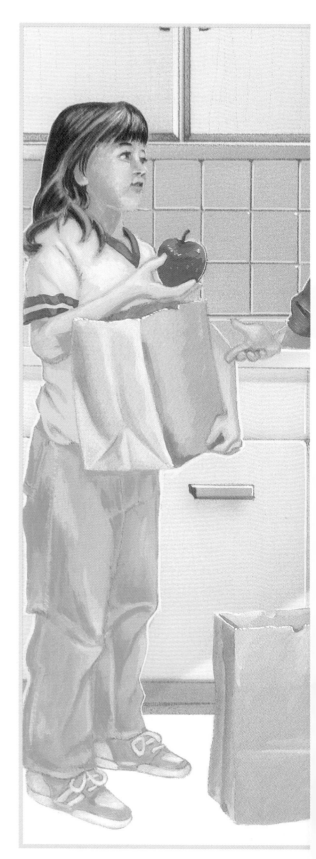

"Whew, is it hot!" said Maria as she sat down next to Joel and Jonathan on the shady steps in front of Jonathan's house.

"This must be the hottest day of the year," Jonathan answered.

"Yeah," agreed Joel. "We've been watching all the people from the park go down the street to buy cold drinks. They pass by on the way to the store. Then they pass by again when they go back to the park."

As Joel spoke, a couple of older boys walked by, drinking cans of cold juice. They dribbled a basketball as they headed toward the park.

"That reminds me of why I came," said Maria. "Do you guys want to work on the Create Your Own Business project for school?"

"Sure," answered Joel.

"Me, too," said Jonathan. "But we can't think of anything to do it on."

"You know, I'm getting an idea sitting here," said Maria. "It's a really hot day, right?"

"Right," said Joel and Jonathan together.

"All those hot people from the park keep passing by to get cold drinks *way* down the street. So all of those people..."

Before she could finish, Jonathan broke in.

"So all of those people *might* just buy their drinks someplace else—if there were a closer spot to get a drink."

"And that closer spot *could* be right here," said Joel, finishing the thought.

"Let's ask your parents if we can set up a juice stand here in front of the house," said Maria excitedly. "We can keep track of how we did it, and then we can write it up for our project."

"Come on, let's go ask," said Jonathan, rising from his seat on the steps. Joel and Maria ran after him through the front door.

Mrs. Tanaka, Jonathan's mom, was in the den, working on her computer.

"It sounds like a good idea," Mrs. Tanaka said. "You can use the folding card table in the hall closet. And you can also use fruit from the kitchen. Just make sure you clean up afterward."

The three friends agreed and happily ran into the kitchen. The Tanakas had just gone to the farmer's market, and there were three bags of fruits sitting on the kitchen counter—apples, grapes, and bananas.

"Well, here are the choices, but they don't look like good ones," said Joel, holding up a banana.

"You're right," answered Jonathan. "We can't make juice from a banana!"

"Apples and grapes have lots of juice," said Maria. "But it would take too many to make enough apple or grape juice to sell."

"And since we don't have a juicer, it'd be hard to press the juice out of these fruits," Jonathan added.

"It looks like we're not going to be making juice today," said Maria sadly.

"Not so fast," said Jonathan, getting an idea.

He went to the refrigerator and opened the door. Then he turned around with a smile, holding two bright, yellow fruits in his hand.

"Lemonade?" asked Maria.

"Why not?" said Joel. "Great idea!"

"Yeah, you're right," Maria said. "It *is* a great idea. Let's do it."

The three friends went to work. They found three pitchers and a bag of lemons. Then they cut the lemons in half. They squeezed the juice from several lemons into each pitcher. Then they filled each pitcher three-fourths full with water. Next they stirred in a couple of scoops of sugar and added ice cubes. The lemonade was ready.

The plan worked well. Lots of people stopped by. They paid 50 cents for a cup of cool lemonade—and saved a walk to the store a few blocks down the street.

"All sold out," said Maria after just about an hour. "And that includes the second batch!"

"We sure make good lemonade," said Joel, holding up an empty pitcher. "We could have sold ten times as much."

"Well, we don't have to," said Jonathan. "We set up our own business, and we sold something that people wanted."

"We had the perfect conditions and the perfect spot," said Joel.

"Now we'd better clean up," said Maria.

"The used lemons can go on the compost pile," Jonathan said, dropping them into an empty pitcher.

"You know, we could plant the seeds," said Maria as she threw used cups into a paper bag for recycling.

"Why do that?" asked Jonathan.

"They make nice plants," said Maria. "My sister grew a lemon tree in school."

"Did it grow lemons?" asked Joel.

"Well, she had to keep it warm indoors for it to grow at all," answered Maria. "Lemons grow only in hot climates. Some lemon trees grown indoors do produce flowers. But my sister's never has. That's okay," Maria said. "I'll be happy with a beautiful lemon plant, even if I can't get lemons from it."

As they finished cleaning up, Joel said, "Gee, it's still really hot out here. I think we need something to drink."

"Do you want to walk down the street and buy some juice?" asked Maria.

"Are you kidding?" said Jonathan. "Let's make some lemonade." The three friends laughed and went into the house.

QUICK CHECK

LESSON 4 REVIEW

Look at the labels on juices and juice drinks you have at home. On each label, the ingredient that the drink has the most of is listed first. The ingredient that the drink has the least of is listed last. List the ingredients. Compare your list with the lists of your classmates. Which ingredients are the most common?

DOUBLE CHECK

SECTION B REVIEW

1. Why are farms that grow grains often found on natural grasslands?

2. Tomato juice is well known as a vegetable juice. Explain why tomato juice is actually a fruit juice.

3. Write down what you would eat and drink if you could have your favorite meal. Then think carefully about each dish. List all the plants and plant parts you would be eating.

SECTION C
Fibers

Plant fibers are all around you. Chances are, you're wearing them. They could make up the sheets you sleep on or the stuffing in your pillow. If you've ever used a rope or swept a floor with a broom, you may have been using plant fibers. The paper of this very page is made of plant fibers.

In this section, you'll get a chance to look at the plant fibers that make up the clothing you wear and the building you live in. You'll see how jeans are made. You'll also make a model house from plants and learn how to decorate a T-shirt with paint and leaves. Keep notes in your Science Log.

1 CLOTHING

Look down at the shirt or dress you're wearing. Can you see the tiny threads running through it? These threads are spun from fabric fibers. Your clothing is made of thousands of these fibers.

There are many types of fibers. In general, fibers are strands that are much longer than they are wide. Some of your clothes are made from natural fibers. Natural fibers come from plants and animals.

Some of your clothes are made of artificial fibers. These fibers are made by people. Most artificial fibers are made from petroleum (puh TROH lee uhm). *Petroleum* is oil that comes from deep inside the Earth. Some artificial fibers are polyester, nylon, and dacron.

▼ **Cotton T-shirt**

◄ **A close look at cotton fibers**

ACTIVITY

Observing Fabrics

Almost all of your clothes are made of fibers. Take a close look at some common fibers in this activity.

DO THIS

❶ Get 3 different pieces of fabric.

❷ Examine each piece closely, using the hand lens. Draw what you see.

THINK AND WRITE

1. How do all of the fabrics look similar?

2. How do the 3 types of fabric differ?

3. **COMPARING** When you carry out an investigation, you often need to compare one object with another. Look at your answers to questions 1 and 2. Use them to write some general rules about how to identify plant fibers and artificial fibers.

MATERIALS
• **3 different pieces of fabric**
• **hand lens**
• **Science Log data sheet**

A66

How Jeans Are Made

As you've seen, your clothes are made of various kinds of fibers. What is one thing you're likely to wear often that contains cotton fibers? It's your jeans! They are usually made of cotton fabric called *denim*.

Cotton denim fabric starts as fibers in fuzzy bolls (BOHLZ). Bolls are the seed pods of the cotton plant. ▶

A cotton gin rakes the seeds from the bolls. Then the cotton is packed in large bales, which are shipped to factories to be made into cotton fibers. ▶

Machines comb the cotton fibers to get out tangles. Then these machines spin many fibers together to make cotton thread. ▶

Weaving machines called looms weave the dyed thread into cotton denim fabric. The fabric is then shipped to factories that make jeans. ▼

▲ For blue jeans, the cotton thread is dyed in large tubs like these. Jeans makers may use a chemical dye to color the thread, or they may use a natural dye from the indigo plant.

Thread can be dyed many different colors. ▶

▲ Threads are put into the loom so cloth can be woven.

▲ At the factory, a patternmaker draws the shapes that will go together to make a pair of jeans. Each shape will be cut from the denim cloth.

◀ Cutters cut many pieces of material at one time. They use the patterns as guides.

◀ Sewing machine operators sew the cut pieces together. Each piece must be sewn separately.

Finally, the jeans are ready for you to buy. ▼

LESSON 1 REVIEW

1 Check the fabric label in one piece of your clothing. With your classmates, make a list on the chalkboard of the fabric fibers that each person finds. What are the most common fabric fibers in your class?

2 Are most of the clothes worn by people in your class made of natural or artificial fibers? Why do you think this is?

2 SHELTER

You depend on plants for more than the clothes you wear. You may depend on them for a home. Most houses are built totally or partly of plants or plant parts. All houses have the same purpose—to provide shelter. So why don't they all look alike?

Types of Homes

Plants that grow in the forests of Minnesota are not the same as those that grow in the grasslands of central Africa. So houses made with wood are common in Minnesota, while grass houses are common in parts of central Africa.

People also build houses to fit the climate where they live. Steep roofs are good for snowy climates because snow can slide off easily. In a hot climate, a house might have an overhanging roof to keep out the sun.

Other factors affect house building, too. In earthquake zones, for example, houses are built of lightweight materials that will give when they are shaken.

◀ In England, grass is sometimes used to make roofs. This type of roof is called *thatch*.

Iroquois Longhouse

The Iroquois lived in deep forests in what is now the northeastern United States. Long before Europeans settled the area in the 1600s, the Iroquois used young trees to make frames for their homes. Then they covered the frames with walls made of tree bark. ▶

Log Cabin

During the 1600s, early European settlers in America also moved into the eastern forests. They chopped down trees to build houses made of logs. Log houses are still being built today. ▼

◄ Prairie Sod House

Many Easterners moved to the grasslands of the Midwest in the 1800s. There were no trees there. So the earliest prairie settlers cut squares of thick grass and soil, called sod, from the ground. They piled them like bricks to make sod houses.

▲ Modern Frame House

Our houses may look different from log cabins or sod houses, but they are still made mostly from plants. Many houses have a frame like this that is made of wood. Trains, boats, and trucks now carry building materials all over the world. So wooden houses can be built even in places where there are no forests.

THINK ABOUT IT

What conditions affect the kinds of shelter that people have?

ACTIVITY

Model of a House

You've read about and seen pictures of several types of houses. Now design and build your own model house.

DO THIS

1 Design a type of shelter to build from plants.

2 Have someone in your group record the steps you took to build the house.

3 Use your plant materials to build a model of your house.

THINK AND WRITE

1. What problems did you have while building your house? How did you solve them?

2. Describe the ways in which the model house you built is suited to a certain environment.

QUICK CHECK

LESSON 2 REVIEW

Describe some things that affect the ways houses are built.

A74

3 DECORATION

How often do you see decorations made from plants? More often than you think. Look at the decorations around you in the room. They are made of materials such as paper, fabric, and wood. You also see plants used in some unusual ways.

Leafing Leopards! Why Am I Green?

from *National Geographic World*

LITERATURE A leopard has been hanging around a garden at the San Diego Zoo in California. In fact the leopard *is* a garden. Its "skin" consists of growing plants. An artist designed this cool cat's wire frame, then covered it with greenery.

The training and cutting of plant material into living sculptures is known as topiary (TOH pee air ee). Traditional topiary involves snipping bushes into shapes—after waiting for them to grow. For faster results people start with hollow frames. They place sphagnum (SFAG nuhm) moss inside, then stuff other plants into the moss.

"We want our stuffed topiary animals to seem as if they've come to life," says Charles Coburn. He organizes the zoo's topiary exhibits. Apparently, he has met his goal. For days a strutting peacock at the zoo tried to attract a topiary flamingo.

A big squirt: That's what this ivy-covered elephant can deliver through a hose in its trunk. The topiary elephant and another just like it greet visitors to the San Diego Zoo. The life-size beasts with concrete tusks stay green with the help of built-in sprinkler systems. "A person could fit inside each of the elephants because they're huge and hollow," says Charles Coburn of the garden staff. 📖

▲ Proud "parents" show off
their babies: stuffed
topiary animals.

A77

Ira Walker
Gardener

You may enjoy topiary sculptures in an outdoor setting like the San Diego zoo. There are other places you can go to enjoy plants. Read on to find out about a man who cares for the plants we enjoy.

New York City has a lot of things that many other big cities have. Those things include tall buildings, subway trains, and lots of people. But New York City also has something that other cities don't have. It has a beautiful 21-hectare (52-acre) garden right in the middle of one of its most crowded neighborhoods. It's called the Brooklyn Botanic Garden.

If you visit the Brooklyn Botanic Garden, you'll find a thousand different kinds of roses. You'll see tall trees and cool ponds. And if you get there at just the right time, you might be able to see Ira Walker tending the plants.

Ira Walker is the gardener in charge of the garden's conifers. Conifers are trees that bear cones. Pine trees and spruce trees are evergreen conifers.

On some days, you'll find Walker planting trees. Sometimes he tends the trees, making sure they get water or fertilizer. At other times, he trims their branches to make sure the trees are healthy and have the right shape.

Walker is not only a gardener. He's a teacher, too. He loves to teach what he knows about gardening to others. So he holds classes at the Brooklyn Botanic Garden for people who want to learn about taking care of plants.

▲ Ira Walker clips one of the garden's bonsai trees.

Bonsai (BOHN sy) trees are one of Walker's specialties. They are miniature trees that look just like full-grown trees. Gardeners must use specific methods to keep the trees small. Walker has the know-how.

The Brooklyn Botanic Garden is a busy place. People like to walk through its flower gardens and its groves of trees. They have Ira Walker to thank for helping to make this garden in the city so beautiful.

THINK ABOUT IT

Why do you think gardens like the one where Ira Walker works are popular in big cities?

Ira Walker ▶

A79

ACTIVITY

Leaf Printing

Using plants for decoration is a career for some people. There are many ways you, too, can decorate with plants. One way is to design and make your own leaf prints.

DO THIS

1 Go to workstation 1. Choose two or three leaves for your prints.

2 Go to workstation 2. Arrange leaves on your shirt or other fabric. If you decorate a T-shirt, put several layers of newspaper inside it before painting.

3 Remove each leaf. Put paint on its underside with a sponge. Put the leaf back onto the material. Once the leaf is in place, don't move it.

MATERIALS

- leaves of different types
- white T-shirt
- newspaper
- containers of acrylic fabric paints
- pieces of sponge
- paper towels
- Science Log data sheet

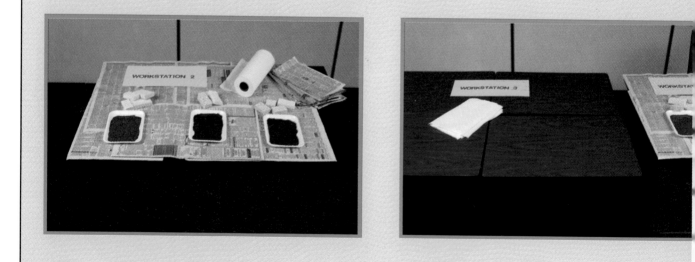

4 Slide your fabric over to work-station 3. Place a piece of paper towel on each leaf. Press on the leaf, but don't rub.

5 When your printed leaves are dry, ask your teacher to run a warm iron lightly over the back of the print. Draw a picture of your decorated fabric.

THINK AND WRITE

Describe other plant parts from which you could make prints. What problems would you have if you used other plant parts?

LESSON 3 REVIEW

How do people use plant parts other than leaves for decoration?

DOUBLE CHECK

SECTION C REVIEW

1. Read clothing labels to find out if the care of natural fibers, such as cotton, differs from the care of artificial fibers, such as polyester. How would this information help you decide which to buy?

2. How are houses where you live built to fit the environment in which you live?

Medicines and Dyes

▲ This yarn was dyed using oak bark.

There are plants on your dinner plate and in your juice glass. Plants are in the walls of your school and in the clothes you wear.

There are other places you can look for plants. You can find them in an aspirin bottle and toothpaste tube. You can also find them in the dyes that make your clothes so colorful.

In this section, you'll read about plants that help you stay healthy. You'll also find out where those bright colors on baseball caps and T-shirts come from. Then you'll dye some materials yourself.

1 MEDICINES

Modern drugstores sell medicines for almost every type of pain or sickness. Many of these medicines come from plants.

RAINFOREST MEDICINES

by **Isaac Asimov**
from *Why Are the Rainforests Vanishing?*

LITERATURE

Some of the plants of the rainforests have proved to be of great importance to people because they provide vital medicines. At least one quarter of the world's most important medicines are based on rainforest plants. The variety of treatments from these tropical products includes painkillers, cough mixtures, drugs that relieve anxiety, anesthetics, antibiotics and cancer-fighting drugs.

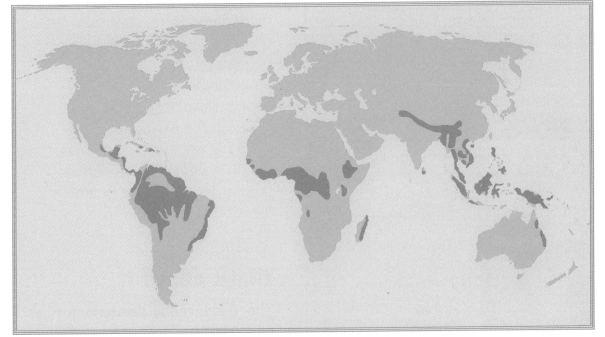

▲ The following rainforest plants provide medicines for illnesses: the rosy periwinkle of Madagascar for leukemia, the calabar bean of West Africa for eye disorders, and the papaya of Latin America for stomach illnesses.

When Amazonian natives hunt, they often use poison-tipped darts shot from blowpipes to kill their food. The poison, known as curare, works by completely stopping the muscles from working. The animal cannot breathe and soon dies. When scientists saw the poison's effect, they used it to develop a powerful muscle relaxant. It is given to people to make their bodies relaxed for surgical operations. Curare is still harvested in the Amazon and helps patients worldwide. ▶

▲ Traditional healers around the world, like this South American healer, employ hundreds of different kinds of plants to treat people.

◀ Madagascan herbalists have long used the rosy periwinkle as medicine, which led Western scientists to discover how useful it could be against leukemia.

Only one percent of tropical plants have yet been carefully tested for their potential as medicines. Some scientists believe that as high as ten percent of untested plants may have the potential to fight cancer. Also, a species of tree found in the Amazon and in Australia contains a substance which is being researched in London as a possible treatment for AIDS.

THINK ABOUT IT

There are many diseases for which we have no cure. How might saving rain forests help bring about cures for these diseases?

Plant Medicines

Long before there were modern medical doctors, people used plants for medicines. Many of the best medicines still come from plants.

Pacific Yew

The bark of the Pacific yew produces taxol. Taxol is used for treating cancer.

Aloe Vera

The aloe vera, a plant, contains an oil that helps heal burns and keep skin soft.

Cinchona

The bark of the cinchona (sin KOH nuh) tree contains quinine (KWY nyn). Doctors use quinine to treat malaria, a disease people get if they are bitten by malaria-carrying mosquitoes.

Opium Poppy

Sap from the seed case of the opium poppy is used to make the strong painkillers morphine (MAWR feen) and codeine (KOH deen).

Willow

Willow bark tea has been used for thousands of years to relieve pain. Several different kinds of willow contain a chemical called salicin (SAL uh sin). A pain reliever called acetylsalicylic (uh SEET uhl sal uh SIL ik) acid was made from salicin in 1899. We call it aspirin.

Cephaelis

Ipecac (IP ih kak) syrup from the cephaelis (suh FAY lis) causes vomiting. Doctors give ipecac syrup to people who have swallowed poison. It helps get the poison out of their stomachs.

Autumn Crocus

The autumn crocus produces colchicine (KAHL chih seen), which is used to relieve pain.

Foxglove

The leaves of the foxglove plant produce a drug called digitalis (dij ih TAL uhs). Digitalis is used as a treatment for some heart conditions.

QUICK CHECK

LESSON 1 REVIEW

Many medicines we use today have been used in some form by traditional healers. These healers use plants to make their medicines. Write a paragraph that tells why learning about traditional healing could help physicians heal people today.

2 DYES

What makes your blue jeans blue? What makes your jacket black? Dyes. The dyes that colored your clothes probably came from a chemist's laboratory. But at one time, almost all dyes came from plants.

ACTIVITY

MATERIALS
- apron
- bowls of prepared plant dyes
- white cotton cloth
- wooden spoon
- water
- Science Log data sheet

Dyeing Cloth with Plants

Use a dye made from plants to color a piece of cloth. See what colors you can create.

DO THIS

❶ **CAUTION: Put on an apron to protect your clothing.** Choose a dye sample from those your teacher has prepared. Look carefully at your sample. Write a hypothesis about what color your dye will make your cloth.

❷ Put the cloth into the dye. Let it stay in a few minutes—until the color is as deep as you want it.

❸ Lift the dyed cloth out of the dye with the wooden spoon.

❹ Rinse the dyed cloth in clear water until no dye comes out. Let it dry.

THINK AND WRITE

1. Most clothing is colored with chemical dyes. Why do you think some clothing makers prefer chemical dyes to natural dyes?

2. **HYPOTHESIZING** A hypothesis is an explanation of why something happens. A hypothesis must be tested by experiment. You wrote a hypothesis before you began this activity. Then you tested your hypothesis.

    Now write a hypothesis about how you might make your cloth a darker shade of the color you dyed it. Write down how you would test your hypothesis.

Looking Ahead You've dyed cloth with dyes from plant parts such as leaves, seeds, flowers, and fruits. Find out next how making dyes was part of the work of a famous African-American scientist.

George Washington Carver (1864–1943)

How long have crayons been part of your life? Probably for as long as you can remember. The dyes that give crayons their colors were first made by George Washington Carver. Carver was born into slavery. By the time he died, he had become one of America's most famous and successful scientists.

 Carver grew up on a farm and was interested in helping farmers grow better crops. He went to college and earned degrees in agriculture. Then he began teaching about farming at Tuskegee Institute and doing experiments with many types of plants.

Carver not only made crayon dyes, he also worked with chemists in the Army to make other dyes from plants. He made dyes from sweet potatoes, grapes, onions, and the vines of tomatoes. He also made dyes from parts of the dandelion and the black oak tree as well as from wood ashes and pecan shells. Carver wanted to make unusual colors. He also wanted to make dyes that wouldn't wash out of cloth.

Although Carver did a lot of other work, people remember him mostly for his work with peanuts. Carver made many products from peanuts in his laboratory. They include bleach, shaving cream, synthetic rubber, and linoleum.

Carver also made many peanut foods. We know about peanut butter, peanut candy, and peanut cookies. However, Carver knew that peanuts could be used for much more. One day, Carver served a lunch in which every food was made from peanuts. First, Carver served peanut soup. He followed this with imitation chicken made from peanuts, served with creamed peanuts and peanut bread. He then gave his guests peanut ice cream and cookies for dessert.

During his career, George Washington Carver also did many experiments to improve the soil. He showed the usefulness of composting to add nutrients to the soil. He also lectured on rotating crops from year to year instead of planting the same crops in the same fields. Carver also experimented with fruit trees to improve their fruit.

Three years before his death, George Washington Carver gave his life savings to Tuskegee Institute to continue research in agriculture. The university has been able to continue Carver's work to find new ways to grow and use plants.

QUICK CHECK

LESSON 2 REVIEW

Before dyes could be made in the laboratory, people had to make their own. Why do you think dyeing yarn and thread was important?

DOUBLE CHECK

SECTION D REVIEW

Look at the label shown on the left. Identify and record the plant ingredients in it. What do these ingredients do?

I REFLECT

It's time to think about the ideas you have discovered during your investigations. Think, too, about your many accomplishments.

SUMMARIZE

Answer the following in your Science Log.

1. What **I Wonder** questions have you answered in your investigations? What new questions have you asked?

2. What have you discovered about plants and the ways people use them? How have your ideas changed?

3. Did any of your discoveries surprise you? Explain.

How People Use Plants

○ People use plants for food. We eat cereal grains in breakfast cereals, breads, and noodles. We eat roots, such as carrots. We eat leaves, such as lettuce. We eat fruits, such as apples.

◉ People also use plants for building things, such as homes. We use plant fibers, such as cotton, in clothes. We get many dyes and medicines from plants. We also make decorations from plants.

○

CONNECT IDEAS

1. How could the pesticides farmers use cause water pollution problems? Report on any problems in your area, and tell what is being done to solve them.

2. Cereal grains are important because they are part of so many foods. What other foods are very important in your diet?

3. People make artificial clothing fibers, fuels, and plastics from petroleum. There is a good chance that the world's supply of petroleum will be used up. Why might that be a problem? What might people do about the problem?

SCIENCE PORTFOLIO

❶ Complete your Science Experiences Record.

❷ Choose one or two samples of your best work from each section to include in your Science Portfolio.

❸ On A Guide to My Science Portfolio, tell why you chose each sample.

I SHARE

Scientists share their discoveries and ideas and learn from one another. How can you share what you've learned?

Decide
▶ what you want to say.
▶ what the best way is to get your message across.

Share
▶ what you did and why.
▶ what worked and what didn't work.
▶ what conclusions you have drawn.
▶ what else you'd like to find out.

Find Out
▶ what classmates liked about what you shared—and why.
▶ what questions your classmates have.

I ACT

Science is more than discoveries. It is also what you do with those discoveries. How might you use what you have learned about how we use plants?

▶ Share with others important information about the uses of plants.

▶ Get involved with a community activity using plants, such as making a garden on a vacant lot.

▶ Help protect plants that are endangered.

▶ Grow some herbs to use in your family's meals.

▶ Find a new way to make plants a part of your life.

THE LANGUAGE OF SCIENCE

The language of science helps people communicate clearly when they talk about plants. Here are some vocabulary words you can use when you talk about plants with friends, family, and others.

chlorophyll—the green substance in plant leaves that absorbs energy from the sun and helps a plant make food during photosynthesis. Chlorophyll is found in chloroplasts. **(A14, A16)**

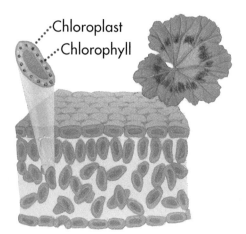

Chloroplast
Chlorophyll

chloroplast—a tiny green structure in plant leaves that contains chlorophyll. **(A16)**

compost—decayed food and plant matter that farmers use to give nutrients to crops. Compost can be used as a fertilizer. **(A28)**

▲ **Backyard compost pile**

fertilizer — a chemical or natural material that is put into soil to give plants the nutrients they need in order to grow. Farmers must often use fertilizer on poor soil or soil that has been used year after year to grow crops. Most fertilizers that modern farmers use are made artificially in factories. Manure and compost are natural fertilizers. **(A28)**

fiber — one of the strands of material that makes up the fabric of clothing and other articles made of cloth, such as sheets, towels, and rugs. Fibers can come from plants, like cotton. Fibers can also come from animals, like the wool from sheep. Fibers from plants and animals are natural fibers. Synthetic fibers, like nylon, are made from petroleum. **(A65)**

grains — a group of plants with tall, stiff stems and long, narrow leaves. Wheat, rice, corn, oats, rye, millet, sorghum, and barley are grains. **(A41)**

nutrient — a substance that plants need in order to live and grow. Plants get nutrients such as calcium, nitrogen, and potassium from soil. **(A22)**

pesticide — a chemical that kills insects or other pests. Farmers often use pesticides to kill pests that eat food crops. Pesticides are usually made from chemicals. Some are made from living things such as flowers. Pesticides kill harmful insects, but they also kill helpful insects. Pesticides can be harmful to people and other animals that eat foods that have been sprayed with them. **(A28)**

photosynthesis — the process a plant uses to make food. Plants use energy from the sun, carbon dioxide from the air, and water from the soil to make sugar. Plants use this sugar as food. Photosynthesis takes place in the parts of plants that contain chlorophyll. It also takes place in some plantlike living things that contain chlorophyll. **(A16)**

Photosynthesis enables plants to make their own food.

CURRENTS AND COASTLINES

Currents and Coastlines

Exploring Ocean Ecosystems

I WONDER

Science begins with wondering. What do you wonder about when you see or think about an ocean? What questions would you like to ask about this picture?

Work with a partner to make a list of questions you may have about the ocean. Be ready to share your list with the rest of the class.

Underwater reef scene, Red Sea
Yaquina Head lighthouse, Newport, Oregon

B3

I PLAN

You may have asked questions such as these as you wondered about oceans. Scientists also ask questions. Then they plan ways to help them find answers to their questions. Now you and your classmates can plan how you will investigate Earth's oceans and other bodies of water.

My Science Log

- What is the ocean like?

- What kinds of plants and animals live near beaches?

- How do oil spills affect the oceans?

- How can oil spills be prevented?

With Your Class

Plan how your class will use the activities and readings from the **I Investigate** part of this unit.

On Your Own

There are many ways to learn about Earth's oceans and other waterways. Following are some things you can do to explore Earth's waters by yourself or with some classmates. Some explorations may take longer to do than others. Look over the suggestions and choose . . .

- **Places to Visit**
- **People to Contact**
- **Books to Read**

PLACES TO VISIT

AQUARIUM

Go to an aquarium in your community or in a nearby city. Observe different kinds of fish and other ocean life. Draw pictures of what you see, and take notes about unusual features of the ocean life you observe. Share and explain your drawings with a family member.

BODY OF WATER

Perhaps there is an ocean, a lake, or a river near your area. With an adult, spend some time studying it. Observe the movement of the water. What kinds of living things can you see? Can you see the bottom? What is it made of? Take photographs or draw sketches. Record the date and time you made the pictures. Make notes about the weather that day. With an adult, return to the same place on a different day. Take or draw more pictures. Compare these pictures with those from your first visit.

PET SHOP

Go to a pet shop and look at the displays of fish. Talk to the store manager about setting up a saltwater or freshwater aquarium. Then plan an aquarium for your classroom. Make a list of the things you would need and how much each item costs. How much will the whole project cost?

PEOPLE TO CONTACT

IN PERSON

To learn about waterways near you, talk to people who have lived in your community for a long time. Find out how waterways have been important to the community and how they have changed over the years. Write a short report about your findings. Find out if your local newspaper or school newspaper would like to print your report.

- American Oceans Campaign
- The Cousteau Society
- The ecology club at your local high school or community college
- Greenpeace
- Sierra Club
- Your state fish and game commission

BY MAIL

There are many agencies and groups that are interested in protecting Earth's water resources. You can write to them for information. To the left is a list of places, agencies, and groups you might try. After you receive the information, share it with your class.

BY COMPUTER

Use a computer with a modem to connect to on-line services or bulletin boards. You can look for information on oceans and other water resources and talk to people to find out about museum exhibits and other projects.

Perhaps the computers at your school are connected to the AT&T Learning Network, an electronic network for students. You may be able to use the Learning Network to share projects about the ocean with students in other parts of the world.

BOOKS TO READ

The Boy Who Lived with the Seals

by Rafe Martin (G.P. Putnam's Sons, 1993). While camped with his people by the great river, a small boy becomes lost. Many weeks later, his parents hear of a boy who lives with seals. He is returned to his people, and he relearns to live as they do. But the boy has new skills that set him apart, and he misses the seals. This story comes from the Chinook people of the Northwest coast. It is a story of both joy and sadness.

Sea Otter Rescue: The Aftermath of an Oil Spill

by Roland Smith (Cobblehill Books, 1990), Outstanding Science Trade Book. Sea otters live in the icy, clear waters of Prince William Sound in Alaska. When a tanker hit a reef and spilled oil, the sea otters living near shore were covered with the poisonous ooze. Read about the people who quickly gathered to save the otters.

More Books to Read

Eskimo Boy: Life in an Inupiaq Village

by Russ Kendall (Scholastic, 1992). This is the true story of Norman Kokeok, an Inupiaq Eskimo. He lives in a village in Alaska. Read this book to find out how Norman and his family get food from the ocean.

I Can Be an Oceanographer

by Paul P. Sipiera (Childrens Press, 1987). More than 70 percent of Earth is covered by oceans. Oceans are important to life on Earth. This book tells you how oceanographers study the oceans and how marine biologists study life in the oceans.

Very Last First Time

by Jan Andrews (Atheneum, 1986). In this story, you'll meet Eva, an Inuit Eskimo. To gather shellfish, the Inuit people climb beneath the ice on the frozen sea and walk on the ocean floor. Today, Eva will do this alone for the first time. She must race to find the way out when she hears the tide coming in. Will she find it in time?

The Seashore

by Joyce Pope (Franklin Watts, 1985). This book will tell you about the seashore. You will learn about different organisms in different zones. You will find animals under rocks, on rocks, and in burrows. There are also activities for you to do. When you visit the shore, be sure to leave everything as you found it.

INVESTIGATE

To find answers to their questions, scientists read, think, talk to others, and do experiments. Their investigations often lead to new questions.

In this unit, you will have many chances to think and work like a scientist. How will you find answers to questions you asked?

▶ **INFERRING** Inferring is using what you have observed to explain what has happened. An observation is something you see or experience. An inference is an explanation of an observation, and it may be right or wrong.

▶ **COMMUNICATING** When you communicate, you give information. In science, you communicate by showing results from an activity in an organized way—for example, in a chart. Then you and other people can interpret the results.

▶ **FORMULATING AND USING MODELS** Objects and events are often too large, too small, or too far away to observe directly. But you can make a model of an object or event and use it to learn more about the real thing.

Are you ready to begin?

SECTIONS

SECTION A
What Are the Oceans?

Suppose you're on a spacecraft. As it zooms through the sky, you look back at Earth. You see a beautiful ball that is mostly blue–the blue of Earth's oceans. What are the oceans made of? How do their waters move? How do people use the oceans? Finding answers to these questions is what this section is all about.

To answer these questions, you will have to do some investigating. You will also need to keep your Science Log nearby, because that's where you will keep track of your important scientific discoveries.

1 HOW BIG ARE THE OCEANS?

Some of Earth is covered by oceans. Some is covered by land. Is Earth covered more by water or more by land? How much more? Here are two activities you can do to find the answers to these questions.

MATERIALS
• world map
• crayons
• 2 sheets of unlined paper
• scissors
• white glue
• Teaching Resources p. 63
• Science Log data sheet

ACTIVITY

Ocean Puzzle

DO THIS

❶ On the map, color the land brown.

❷ Color the oceans blue.

❸ Label one sheet of paper *Land*. Label another sheet of paper *Oceans*.

❹ **CAUTION: Be careful when you use scissors.**
Use scissors to cut out all the pieces of land on the map. Cut the pieces into squares. Paste these together to make a big square on the sheet of paper labeled *Land*.

❺ Now cut out the oceans, which you colored blue. Cut the pieces into squares. Paste these together in a square on the sheet labeled *Oceans*.

❻ Compare the two sheets of paper. Record your observations.

THINK AND WRITE

1. Which square is larger?

2. About how much larger is one square than the other?

3. What does this tell you about Earth's oceans?

B13

ACTIVITY

Ocean Tossup

DO THIS

1 Make a data table like the one below.

2 Form a circle with your classmates. Toss the inflatable globe from person to person.

3 Each time someone catches the globe, observe where the person's right hand touches it.

4 Make a mark on your data table in the column labeled *Water* if the tip of the person's little finger is touching water. If the person's fingertip is touching land, make a mark in the *Land* column.

5 Keep tossing the globe until you have completed 50 tosses.

6 Count the number of marks in each column. Record your totals.

MATERIALS

- inflatable globe
- Science Log data sheet

THINK AND WRITE

After completing your observations, write a paragraph telling what you found out. Tell how much of Earth you think is covered with water and how much you think is covered with land. You can use expressions such as these—*about half as much, about the same amount, about twice as much, about three times as much.*

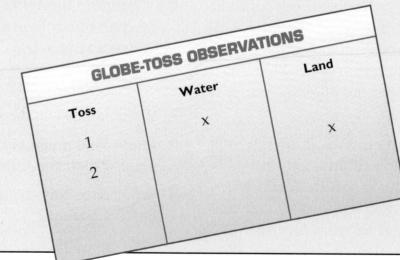

GLOBE-TOSS OBSERVATIONS		
Toss	Water	Land
1	X	X
2		

LESSON 1 REVIEW

❶ In the Ocean Puzzle activity, you found that a certain amount of Earth was covered by oceans and another amount by land. In the Ocean Tossup activity, you found information on the same topic but in a different way. Compare the results of the two activities.

❷ There are many small pieces of rock floating through the solar system. Some of these rocks, called *meteors*, come through Earth's atmosphere. Most burn up in the atmosphere but some, called *meteorites*, make it to Earth's surface. Would a meteorite be more likely to crash on land or in the water? Why?

2 EXPLORING THE OCEANS

Oceans are mysterious and ever-changing places. The surface of an ocean can be as flat and smooth as a sheet of glass. At other times, the same ocean may have waves that seem like huge, leaping, gray mountains. At their deepest points, oceans can be as black as the blackest night. Sometimes sea animals and plants twinkle and glow in the deep darkness. Why is the ocean so dark? What secrets does it hide? What makes water in the ocean move? A sailor may be able to help you find answers to these questions. Read on.

The Sea Challenger

 A small sailboat bobbed gently at a wooden dock in Bar Harbor, Maine. Across its stern, two words announced its name, *Sea Challenger*.

Lisa Candalas had chosen that name for her boat for two reasons. For one thing, she saw herself as a challenger of the sea because she was an expert sailor. For another thing, a great scientific exploration of the sea had been made more than 100 years earlier by a ship called the HMS *Challenger*. Lisa had learned all about the HMS *Challenger* in college.

A soft breeze tangled Lisa's hair as she raised the sails of the *Sea Challenger*. Then a puff of wind snapped the sails outward. The *Sea Challenger* gathered speed. Lisa carefully guided the small boat out of the sheltered harbor and into the Atlantic Ocean.

As the wind picked up speed, the boat bounced higher and harder. The waves got bigger, and the ocean slapped the sides of the small boat. Lisa had learned in school that wind made ocean waves. The stronger and longer the wind, the higher the waves.

The *Sea Challenger* moved up and down as the waves rose and fell. The wind whipped a fine spray off the waves and onto Lisa's face. Lisa tasted the salty water. She was thirsty. But the water was too salty to drink. Lisa reached for a bottle of fresh water she had put nearby and took a large gulp.

Looking back over her shoulder, Lisa could no longer see the land. She was surrounded by water. Soon the wind grew calmer and the waves less wild. Now the ocean looked more like a huge landscape of rolling hills.

These "rolling hills," called *swells*, are giant ripples. If nothing gets in their way, swells will spread out in all directions for thousands of kilometers. From off the coast of the United States, they can travel east all the way to Europe. They might also find their way south to a sandy beach in Africa or South America. They could move north to break eventually on the icy shores of Greenland. To the west, the swells don't travel far before spilling over the rocks of Lisa's home state of Maine.

Lisa tied the tiller in place and headed for the cabin of the boat. A tiller is used to steer a sailboat. Before ducking into the cabin, Lisa checked the sky for signs of bad weather. But she saw only one small cloud. As the *Sea Challenger* passed beneath it, it began to rain gently.

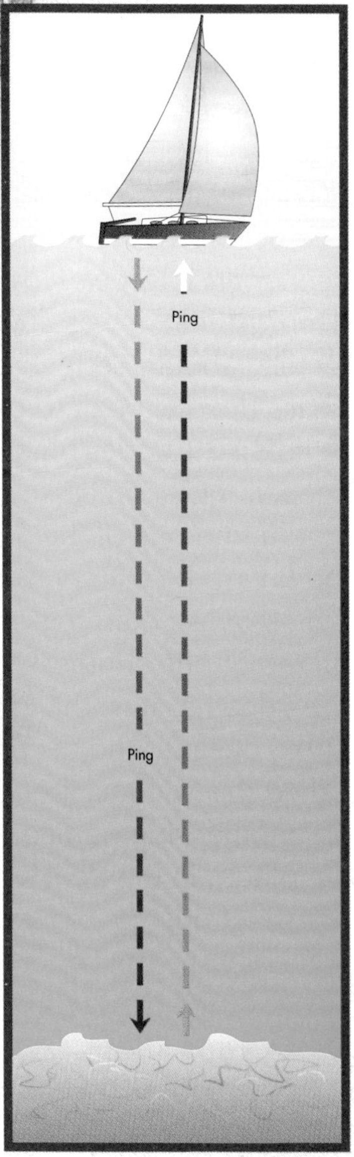

Rain is fresh water. Lisa knew that the rainwater in the clouds overhead came from the oceans. When she was younger, she had wondered why the rainwater over the oceans isn't salty. But in school she learned that when water evaporates from the oceans into the air, it leaves the salt behind.

In the cabin, Lisa switched on an instrument her parents used for fishing. It is called *sonar*. The sonar sent a "ping" of sound streaking down into the ocean. In less than a second, the ping echoed back into the cabin. *Ping…ping!*

The sound had bounced off the ocean bottom and returned to the boat. The sonar instrument timed how long it took for the sound to make the round trip. Lisa knew that the sonar instrument used the speed of sound through sea water to give her a reading that had calculated how far down the ocean bottom was.

Ping

Ping

As the *Sea Challenger* moved farther and farther into the Atlantic Ocean, the pings sounded like this:

ping . . . ping!
ping . . . . ping!
ping . . . . . ping!
ping . . . . . . ping!

The pauses between the pings got longer and longer.

Lisa knew that as the pauses between pings got longer, the ocean became deeper. The ocean was getting deeper and deeper. How deep? At first, it was about 100 meters (about 300 feet) deep. That's deep enough to cover a building 29 stories high. But parts of the ocean are much deeper. If Lisa sailed south to a spot near Puerto Rico, she would find one of the deepest places in the Atlantic Ocean, the Puerto Rico Trench. The Puerto Rico Trench is so deep that the 30 tallest buildings in the United States could fit in it stacked on top of one another!

As deep as it is, the Puerto Rico Trench is not the deepest spot in the oceans. The deepest spot lies in the Pacific Ocean. It's called the Mariana Trench and it was first discovered by scientists on another ship named *Challenger*. In fact, one of the places in the trench is called Challenger Deep.

Lisa wondered about the Challenger Deep. Someday she might get the chance to go there. For now, the orange sun dipping slowly in the west let Lisa know it was time to head home. She turned the *Sea Challenger* around and headed west toward the setting sun.

THINK ABOUT IT

If Lisa were sailing over the Puerto Rico Trench and using her sonar, would the time between the pings be longer or shorter than they were in the story? Why?

What's What with the Ocean?

Use the drawing on this page and the *Sea Challenger* story to answer these questions.

1. Over which spot would the pings of sonar take the longest to make a round trip?

2. Which spot is an island?

3. At which spot or spots will the boat be docked?

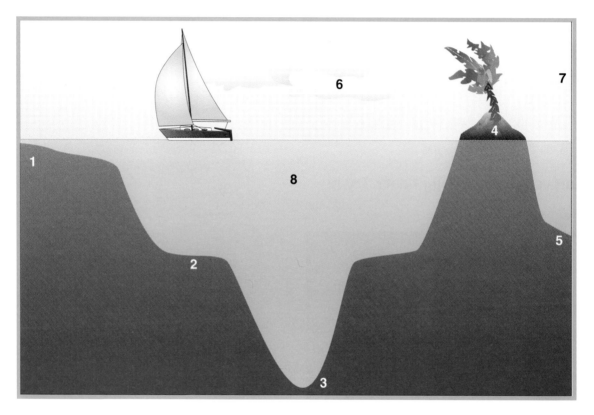

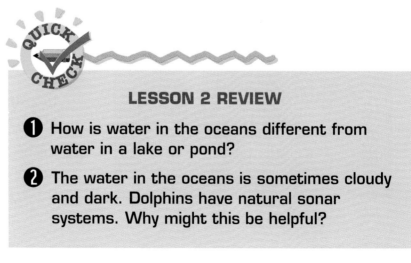

LESSON 2 REVIEW

❶ How is water in the oceans different from water in a lake or pond?

❷ The water in the oceans is sometimes cloudy and dark. Dolphins have natural sonar systems. Why might this be helpful?

3 WORTH ITS SALT

Anyone who has tasted ocean water knows that it's different from lake water. Ocean water tastes salty. Fresh water doesn't. But salt changes water in other ways, too. Do the following activities to see what you can find out about the differences between salt water and fresh water.

ACTIVITY

An Egg-cellent Detective

Can you make an egg float? Try it!

DO THIS

1 Fill the cup about two-thirds full of warm tap water. Gently put the egg into the water.

2 Observe what happens to the egg and record your observations.

3 Remove the egg. Add a heaping spoonful of salt to the water.

4 Stir until the salt dissolves. Gently replace the egg in the water.

5 What does the egg do now? Record your observations.

6 Repeat steps 3 through 5 until you've added 5 spoonfuls of salt. Make sure you record your observations each time.

THINK AND WRITE

1. Which would be easier to do— float on an ocean or float on a lake? Explain how the Egg-cellent Detective investigation helps you answer this question.

2. INFERRING You often draw conclusions from your observations. When you infer, you use those conclusions in cases similar to the ones you observed. For example, in this investigation, you had to infer which would be easier to do— float on an ocean or float on a lake. What would you have to do to make sure that your inference was correct? Look at the pictures. Infer which body of water has more salt. Why is inferring useful?

ACTIVITY

Have an Ice Time

Salt helps things float. What else does it do?

DO THIS

1 Measure 2 cm from the bottom of each cup. Make a mark on the cup at that height. Fill each cup with water to the mark. This is the water level.

2 Add 3 spoonfuls of salt to cup A and 1 spoonful to cup B. Stir to dissolve the salt. The water level may change after you add the salt. If it does, make another mark on the cup to show the new water level.

3 Label each of the cups with its cup letter and the amount of salt you added. For example, cup A should be labeled *Cup A, 3 Spoonfuls of Salt*. Cups C and D should be labeled with their letters and *No Salt*.

4 Put all 4 cups in the freezer. Record the time.

5 Look at the cups 3 hours later. Write what the water in each cup looks like.

MATERIALS

- ruler
- marker that writes on plastic
- 4 clear plastic cups
- water
- salt
- spoon
- watch
- Science Log data sheet

THINK AND WRITE

1. Which cups had the most ice?

2. How did freezing affect the space the water took up? HINT: Look at the water-level marks on each cup.

3. Why would it be a bad idea to place an unopened bottle of water in a freezer?

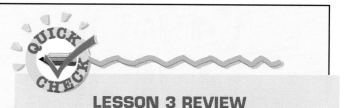

QUICK CHECK

LESSON 3 REVIEW

❶ A cargo ship carries food, fuel, or items that have been made in factories. When cargo ships sail on the oceans, they are often loaded with heavier cargo than when they sail on lakes or rivers. Why do you think this is so?

❷ During the winter, people often put salt on their front steps and sidewalks after a snowstorm. Why do you think they do that?

▲ Cargo ship

4 OCEAN MOTIONS

Have you ever tried to rub your stomach while patting your head? It's sometimes difficult to do because you have to move two different ways at the same time. The water in the oceans has no trouble moving in two different ways. In this lesson, you will have the chance to investigate both kinds of movement.

ACTIVITY

MATERIALS
- large plastic pan
- water
- cork
- sheet of cardboard
- pebble
- Science Log data sheet

Making Waves

Picture yourself standing waist-deep in an ocean. You gaze out to sea. You spot a blue hump of water rolling toward you. As the wave passes you, it lifts you up off your feet and then sets you down again. Finally, the wave breaks on the shore and is gone. Where do waves come from? This activity may help you find out.

DO THIS

❶ Fill the pan half full with water. Place the cork in the water. Let the water stand for a few minutes so it becomes still.

❷ Fan the water with the sheet of cardboard as fast as you can, but make sure you don't touch the water or the pan.

3 Observe what happens to the water and the cork. Record your observations.

4 Wait for the water to become still. Then tap on the side of the pan several times.

5 Again, observe what happens to the water and the cork and record your observations.

6 Once again, let the water become still. Then drop the pebble into one end of the pan.

7 Write a paragraph to explain what the pebble does to the water and the cork.

THINK AND WRITE

1. What happened to the water in the pan every time you disturbed it? How was the cork affected each time?

2. What does the movement of the cork tell you about the movement of the water?

What Causes Waves?

The oceans are much, much larger than the pan you used. The disturbances you made in your pan and those in the ocean are called **waves.** Some ocean waves are made by underwater earthquakes. Others are made by landslides that dump great slabs of rock and soil into the sea. However, most ocean waves are made by the wind.

The more the water is disturbed, the higher the waves will be. That's why the waves caused by the strong winds of a hurricane are much larger than the waves caused by a gentle breeze. But even gentle breezes can cause large waves if the winds blow on the water for a long time.

As you saw in the activity, no matter what causes waves, they don't move water from place to place. All they really do is move the water up and down.

THINK ABOUT IT

Name two things that cause waves.

Fishing boat on the ocean

ACTIVITY

Current Events

Since waves don't move water from place to place, you might think that the water in the oceans doesn't move around very much. But before you draw this conclusion, try this activity and look at the map on the following pages.

DO THIS

1. Fill the pan half full with water. Place the cork in the water.

2. Let the water stand for a few minutes so it becomes still.

3. Put your hand in the water at one end of the pan.

4. Slowly move your hand to the other end of the pan, pushing the water as your hand moves through it.

5. Take your hand out of the pan.

6. Observe what happens to the cork. Record your observations. Make a drawing of the path the cork takes. What does your drawing tell you?

MATERIALS
- large plastic pan
- water
- cork
- Science Log data sheet

THINK AND WRITE

1. What happened to the cork when it reached one end of the pan?

2. Why did the cork move?

3. **COMMUNICATING** In the activity, how did you communicate the data? Why is it important for scientists to communicate their results?

Explore the Map

Think about how the water moved in the last activity. Now suppose that you are on a sailboat far out in the North Atlantic Ocean. A storm comes up and breaks the pole that holds the sail. Will you be stuck in one spot forever? No! You will drift in a big circle. Why? Because you will be carried by an ocean current.

The map on this page shows the world's ocean currents. A **current** is a strong flow of water, much like a great river of water in an ocean. However, no river on land is as long as the longest ocean current. The blue arrows on the map show currents that are very cold. The red arrows show warm currents.

What does the map below show about ocean currents? Answer the questions to find out.

1. From where do most warm currents flow?
2. If you were drifting on a raft east of Florida, where might you end up?
3. Would you rather swim off the coast of California or off the coast of North Carolina? Explain your answer.

ASIA

NORTH

AMERICA

California

Equator

AUSTRALIA

In the Current Events activity on page B29, you made a current in the pan by using your hand. However, there are no giant hands in the oceans, pushing the water around. What *does* cause ocean currents?

Winds are one of the main causes. But these winds don't change direction and speed hour by hour or day by day, like the winds do where you live. Instead, they are steady, slow winds that follow the same paths most of the time. They cause surface currents in the oceans. So if you were drifting in the North Atlantic, you probably would be carried along by a current.

QUICK CHECK

LESSON 4 REVIEW

❶ What is the difference between waves and currents?

❷ In the Current Events activity, how was the movement of your hand similar to the wind blowing on an ocean?

EUROPE

North Carolina

Florida

AFRICA

SOUTH AMERICA

5 RIVERS: WATERWAYS TO THE OCEANS

Ships need water to get from place to place, so they can go only to places that are near oceans—right? Maybe. Maybe not. Find out in this lesson.

Gateways to the World

People built many of the world's greatest cities along rivers or at their mouths. Why do you think they built along rivers?

Rivers were natural highways long before artificial highways or railroads existed. What's more, rivers linked cities with the oceans. The oceans were the grandest highways of them all. After all, before the invention of airplanes, the oceans were major pathways between the world's continents.

Today rivers are still important links between seaports and communities far from the oceans. Tugboats pull barges up and down these rivers, hauling such resources as lumber, minerals, cotton, and manufactured goods back and forth.

▲ **Corn**

Tugboat and barges on the Mississippi River ▶

▲ Wheat

▲ Coal

B33

This map shows some of the major rivers in the United States.

1. If you were a tugboat captain, what rivers would you travel to take steel from Cincinnati, Ohio to Memphis, Tennessee?

2. You've got a load of lumber to ship from Bismarck, North Dakota, to New Orleans, Louisiana. But a storm has knocked out railroad bridges and roads between the two cities. Which rivers might you use to ship your lumber?

3. A ship loaded with cars is on its way from Germany to Albany, New York. The captain doesn't want to stop in New York City to transfer the cars to trucks or trains. How could the ship get to Albany?

Missouri River

Bismarck

Yellowstone River

Snake River

Platte River

Colorado River

Arkansas River

Gila River

Pecos River

Rio Grande River

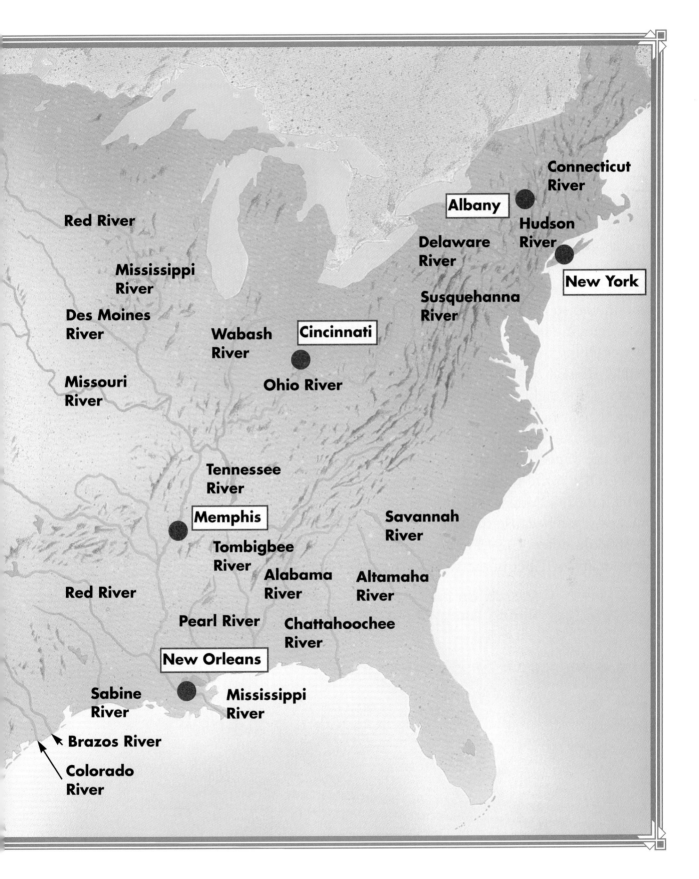

Red River

Mississippi River

Des Moines River

Missouri River

Wabash River

Cincinnati

Ohio River

Albany

Connecticut River

Delaware River

Hudson River

New York

Susquehanna River

Tennessee River

Memphis

Tombigbee River

Savannah River

Alabama River

Altamaha River

Red River

Pearl River

Chattahoochee River

New Orleans

Sabine River

Mississippi River

Brazos River

Colorado River

Rivers in Other Countries

On these two pages, you will read about Wong Yin-Chin and his life in Tibet. You will read about a river that is very important to him and to all the people of China.

Wong Yin-Chin once climbed high into the T'ang-ku-la Mountains in Tibet near where his family raises cattle. Up there it is very cold, and ice and snow are everywhere. Wong was tired after climbing up the mountain, so he stopped to rest. As he was catching his breath, he saw a drop of water falling from the pointed end of an icicle. He realized that the drop of water was his first sight of what is the third-largest river in the world.

People outside of China call this great river the Yangtze. But the Chinese call it the *Chang Jiang* (CHAHNG • ZHYAHNG), which means "long river." This name makes sense because the river winds 6,300 kilometers (3,915 miles) from the mountains of Tibet in the west to the East

Vessels on the Upper Chang Jiang, China ▶

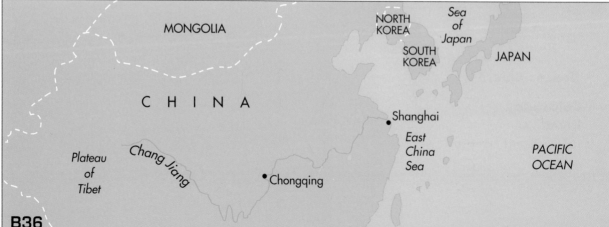

▲ **Grain barges at Wuhu, city on Chang Jiang, China**

China Sea. That's longer than the United States is wide. As the Chang Jiang snakes down through the mountains, it cuts through one of the most startling landscapes in the world. In the Szechwan province, the river rushes past natural stone towers that rise hundreds of meters above the tumbling waters. A bit farther on, it sweeps between two steep walls of rock that rise equally high.

But the Chang Jiang is more than a beautiful ribbon of water. It is China's biggest liquid highway. Ships and boats of all kinds carry goods up and down the river. Some of the vessels go from one port to another inside China. Others bring in cargo from foreign countries. Still others carry goods like rice, coal, copper, gold, and oil from Chinese cities to the ocean and then to countries around the world.

QUICK CHECK

LESSON 5 REVIEW

Many cities and towns in the United States are on or near rivers. Choose a river that is near where you live. Write a paragraph telling how it is the same as or different from the Chang Jiang.

✔ DOUBLE CHECK

SECTION A REVIEW

1. Draw a circle. Write the word *OCEANS* in the circle. Draw lines from the circle, and write words or sentences next to the lines to show what you have learned in this section about oceans.

2. In your own words, write a paragraph, poem, or song that answers the following question: What is an ocean?

What Lives in Coastal Waters?

▲ **Portland Head lighthouse, Cape Elizabeth, Maine**

If you were to sail down the East Coast of the United States, you would see great changes in scenery. You might watch crashing waves on the rocky shore of Maine. Between Maryland and Virginia, you might see the choppy waters of Chesapeake Bay. In Florida, you might spot the still waters of a mangrove swamp. Although these areas are very different from each other, they are also alike in some ways. Their waters are shallow and salty, and they are home to many different kinds of plants and animals.

Why are these different areas so rich with life? What kinds of things live there? You'll find answers to these questions as you do the following investigations. Keep notes about your discoveries in your Science Log.

1 EXPLORING ESTUARIES

You know that ocean water is salty and that the water in most rivers and lakes is not salty. The fresh water in some rivers flows into the salt water of the ocean. What happens when the fresh water and the salt water mix?

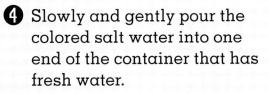

Mixed-Up Water

This activity will help you see what happens when salt water and fresh water mix.

DO THIS

 1 Put tap water into the plastic container until it is half full. This is fresh water.

2 Make salt water in the measuring cup. Get a cupful of tap water. Add a few spoonfuls of salt to it.

3 Stir the solution to dissolve the salt. Add food coloring to the salt water.

4 Slowly and gently pour the colored salt water into one end of the container that has fresh water.

5 Observe what happens, and record your observations.

MATERIALS

- tap water
- clear plastic container
- measuring cup
- salt
- spoon
- food coloring
- Science Log data sheet

THINK AND WRITE

Diagram what happened to the salt water when you poured it into the fresh water. What does this tell you about what happens where a river meets an ocean?

The Amazon River

The place where fresh water in a river mixes with salt water in an ocean is called an *estuary* (ES tyoo er ee). Rivers form estuaries where they meet the ocean. The Chesapeake Bay in Virginia and Maryland is an estuary. The mouth of the Amazon River in South America is a huge estuary.

The estuary of the Amazon River is on the north coast of Brazil, at the Atlantic Ocean. More fresh water pours into the ocean from this river than from any other river on Earth.

▲ **Giant Amazon water lily**

Many unusual plants and animals live in and around the Amazon. Water lilies the size of mattresses float on its waters.

The largest snake in the world, the anaconda, hides in the Amazon's waters. It can be over 9 meters (30 feet) long.

Mouth of the Amazon River ▶

▲ **Anaconda snake**

The strongest bird of prey in the world, the harpy eagle, soars over the Amazon's banks.

The biggest rodent on our planet, the capybara, suns its 50-kilogram (110-pound) body on the shore.

THINK ABOUT IT

What is an estuary?

Harpy eagle ▶

▲ **Herd of capybaras (kap ih BAHR uhs)**

Let's Explore an Estuary

The world is full of estuaries. They're not quite like oceans. They're not quite like lakes. And they're often very different from each other. What makes estuaries different? How do the differences affect the kinds of things that live in them?

Pass the Salt

If you have ever visited an ocean shore, you may have observed that the water is farther up on the shore at some times and farther down at other times. This change in ocean water levels is caused by the *tide.* When the tide comes in, ocean water moves into an estuary. So all the water in the estuary becomes saltier. When the tide goes out, water rushes back into the ocean. River water moves in, and all the water in the estuary becomes less salty.

In spring, when snow melts and rainfall is heavy, an estuary becomes less salty. If there is a long, dry hot spell, an estuary becomes more salty. This happens because in dry weather, water evaporates from the estuary, leaving the salt behind. The amount of salt in an estuary changes all the time.

▲ **High tide at Chesapeake Bay, Sandy Point, Maryland**

▲ **Low tide at Chesapeake Bay, Sandy Point, Maryland**

Mix 'em Up

The saltiness also varies in different parts of an estuary. In the Mixed-Up Water activity on page B39, you found that salt water sinks below fresh water. When ocean water enters an estuary, it slips under the fresh river water. So the muddy bottom of an estuary tends to be more salty than the surface.

As fresh water moves out of an estuary and salt water moves in, they slide against each other. This makes the water swirl in little up-and-down currents. The currents move salty water up and fresh water down. This reduces the difference in saltiness between the top and the bottom.

Life in an Estuary

What characteristics do plants and animals that live in an estuary need to have? Think about the water in an estuary. The salt content changes often. Therefore, animals and plants that live there must be adapted to life in water that doesn't always contain the same amount of salt. Are there animals and plants that have these adaptations? Yes!

Clams and oysters live on the bottom of estuaries. They can suck up the rich mud, filter out the nutrients, and pass the remainder through their bodies.

▲ Blue crabs live in estuaries.

The gray mullet is a fish that feeds on the algae in estuaries. It takes in the mud and mixes this in its thick-walled, muscular stomach. There, particles of food are removed and digested.

Plants like marsh grass, eel grass, and all sorts of algae grow in estuaries. Cord grass, also known as *spartina,* has an important role in estuaries. It grows quickly in the shifting mud. Because its roots hold the mud in position, materials on the bottom of the estuary can build up. These materials may eventually form mud flats or salt marshes as other plants begin to take hold and grow.

▲ Birds skim over the water.

Menhaden ▶

▲ Grasses grow at the edge of estuaries.

Sea birds make their nests in the grasses and swoop over the water in search of a seafood meal. The meal might be the young of a fish called *menhaden* (men HAYD uhn). Although these fish are hatched in the ocean, they spend part of their early days in estuaries, as other young fish do, also. That's why scientists often refer to estuaries as nurseries.

LESSON 1 REVIEW

The saltiness of estuary water changes. What things happen that make the saltiness change? Compare the effects of these things on the fish and the grasses.

2 TIDAL COMMUNITIES

Suppose you had to live half your life under water and half above water. You'd have to make some enormous changes. This is what plants and animals on the shores of the ocean do every day. How do they survive, and what dangers do they face?

ACTIVITY

Changing Pools

When the tide goes out, ocean water remains in hollowed-out parts of rocks and in low places in the sand. Each hollow is left with a little pool. These pools are called *tidal pools*. Small plants and animals live in them. How do living conditions in tidal pools change as the tide moves in and out?

DO THIS

❶ Put each ice cube tray in an aluminum pan, with the "cups" facing up.

❷ Measure and record the temperature of the cold salt water.

❸ Fill one pan with cold salt water. The water should be at least a few centimeters over the top of the tray.

B46

Add cold salt water only to the cups in the second ice cube tray. The pan should not have any water in it.

 Place both pans in direct sunlight or in a warm spot in your classroom.

 Every 10 minutes, for 30 minutes, find the temperature in the cups in each tray. Record the temperatures.

THINK AND WRITE

1. In what ways did this investigation model the way the ocean goes in and out?

2. How did the temperature vary in step 6? What would this variation mean to animals living in a tidal pool?

3. **FORMULATING AND USING MODELS** In this investigation, you made a model of a tidal pool. The model represented two conditions in nature. What were those two conditions?

ACTIVITY

Wet Barnacle

Barnacles are animals with shells. Barnacles do not move around. Instead, they attach themselves to anything solid, such as rocks. When the tide goes out, the barnacles are exposed to the air, but they don't dry out. Why do you think this is so?

DO THIS

❶ Fold one napkin in half four times. Put a rubber band around it to keep it folded.

❷ Use the measuring cup to pour the same amount of water on the folded and the unfolded napkins. Spread the water evenly over each napkin. Pour the water in small amounts so that none drips off.

❸ Place the folded napkin on one side of the balance. Drape the unfolded napkin over the other side.

❹ Observe the balance over a period of a few hours. Record your observations.

THINK AND WRITE

1. What happened to the balance?

2. Why do you think this happened?

3. Look at the picture of the barnacles. In what way was the folded napkin like a barnacle?

4. How do you think the shape of a barnacle helps it survive during low tides?

5. **FORMULATING AND USING MODELS** In this investigation, you used napkins to make two models. Which napkin represented a barnacle? How was the shape of the napkin like the shape of a barnacle? Was this a good model? Why or why not?

Beachcombing

You just made a model of a barnacle. Now you will be able to read about barnacles and other animals that live along the ocean shore.

Todd and his aunt Joan loved to explore the Oregon coast. They watched the waves of the Pacific Ocean sweep over the rocky shore. In some places, the waves dashed into great bowls that waves had worn in the rocks. White foam flew into the air. The spray hit rocks that not even the highest tide could reach.

The rocks on the shore were the habitats of many small animals. Todd and Aunt Joan spotted a group of snails huddled together between two smooth, gray rocks. The snails needed a little moisture to live. All of a sudden, a fine, gentle spray fell on the snails. Off they went in search of a meal.

Todd and Aunt Joan watched the tide gradually go out. As it did, they climbed down the rocks, toward the ocean. They walked carefully because they didn't want to step on the barnacles and mussels that clung to the rocks in thick bunches.

A group of snails ▶

▲ **Climbing over rocks at the Oregon coast**

Many of the mussel shells were empty. Aunt Joan asked Todd if he could figure out why this was so. He bent down to get a better look at the shells. Todd saw that they had little holes in them. He guessed that some animal must have drilled into the mussel shells and sucked out the meat inside. Todd was right. Aunt Joan told him that meat-eating snails called *whelks* feed on mussels. Todd had eaten mussels at his aunt's house, but the mussels had been cooked and served in a spicy tomato sauce.

▲ **Blue mussel shells**

A moving shell caught Todd's eye. Something is wrong, thought Todd to himself. That whelk is moving too fast. Todd quickly figured out why the shell was so speedy. It didn't have a slow-moving whelk inside it. Instead, the shell had become the mobile home of a hermit crab. The shell provided extra protection against predators, such as sea birds.

▲ **Hermit crab in a whelk shell**

The tide kept moving out. Todd and Aunt Joan kept following it. A garden of sea palms appeared as the ocean backed away from the land. This green seaweed came up only to their ankles. The plants did look a little like tiny palm trees, though they were not nearly as tall. The movement of the tides and even the pounding of the waves hadn't knocked the sea palms off the rocks.

▲ **Sea palms**

The stalks of the sea palms bent without breaking, and their bottoms gripped the rocks tightly.

A pink sea spider crept out from under a sea palm. This made Todd and Aunt Joan look for another animal that lived on this part of the shore, a sea anemone (uh NEM uh nee). Sea anemones had to be nearby because they are one of the things sea spiders eat.

Within seconds Todd found a purple sea anemone resting in the water of a tidal pool. Its poisonous tentacles floated lazily in the water. Sea spiders that shared the tidal pool were not harmed by the anemone's stinging tentacles. Maybe a sea spider's hard outer skeleton provides it with enough protection, thought Todd.

Eventually, the tide reached its lowest point. Now a whole new community of living things came into view. A red starfish inched across the glistening rocks and dipped into a tidal pool in search of a clam. If the starfish found its prey, it would wrap its arms around the clam's shell and pull. The pull would pry open the shell. Then the starfish would have a meal.

▲ Sea spider

Sea anemone ▶

▲ Red starfish eating an oyster

Looking like black pincushions, animals called *sea urchins* crowded into cracks between the rocks. Although Todd and Aunt Joan were wearing tough shoes, the thought of stepping barefoot on a sea urchin's spines made them shiver. Like the two humans, animals in the water usually stay clear of sea urchins' spines.

As Todd and Aunt Joan watched the sea urchins, a wave splashed on Todd's shoes, reminding him that what goes out comes back in. The tide had turned, and it was time to leave the shore for home.

QUICK CHECK

LESSON 2 REVIEW

Describe how animals are adapted to living in tidal communities.

▲ **Black sea urchins on a reef at low tide**

3 MANGROVE SWAMPS

You may never have seen a tree growing in the ocean. But some trees do grow in ocean water. These trees are called *mangroves.* Mangroves grow along the coasts of southern Florida and of northern South America and West Africa. Mangroves also grow along the coast of Australia. How do mangrove trees survive in ocean water? How do they change the land? What kinds of animals and plants live among mangrove trees? Hunt down the answers to these questions.

ACTIVITY

Mangrove Seed Mystery

Most of the trees you know about drop their seeds on soil. There the seeds can sprout and grow into new trees. Mangrove seeds sprout from the soil, too, though the soil is under water. However, mangrove seeds don't fall through the water to the soil beneath. They float. So how do you think the seeds find their way to the soil? You might learn the answer by first making and then investigating a model of a mangrove seed.

▲ **Mangrove seeds**

DO THIS

1 Seal both ends of the plastic straw with the tape. Place a small ball of clay on one end of the straw. The straw must be watertight.

2 Pile the aquarium gravel on one side of the pan until it is about 2 centimeters from the top. Slowly pour in the water on the side where there is no gravel. Do not cover the gravel completely. A small amount of gravel should stick up out of the water.

3 Place the straw "mangrove seed" clay-end first into the water, away from the gravel.

4 Without touching the mangrove seed, try doing different things to move it toward the gravel.

THINK AND WRITE

1. Describe the behavior of the seed in the water.

2. How might mangrove seeds in a real mangrove swamp reach the soil?

3. FORMULATING AND USING MODELS In this investigation, you explored how the seeds of mangrove trees find places to sprout. How was your straw mangrove seed like a real mangrove seed? How was it different? Was the pan a good model of a mangrove swamp? Why or why not?

Looking Ahead Now turn the page to read about a real mangrove forest in Australia. As you read, think about the activity you just did.

MATERIALS
- plastic straw, cut into 6.5-cm pieces
- transparent tape
- modeling clay
- aluminum pan
- aquarium gravel
- pitcher
- water
- Science Log data sheet

AN AUSTRALIAN MANGROVE FOREST

by **Rebecca L. Johnson**

from *The Great Barrier Reef: A Living Laboratory*

LITERATURE A mangrove forest is different from any other kind of forest on Earth. Right now the tide is out. The sea has drained away from around the bottoms of the trees, and their roots are exposed. Mangrove trees have some roots that grow *above* the ground. When the tide is high, these roots are covered by water. But at low tide, the trees look as if they are standing on a tangled mass of spindly legs.

The ground looks firm, but as you step out of the boat, you sink deep into mud. Lots of mud. Soft, gooey, black mud that smells terrible. You take another step and sink even deeper. As you lift your foot to try again, your shoe nearly stays behind in the black muck below. You will never get anywhere this way. So you do what the scientists who work in the mangroves do—you walk on the roots of the mangrove trees!

Above your head are the green, leafy tops of the mangrove trees.

▲ Close-up of a mangrove tree

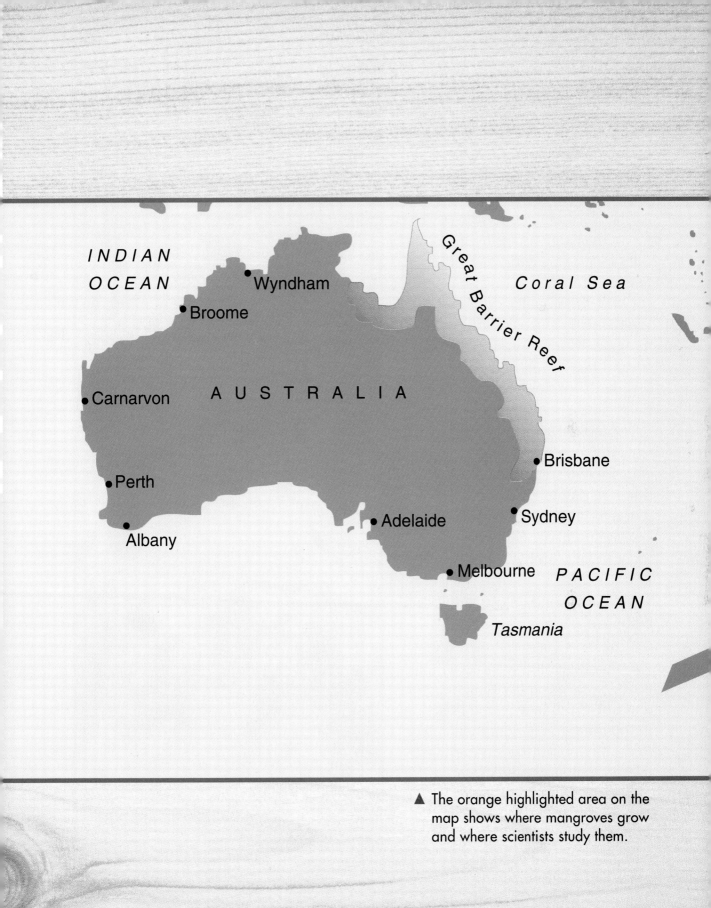

INDIAN
OCEAN

• Wyndham

• Broome

Great Barrier Reef

Coral Sea

• Carnarvon

A U S T R A L I A

• Perth

Albany

• Adelaide

• Brisbane

• Sydney

• Melbourne

PACIFIC
OCEAN

Tasmania

▲ The orange highlighted area on the
map shows where mangroves grow
and where scientists study them.

They are so close together that they cut out much of the sunlight, but it is still very hot and humid in the forest. Moving up and down the trunks of the trees are ants and beetles and other insects. Spiders have spun strong webs between some of the trees. Huge wasps fly in and out of a nest hanging beneath a twisted branch.

Off in the distance, you can see the dark shapes of fruit bats hanging from the branches of several trees. Fruit bats hang upside down from tree branches during the day. They are supposed to be resting. But instead they screech and squawk and squabble with each other all day long. At sunset, when the light fades from the sky, the fruit bats will fly off together in search of ripe fruit to eat.

On the ground below, small crabs are scurrying around, darting here and there across the mud beneath the tangled roots. Some keep popping in and out of the little round holes in the mud that lead to their underground burrows. When the tide comes in, the crabs will disappear down these holes. The muddy ground and the roots you are now standing on will gradually be covered by sea water. With the water will

▲ **Fruit bats hanging from mangrove branches**

come other kinds of animals. Smooth, flat rays will appear, to dig for food in the soft mud. Tiny fish will arrive by the thousands.

As you stand perched on the mangrove roots, you notice something else going on in the forest. A yellow mangrove leaf falls from a tree and drifts past your face. A moment later, another one lands on your head. Suddenly you realize that everywhere around you, leaves are falling from the branches of the mangrove trees.

What happens to all the leaves that constantly rain down from the branches of the mangrove trees? Each time the tide goes out and the water retreats, some of the fallen leaves wash out to sea. They are gone before they have a chance to rot and return their nutrients to the forest floor.

▲ **Mangrove leaves and seeds**

Mangrove forest on the northeastern coast of Australia ▼

Alistar Robertson is an Australian scientist who studies mangroves in tropical places such as the northeastern tip of Australia and Papua New Guinea. Alistar began his research with some simple experiments. For one experiment, he collected fallen mangrove leaves and put some into mesh bags. He tied strings to a number of individual leaves and secured the other ends of the strings to mangrove roots.

▲ **Mangrove forest crab**

Several days later, when he came back to check on his experiment, the leaves that had been tied with strings were gone. When Alistar followed the strings, he found that each one disappeared down a small hole in the mud. These holes looked like the entrances to the underground burrows of crabs. Could crabs have taken the leaves underground and eaten them?

Scientist Alistar Robertson at work in the mangrove forest ▶

To find out, Alistar tied more leaves to strings and then simply watched and waited. It wasn't long before the "thieves" appeared. They *were* crabs!

After doing some additional experiments, Alistar and other scientists learned that these little crabs play a remarkably important role in the mangrove forests. Crabs collect at least a third of all the mangrove leaves that fall to the forest floor.

What's more, leaves carried underground rot faster than those left on the surface. When the leaves are eaten, the nutrients they contain return to the soil especially fast, since it doesn't take long for crab wastes to break up and decay. Because of the crabs, nutrients that would otherwise be lost from the mangrove forest are returned to the soil so that the trees can reuse them again and again.

LESSON 3 REVIEW

1 Tell how a mangrove forest is unusual.

2 Tell how crabs keep a mangrove forest healthy.

DOUBLE CHECK

SECTION B REVIEW

1. Make a chart that explains how estuaries, tidal areas, and mangrove swamps are similar to and different from one another.

2. The title of this section is "What Lives in Coastal Waters?" Write a paragraph to answer that question. In your paragraph, include descriptions of the plants and animals that live in coastal waters and their adaptations.

SECTION C
Oil Spill

▲ Oil tanker

▲ Alaska pipeline

When you hear the word *oil,* you probably think of a liquid that people put in cars. But the word *oil* describes several things. One of these is the material taken from the ground or from under the ocean by drilling.

This oil is also called *petroleum.* The oil in a car is made from it. In this section, the word *oil* will mean "petroleum."

Oil is important, but sometimes getting it to where people can use it is a problem. Where do we get oil? How does it get to where we need it? What can happen to it as we move it from place to place?

In this section, you'll investigate these questions and others. In your Science Log, write about what you discover.

1 GETTING AND USING OIL

Our lives would be very different if we did not have oil products. In this lesson, you will learn about the ways we get oil and the many uses of oil. As you read about how much we depend on oil, think how your own life would be different without it.

Where Does Oil Come From?

You can buy oil in cans at a gas station or auto parts store. How did it get there? Read on to find out.

Oil lies deep in the ground in different places on Earth. Although there is a great deal of oil under the ground in the United States, we use more than we produce. So the United States imports, or brings in, some oil from other countries.

As you can see on the map, many oil-rich countries lie far away from the United States. There often is an ocean or other large body of water between an oil-rich country and our own. Look at the map carefully. You can see **tankers,** or oil-carrying ships, next to some countries. The bigger the tanker symbol, the more oil we import from that country.

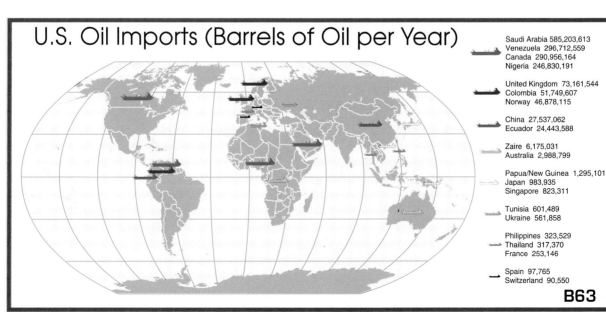

U.S. Oil Imports (Barrels of Oil per Year)

Saudi Arabia 585,203,613
Venezuela 296,712,559
Canada 290,956,164
Nigeria 246,830,191

United Kingdom 73,161,544
Colombia 51,749,607
Norway 46,878,115

China 27,537,062
Ecuador 24,443,588

Zaire 6,175,031
Australia 2,988,799

Papua/New Guinea 1,295,101
Japan 983,935
Singapore 823,311

Tunisia 601,489
Ukraine 561,858

Philippines 323,529
Thailand 317,370
France 253,146

Spain 97,765
Switzerland 90,550

B63

Oil on the Move

There are two main ways to move oil from one place to another. One way is over land through pipes. This is how oil gets from wells in northern Alaska to seaports on Alaska's southwest coast.

▲ This cutaway view of an oil tanker shows where oil is stored.

◀ Tanker loading oil

Most of the oil taken from the ground, however, is moved on tankers. Some of these ships are so huge that they're called **supertankers.** Supertankers can be longer than three football fields. They can carry more than 200 million liters (53 million gallons) of oil across the ocean.

If all the oil carried by a supertanker were put into barrels and the barrels were laid end to end, they would reach from Seattle, Washington, almost to San Francisco, California! ▶

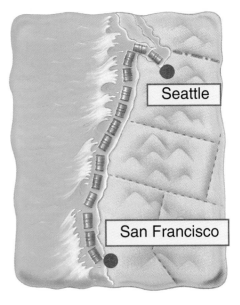

Seattle

San Francisco

A barrel is the liquid unit of measurement for oil. It is equal to about 160 liters (about 42 gallons). Altogether, more than 7,000 tankers, big and small, move more than one trillion liters (264 billion gallons) of oil every year.

Unfortunately, some of that oil gets dumped into the ocean when tankers have accidents. The oil spreads over the water and, as you will soon discover, may cause great harm.

THINK ABOUT IT

Describe the two ways oil can be transported.

▲ Caribou grazing on the tundra next to the Alaska pipeline

How Oil Is Used

Now you know where oil comes from. But how do people use oil? Read on and look at the photographs. You may be surprised.

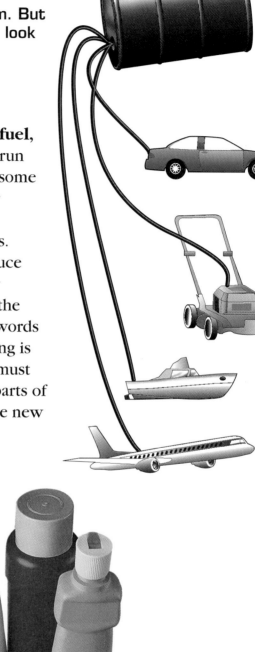

When you go to the gas station, the person you're with pumps gasoline, a **fuel,** into the car's tank. The fuel is used to run the engine. Look at the picture to see some of the ways fuels are used. What other things use fuel to make them run?

Oil is a mixture of different materials. Some materials in oil are used to produce plastics that can be made into cloth or molded into different shapes. Look at the labels in your clothing. If you see the words *polyester*, *nylon*, or *acrylic*, the clothing is made from oil. Sometimes physicians must operate on people to replace certain parts of the body that don't work anymore. The new parts they put in are often artificial. The plastic in these parts, such as heart valves or hip replacement joints, may be made from oil.

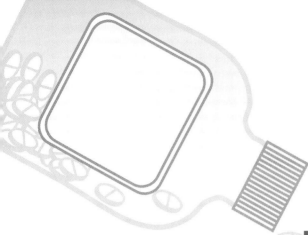

The next time you catch a cold or get an infection, your parents may give you a medicine that is made from oil. The colors in your school flag probably come from dyes made from oil. There are all kinds of materials made from oil in the paints that decorate houses and protect them from the weather.

There is oil in paints such as these. ▶

Dyes, such as the ones from this textile dye machine, are used to color fabrics. ▼

QUICK CHECK

LESSON 1 REVIEW

❶ Why must some countries import oil?

❷ Why does much of the oil used in the United States have to come by tanker?

❸ How is oil important to you?

This is the story of how an accident at sea caused one of the worst oil spills in American history.

SPILL!

by **Terry Carr**
from **Spill! THE STORY OF THE EXXON VALDEZ**

Collision

LITERATURE On the windless night of March 23, 1989, a light snowy mist settled over Port Valdez on Alaska's southern coast. From the town of Valdez, snuggled deep in the port, the lights of boats on the water hung like faint twinkles in the haze. The people of Valdez were turning in for the night.

Across the water from Valdez, at the Valdez pipeline terminal, the job of loading the oil tanker *Exxon Valdez* ended. About 53 million gallons of oil had been pumped into the huge vessel.

At 9:26 P.M., the *Exxon Valdez* pulled away from the pipeline terminal. The plan was to steam south away from Alaska, travel along the western coasts of Canada and the United States, and deliver the oil to Long Beach, California.

The tanker was under the command of Captain Joseph Hazelwood. The *Exxon Valdez* is among the largest vessels on water anywhere. Almost a thousand feet (304 m) long, it plows the water with tremendous force.

Tankers loading oil at the pipeline terminal in Port Valdez ▶

B69

While moving at her top speed of about 15 miles (24 km) an hour, the ship takes 3 miles (4.8 km) to stop.

A little over an hour after leaving the pipeline terminal, the *Exxon Valdez* passed through Valdez Narrows. This narrow opening connects Port Valdez with Prince William Sound.

The tanker route through the Sound is like a divided highway. The lane on one side is for ships traveling south. The other lane is for northbound ships. A separation zone, a sort of median strip, divides the two lanes. When Captain Hazelwood reported that he was changing course because of floating ice, he meant he was going to swing left across the separation zone to the other lane. The Coast Guard radioed that no other tankers were on the "highway," so it was all right for the *Exxon Valdez* to cross the zone.

Ice that has broken off from the Columbia Glacier and drifted into the Sound ▶

Icebergs are formed when ice breaks off from a glacier in a process called *calving.* ▼

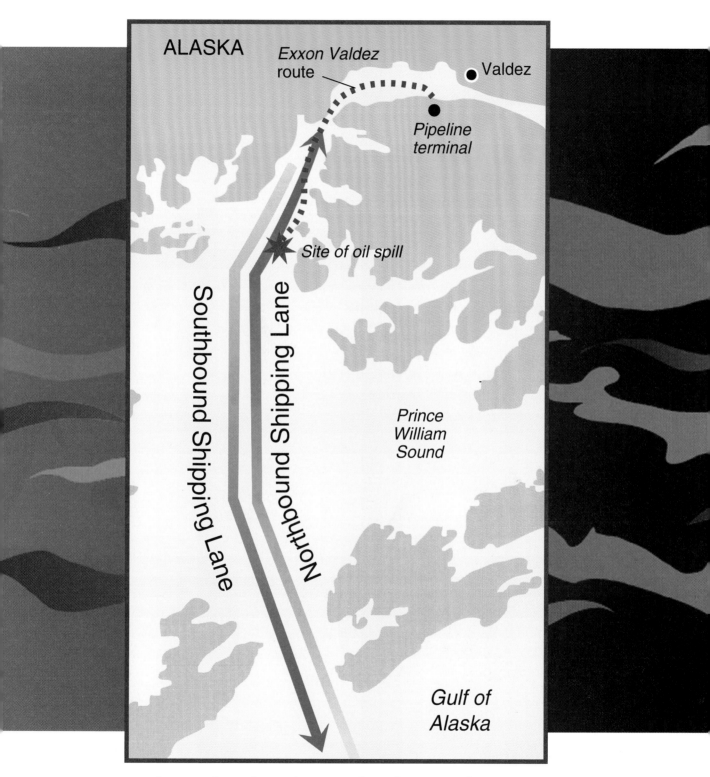

ALASKA

Exxon Valdez route

Valdez

Pipeline terminal

Site of oil spill

Southbound Shipping Lane

Northbound Shipping Lane

Prince William Sound

Gulf of Alaska

▲ This map shows that tanker routes through Prince William Sound are like a divided highway.

In the tanker's control room, Captain Hazelwood instructed his third mate, Gregory Cousins, to steer the tanker back into the correct shipping lane once the tanker reached Busby Island. Then the captain went below to his cabin. A few minutes later, Third Mate Cousins gave the order to the helmsman, who steers the vessel, to turn the tanker to the right. This turn would begin taking the ship back into the correct shipping lane. Another few minutes passed. Third Mate Cousins gave the order for another turn.

Something was seriously wrong. The vessel was not turning sharply enough. Either Third Mate Cousins had given the orders to turn too late, the helmsman had not carried out the command properly, or something was wrong with the way the ship was responding.

It was now about midnight. The tanker had crossed the other lane and was heading toward a submerged rock called Bligh Reef. On deck the tanker's lookout warned that the light marking Bligh Reef was to the right of the tanker, not to the left, where it would be if the ship was in safe water.

The tanker was turning, but it was too late. The third mate phoned Captain Hazelwood, who was still in his cabin, telling him, "I think we're in serious trouble." Immediately after he said the words, those aboard felt the first impact of the tanker with Bligh Reef. It was 12:04 A.M., Friday, March 24, 1989.

The tremendous impact of the tanker hitting the reef ripped open her steel cargo holds as if they were plastic. Tons of oil poured out, so fast and with such force that it created a wave of oil three feet high on the water.

▲ Closeup of the rip in the hull of the *Exxon Valdez*

Once in the water, the oil fanned out, spreading like thick black ink in a bathtub.

In all, 11 million gallons of crude oil bled from the tanker into the waters of Prince William Sound. By the time the leaking stopped, it became the worst oil tanker catastrophe in American history.

THINK ABOUT IT

What conditions were present that help explain the *Exxon Valdez* accident?

The *Exxon Valdez* pinned on Bligh Reef and pouring oil into the sound

ACTIVITY

What Happens When Oil Spills in Water?

Why is an oil spill a disaster? You can begin to answer this question by exploring how oil acts in water.

MATERIALS

• clear plastic container
• water
• self-sealing plastic bag
• vegetable oil
• spoon
• Science Log data sheet

DO THIS

❶ Fill the plastic container with water.

❷ Put some vegetable oil in the plastic bag, and close the bag tightly. Place the bag in the water.

❸ Open a corner of the bag so oil escapes into the water.

❹ Observe what the oil does, and record your observations. Make drawings of what happens to the oil.

❺ Stir the water gently. The stirring represents currents in the water. Observe what the oil does, and record your observations. Make new drawings of what happens to the oil. How do the drawings compare with your first set?

THINK AND WRITE

1. Describe what the vegetable oil did as it entered the water.

2. How is the investigation you just did similar to the *Exxon Valdez* accident?

3. **INFERRING** When you use your observations to reach a conclusion, you're inferring. You can make an inference about an oil spill by using the data from the activity. Look at the information you recorded and the drawings you made. What inferences can you make about tankers and oil spills?

LESSON 2 REVIEW

❶ What happens when oil tankers have accidents?

❷ Make a list of problems you think there would be in cleaning up an oil spill.

3 AFTER THE SPILL

Ocean plants and animals live in or near water. They feed in it. They move around in it and on it. But as you discovered in the last lesson, oil is very different from water.

After an oil spill, oil sticks to the feathers of birds, making the birds so heavy that they can't fly. When birds try to clean oil off their feathers, it gets stuck in their beaks. Oil seeps into the fur of sea otters, so they can't stay warm in icy water. And fish swallow oil, which, unlike vegetable oil, is made of materials that are poisonous.

An oil spill is a deadly event. People are needed to help clean up when oil has spilled into the ocean.

▲ **Western grebe soaked in oil**

Oil-covered otter ▶

▸ Villagers clean an oil-covered beach

THINK ABOUT IT

How can people help clean up oil spills?

ACTIVITY

Cleaning Up an Oil Spill

Oil spills happen. When they do, they have to be cleaned up. What's one way to clean up oil? This investigation will help you reach your own conclusions.

DO THIS

1. Label the bowls *A*, *B*, and *C*.

2. Add water to the same depth in each bowl.

3. Add a large spoonful of vegetable oil to each bowl. Observe and record what the oil looks like.

4. Add a small spoonful of liquid dishwashing detergent to bowl B. Stir and let stand.

5. Add the same amount of detergent to bowl C. Do not stir.

Compare bowls A, B, and C. Write your observations. Make a data table to organize your results. Share your results with your classmates.

THINK AND WRITE

1. How did the detergent affect the way the oil looked in bowls B and C?

2. Suppose detergents were used to clean up an oil spill in the ocean. Would a strong wind help or work against the cleanup?

3. **COMMUNICATING** In the activity, how did you record your observations? How did you communicate your findings? What did you discover about communicating?

Looking Ahead Now you will read about some people who volunteered their time to help clean oil off animals. These animals were caught in the *Exxon Valdez* oil spill.

▲ **Worker using detergent to clean up oil from the *Exxon Valdez* oil spill**

Volunteers to the Rescue

by **Terry Carr**

from **Spill! The Story of the *Exxon Valdez***

LITERATURE Animal rescue workers from all over the world poured into Valdez. Many came as volunteers.

These people quickly set up bird and otter rescue centers. They spent hours out on the water, trying to capture the animals and bring them in for cleaning.

It was a difficult and sad fight. The workers could help only a tiny number of the creatures harmed by the oil. Still, they worked night and day, sometimes without stopping.

It took hours to clean a single bird. First, workers gently scrubbed it with soap and toothbrushes. They used Water Piks, which squirt tiny jets of water and are normally used to clean teeth, to wash around its eyes. Once washed, the bird would be dried and then, if necessary, washed again. The washing-drying-washing cycle might be repeated three or four times before a bird was clean enough to be released to the wild.

Otters presented even more problems than the birds. Bigger and stronger, they were harder to catch. Several even bit people trying to rescue them. They were also more difficult to clean. Workers would spend hours trying to scrub the oil off a single animal. Otters got the same wash-dry-wash treatment as the birds.

Plywood cages were built to hold the otters while they were being cleaned and treated. Many of the animals were very sick. They lay helplessly in their cages. Some shivered constantly. Some didn't move at all. The oil's poisons damaged the otters' lungs, stomachs, and livers. Half the otters treated during the first weeks of the spill died anyway. But, during the first summer, 348 otters were treated at the centers and 226 of them were saved.

THINK ABOUT IT

Volunteers are people who give of their time without being paid. Why do you think people volunteered to help clean the birds and otters who had been caught in the spilled oil?

▲ Volunteers at the Otter Rescue Center wash otters two weeks after the *Exxon Valdez* oil spill.

ACTIVITY

A Feathery Mess

This investigation will give you some idea of how an oil spill can affect birds.

DO THIS

1 Work with a partner.

2 Look at the feather carefully without the hand lens. Then use the hand lens to observe the feather. Record your observations.

3 Fill a container halfway with water. Dip the feather into the water. Place the feather on a paper towel. Observe the feather without the hand lens and with it. Write what you observe.

4 Pour some cooking oil into the other container. Dip the feather in the oil. Place the feather on a paper towel. Observe the feather without the hand lens and with it. Write what you observe.

THINK AND WRITE

1. What happened when you dipped the feather into the water?

2. What happened when you dipped the feather into the oil?

3. How might oil on birds' feathers affect them?

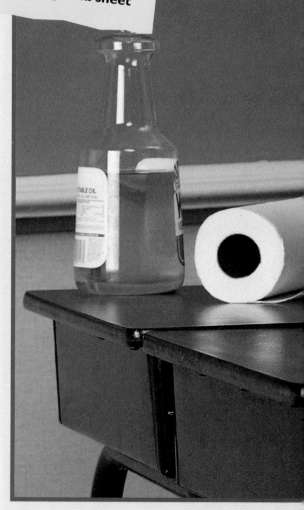

MATERIALS

• feather
• hand lens
• 2 clear plastic bowls
• water
• paper towels
• cooking oil
• Science Log data sheet

LESSON 3 REVIEW

1 Discuss how oil spills endanger living things.

2 What can be done to rescue animals covered with oil?

4 PREVENTING SPILLS

No one has a perfect solution on how to stop tankers from having accidents. Every now and then, a tanker is going to run into a reef or perhaps another ship. The tanker's hull, its metal outer shell, may rip open. If this happens, oil will come gushing out of most tankers, and the result will be a great natural disaster. This is exactly what happened in the case of the *Exxon Valdez.*

Safety at Sea

You have seen that an oil spill causes serious problems. There are ways to make transporting oil safer. In the following activity, you'll have a chance to investigate this as you make a model of a tanker and an oil spill.

MATERIALS
- clear plastic container
- water
- 2 different sized self-sealing plastic bags
- vegetable oil
- straightened paper clip
- Science Log data sheet

DO THIS

❶ Fill the container with water.

❷ Fill the smaller of the plastic bags with vegetable oil, and close the bag tightly.

❸ Put the oil-filled bag inside the larger bag. Blow as much air as you can into the second bag, and then seal it quickly.

❹ Place the bags in the water. Use the paper clip to make a hole in the outer bag of the "tanker." What happens?

❺ Jab the paper clip into the bags to make holes in both of them. Wait a few minutes. Record your observations.

Two Hulls Are Better Than One

To make hauling oil safer, engineers have designed tankers with two hulls. These ships are similar to the model you made in the activity.

Tankers that are made with two shells of metal and an air space in between are called double-hulled tankers. If a double-hulled tanker hits something, there is a good chance that only the outer hull will break open. The inner hull may not be damaged, so the oil would be safely contained.

Double-hulled tankers have been crisscrossing the oceans for more than 20 years. However, for every double-hulled tanker on the sea, there are still about six tankers that have only a single hull.

Outer hull   Inner hull

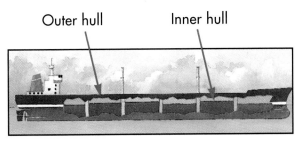

▲ This cutaway view shows you the two hulls of a double-hulled tanker.

THINK AND WRITE

1. How was the air between the bags useful?

2. Are there any advantages to a "double-hulled" tanker when both hulls are damaged? Explain.

THINK ABOUT IT

What is the advantage of double-hulled tankers?

Margarita Colmenares
She Helps Keep the Environment Clean

You've just read about an oil spill and the people who helped clean it up. The oceans are just one part of the environment that must be kept clean.

The air we breathe and the soil under our feet are also important parts of the environment. What can be done to improve the air we breathe? How can harmful materials be thrown away without harming the environment?

These are some of the questions Margarita Colmenares tries to answer. She is an environmental engineer.

When Colmenares started college, she discovered engineering by accident. She had planned on studying business. But engineering was more challenging to her. During college she began to work part time for a water resources company. She put on a hard hat and boots to inspect dams and water-pumping plants. Colmenares says this job was good experience. It gave her the chance to apply what she learned in class to real life.

After college Colmenares started her engineering career with an oil company. One of the jobs she had was to lead an environmental

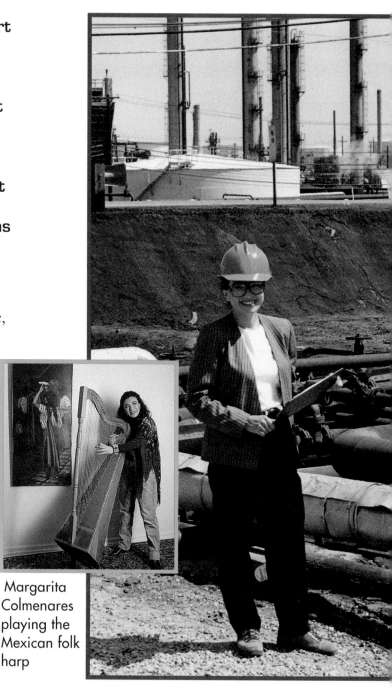

▲ Margarita Colmenares playing the Mexican folk harp

▲ Margarita Colmenares on a job site

cleanup project at an oil refinery. A refinery is a factory where chemicals are made from oil. The chemicals are then used to make products such as gasoline, jet fuel, grease, and wax.

Colmenares helped design a plan for the removal of gasoline from the water and the soil underneath the refinery. In addition, she helped put together the plan to reduce air pollution from the refinery furnaces.

Margarita Colmenares has many interests. She was the first woman elected as president of the Society of Hispanic Professional Engineers. She has also taught and performed in Mexican folk-dance groups and is learning how to play a Mexican folk harp. Colmenares has always found a way to balance work and play!

One of her great interests is improving science and math education. Colmenares was appointed by the President to work with the Department of Education in Washington, D.C. Among other responsibilities, she met with officials from other Federal agencies to discuss how math and science education might be improved. She wants more young people to have the chance to become scientists and engineers. Margarita Colmenares believes young people can make a difference and help make the environment cleaner for everyone.

LESSON 4 REVIEW

What can people do to help clean up oil spills and protect the environment? Give reasons for your ideas.

DOUBLE CHECK

SECTION C REVIEW

1. Explain why Americans import oil from other countries.

2. The feathers of birds contain natural body oils that make the feathers waterproof. What problem might result from using detergent to clean birds coated with oil from a tanker?

3. If there were an oil spill in a lake, river, or ocean near where you live, how might it affect your life?

I REFLECT

It's time to think about the ideas you have discovered during your investigations. Think, too, about your many accomplishments.

SUMMARIZE

Answer the following in your Science Log.

1. What **I Wonder** questions have you answered in your investigations? What new questions have you asked?

2. What have you discovered? How have your ideas changed?

3. Did any of your discoveries surprise you? Explain.

Oceans and Oil

Big ships called supertankers carry oil. The ships travel all over the world. I found out that we need oil for lots of things. I also found out that oil can spill into the ocean when tankers have accidents. When this happens animals can get hurt or die.

CONNECT IDEAS

1. What causes ocean water to move?

2. Compare an estuary with an ocean and with a river.

3. Explain how oil from a tanker can harm living things.

4. How can oil spills be prevented? Add your own ideas to those you have learned.

SCIENCE PORTFOLIO

 Complete your Science Experiences Record.

❷ Choose one or two samples of your best work from each section to include in your Science Portfolio.

❸ On A Guide to My Science Portfolio, tell why you chose each sample.

I SHARE

Scientists share their discoveries and ideas and learn from one another. How can you share what you've learned?

Decide
▶ what you want to say.
▶ what the best way is to get your message across.

Share
▶ what you did and why.
▶ what worked and what didn't work.
▶ what conclusions you have drawn.
▶ what else you'd like to find out.

Find Out
▶ what classmates liked about what you shared—and why.
▶ what questions your classmates have.

I ACT

Science is more than discoveries—it is also what you do with those discoveries. How might you use what you have learned about oceans?

▶ Help solve a water-pollution problem. Write a letter to the editor of your local newspaper, explaining the importance of clean water.

▶ Get involved with a community cleanup of a riverbank, a lakeside, or an ocean shore.

▶ Make posters reminding people about the dangers of dumping trash into oceans or other waterways.

THE LANGUAGE OF SCIENCE

The language of science helps people communicate clearly when they talk about nature. Here are some vocabulary words you can use when you talk about the oceans with friends, family, and others.

current—a stream of water that moves like a river through the ocean. The Gulf Stream is a warm ocean current that flows from the Gulf of Mexico, along the east coast of the United States. **(B30)**

CANADA
UNITED STATES
GULF STREAM
ATLANTIC OCEAN

double-hulled tanker—tanker that is made with two shells of metal and an air space in between. If a double-hulled tanker hits something, the inner hull will usually remain undamaged. Only one out of seven tankers on the oceans is double-hulled. **(B85)**

Outer hull   Inner hull

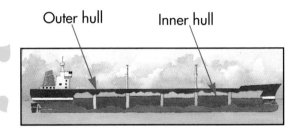

▲ Cutaway view of a double-hulled tanker

estuary—a place where fresh water flowing off the land in rivers and streams mixes with salt water from an ocean. The amount of salt water in an estuary depends on tides and weather. The amount of salt in an estuary changes all the time. Plants and animals that live in an estuary must be able to live in both salt water and fresh water. **(B40)**

▲ Avocets in a shallow estuary

Exxon Valdez—The name of the tanker that ran into a reef in Alaska's Prince William Sound on March 24, 1989. It was the worst oil spill in the history of the United States. Thick, black oil seriously harmed the ocean ecosystem. **(B68)**

Tanker routes through Prince William Sound ▶

Wind and current drove the oil slick from the *Exxon Valdez* accident more than 483 km (300 miles) past the site of the oil spill. ▼

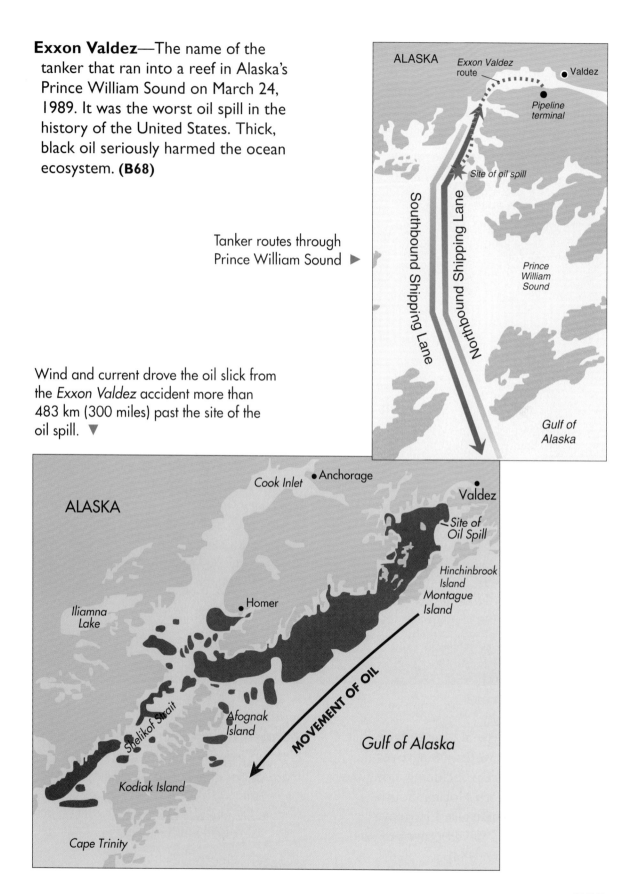

fuel—a substance that gives off energy when it burns. Fuels are used to run the engines of cars, trucks, buses, jet planes, and ships. **(B66)**

oil—material taken from under the ground or under the ocean. We use more oil than we can produce. So the United States imports oil from other oil-rich countries. **(B62)**

▲ **Mangrove trees**

mangrove trees—a type of tree that grows in ocean water. Mangroves grow in many areas including along the coasts of southern Florida, South America, and Australia. Mangrove trees help in the development of soil, land, and islands. **(B54)**

petroleum—another name for oil that is taken from under the ground and from under the ocean by drilling. **(B62)**

B94

supertanker—a tanker the size of three football fields. A supertanker can carry more than 200 million liters (53 million gallons) of oil. **(B64)**

tanker—ship used to carry oil. **(B63)**

waves—disturbances in the ocean caused by earthquakes, landslides, or wind. **(B28)**

tidal pool—a water-filled hollow in the rocks left behind when the tide goes out. Small plants and animals live in them. The living conditions in tidal pools change as the tide moves in and out. The barnacle is one animal that has adaptations that help it survive in this habitat. **(B46)**

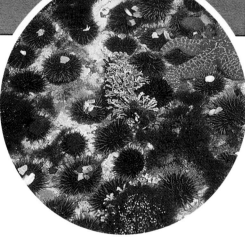

▲ **Tidal pool**

trench—a very deep place in the ocean. The deepest spot, the Challenger Deep, lies under the Pacific Ocean. **(B20)**

Unit C

Pass the Word

Using Energy and Technology

I WONDER

Science begins with wondering. What do you wonder about telephones or computers? This map of the United States shows some of the places connected by telephone systems. Systems like these use electricity, light, and sound to link hundreds of thousands of people.

Work with a partner to make a list of questions you may have about electricity, light, and sound and how they are used. Be ready to share your list with the rest of the class.

This photograph shows how the United States is connected by telephones.

Computers can be linked by phone lines, too.

I PLAN

You may have asked questions such as these as you wondered about electricity, light, and sound. Scientists also ask questions. Then they plan ways to help them find answers to their questions. Now you and your classmates can plan how you will investigate electricity, light, sound, and ways our ability to communicate has changed because of new uses of electricity, light, and sound.

My Science Log

- Why do the lights in a building stay on, even if one bulb is burned out?

- What causes shadows?

- Why can you sometimes feel the sound of loud music?

- How do we use electricity, light, and sound to communicate?

Plans

With Your Class

Plan how your class will use the activities and readings from the **I Investigate** part of this unit.

On Your Own

There are many ways to learn about electricity, light, and sound. As you study this unit, you will read and do activities during class time. Following are some things you can do to explore electricity, light, and sound by yourself or with some classmates. Some explorations may take longer to do than others. Look over the suggestions and choose…

- **Projects to Do**
- **Places to Visit**
- **Books to Read**

PROJECTS TO DO

SCIENCE FAIR PROJECT

Investigate shadows. Observe them at different times of the day. Observe shadows made by different objects. Find out why some shadows are darker than others. Take photographs of interesting shadows. Then write captions for the photographs, explaining what you have found out about shadows. Have people guess what made the shadows in your photographs.

TIME LINES

Work with a partner. Choose one invention, such as the telephone, the camera, or the computer. Read about how this invention was developed and how it has been changed over the years. Use information from your reading to make an illustrated time line showing the development of the invention. You may also want to extend your time line into the future and predict what future improvements will be.

BROADCAST STATION

Set up a broadcasting station in your classroom. Use what you learn about sound, light, and electricity to develop a code and a method for communicating with others.

PLACES TO VISIT

NEWSROOM

Go to a local newspaper office or television station. Observe different kinds of communication equipment reporters use to find and report the news. Watch someone working on a computer to write a story or design a page. Take notes about the things you see. Then write several paragraphs comparing what the newsroom is like today with what it might have been like before the telephone, computer, and fax machine were invented.

ELECTRONICS STORE

Is there an electronics store or a telephone store in your neighborhood? With an adult, spend some time studying the electronic equipment for sale there. If the store has a videophone, observe how it works. Draw a picture of something you see there that is new to you. Write a few sentences telling what makes the invention unique.

MUSEUM

Many science and other museums have exhibits about electricity, magnets, sound, light, and electronics used for communication. Visit a nearby museum or science center where you can see exhibits of the inventions of the twentieth century.

BOOKS TO READ

In the Middle of the Night

by Kathy Henderson (Macmillan, 1992). Many people work at night while you sleep. People use light and electricity to travel, clean, cook, send mail, and do many other jobs at night that make your days better. Watching these people and listening to the sounds of the night, shows that night isn't a restful time for everyone. After a busy night, you find clean streets, fresh food, and mail in the mailboxes. In this book, you will read about the people who work at night and how light, sound, and electricity help them do their jobs.

IN THE MIDDLE OF THE NIGHT

Kathy Henderson ◆ Jennifer Eachus

Mom Can't See Me

by Sally Hobart Alexander (Macmillan, 1990). Can you imagine a world without light? How would you find things? In this book, you'll read about Leslie's mother, Mrs. Alexander. She lives in a world without light, yet she cooks, takes dancing lessons, and writes stories. Find out how she uses senses other than sight to do these things and many others.

Mom Can't See Me

Sally Hobart Alexander
Photographs by George Ancona

More Books to Read

The Little Pigs' Puppet Book

by N. Cameron Watson (Little, Brown, 1990). On a rainy day, the three pig brothers decide to put on a puppet show. After you read this book, you will be able to put on a puppet show, too. You will learn about the stage, lighting, special effects, and even how to make refreshments for the audience.

Samuel Todd's Book of Great Inventions

by E. L. Konigsburg (Atheneum, 1991), Outstanding Science Trade Book. Inventions make our lives easier and better in many ways. In this book, you will find out that Samuel Todd thinks the greatest invention is the box—or maybe the mirror, the backpack, or French fries.

Here Comes the Mail

by Gloria Skurzynski (Bradbury, 1992). This book takes you on a visit to the post office to see what happens to the letters you mail. With the help of machines, postal workers sort the mail, scan it, and put it on a truck. Post office employees work night and day to deliver the mail.

The Science Book of Electricity

by Neil Ardley (Harcourt Brace, 1991). There are two kinds of electricity—static electricity and current electricity. This book shows you how to do experiments that will help you discover something about both kinds of electricity.

I INVESTIGATE

To find answers to their questions, scientists read, think, talk to others, and do experiments. Their investigations often lead to new questions.

In this unit, you will have many chances to think and work like a scientist. How will you find answers to questions you asked?

▶ COMMUNICATING When you communicate, you give information. In science, you communicate by showing results from an activity in an organized way—for example, in a chart. Then you and other people can interpret the results.

▶ HYPOTHESIZING You form a hypothesis when you want to explain how or why something happens. Your hypothesis is an explanation based on what you already know. A hypothesis should be tested in an experiment.

▶ EXPERIMENTING You experiment to test hypotheses. In a test, you must control variables and gather accurate data. You also must interpret the data and draw conclusions.

Are you ready to begin?

SECTIONS

SECTION A
Electricity

▲ Fax machine

You are listening to the radio when the telephone rings. It's a friend who moved away last month, and you are very glad to hear from her. She tells you that her dad's new job allows him to work at home two days a week. He has bought a fax machine so that he can receive important papers from the office.

Electricity was first used for things like electric lights. Today there are many things that require electricity to work. Communication depends a great deal on electricity, as it has ever since the telegraph was invented more than 150 years ago.

In this section, you will explore ideas about electricity and discover how it has improved our ability to communicate.

1 ELECTRIC CHARGES

You probably use electricity to run many things—radios, compact disc players, and televisions, for instance. But did you know that you can use electricity to pick up confetti with a balloon? In this lesson, you will have a chance to see why.

ACTIVITY

Charge It

By doing the following activity, you will find out some interesting things about balloons.

DO THIS

❶ Blow up the balloon so it is completely filled. Tie it closed.

❷ Place the confetti on a table. Hold the balloon directly over the confetti. Move the balloon closer and closer to the confetti. Observe what happens. Record your observations.

❸ Now rub the balloon with the piece of wool about 20 times. This works best if you rub in only one direction.

❹ Hold the rubbed balloon directly over the confetti. Move the balloon closer and closer to the confetti. Record your observations.

THINK AND WRITE

1. Describe what happened to the confetti each time the balloon was held over it.

2. What other materials do you think might interact with the balloon the way the confetti does? Experiment to find out.

Positive and Negative Charges

Even before you experimented with balloons and confetti, you probably experienced similar things. Perhaps you've seen a shirt come out of a clothes dryer with a sock stuck to it. Maybe while taking a sweater off, you pulled it over your head and your hair stood up. You may have walked across a carpeted floor, touched a doorknob, and gotten a shock. All of these things are related. Why do they happen?

It all has to do with electric charges. Every object has electric charges, but they are too small to see. There are two kinds of electric charges. Some charges are positive (+), and some are negative (−). If an object has more positive charges than negative charges, we say that it is *positively charged*. If it has more negative charges than positive charges, we say that it is *negatively charged*. If an object has exactly the same number of positive charges and negative charges, we say that it is *neutral*. Most objects are neutral. They have the same number of positive and negative charges.

Think back to the activity. When the balloon, the wool, and the confetti each had the same number of positive and negative charges, they were neutral. They didn't pull on one another. Then, when you rubbed the balloon with wool, some negative charges moved from the wool to the balloon. The balloon then had extra negative charges. The balloon was negatively charged. The wool was left with a greater number of positive charges—it was positively charged. The confetti was still neutral.

The charged balloon pulled on the neutral confetti, and some of it stuck to the balloon. Charged objects attract neutral objects. The balloon and the wool were attracted to each other. Objects with opposite charges are also attracted to each other.

THINK ABOUT IT

How are charged balloons like magnets? How are they different?

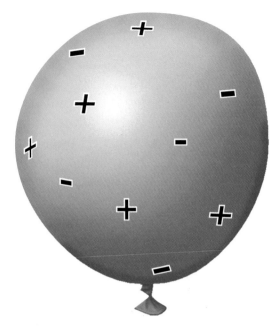

▲ **Neutral balloon**

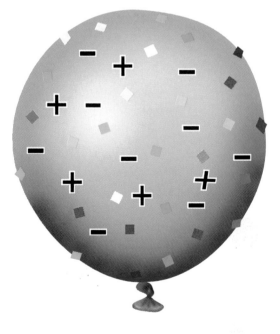

▲ **Charged balloon**

ACTIVITY

Two Charged Balloons

You've seen how a charged balloon attracts uncharged objects. What do you think would happen if two charged balloons were brought together? Try this activity to find out.

DO THIS

1 Predict whether two charged balloons will attract each other. Write down your prediction.

2 Blow up the balloons and tie them closed. Tie a piece of thread to each balloon. Tape the threads to a desk or table, so the balloons hang about 5 cm apart.

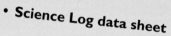

MATERIALS

- 2 balloons
- 2 pieces of thread (30 cm)
- transparent tape
- piece of wool (5 cm x 5 cm)
- cardboard
- Science Log data sheet

3 Rubbing in only one direction, rub both of the balloons with the wool. This will place charges on the balloons. Record what happens to the balloons.

4 Repeat step 3. This time, put the cardboard between the balloons. Record what happens to the balloons.

THINK AND WRITE

1. Describe what happened to the two balloons.

2. How did placing the cardboard between the two charged balloons affect them? Explain why you think this happened.

Like and Unlike Charges

Look at the photos of two charged balloons. Think about what kind of charges attract, and what kind push away.

◀ Nothing happens when both balloons are neutral— that is, when each balloon has the same number of positive and negative charges.

When you rub the balloons with wool, both balloons gain negative charges. The balloons push away, or repel, each other. That's because they have the same, or like, charges. ▶

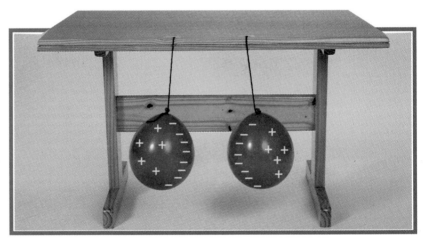

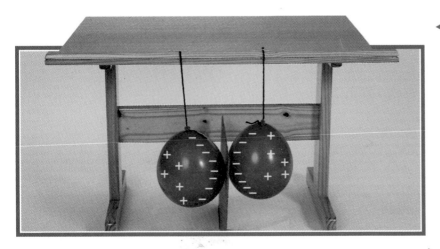

◀ Notice what happens when cardboard is placed between the balloons. The cardboard is neutral at first. Then the negative charges on the balloons push the negative charges in the cardboard away from the surface. There are more positive charges near the surface of the cardboard, and the negatively charged balloons are attracted to it.

How do charged balloons relate to your life? Think about when you pull a sweater over your head. The friction, or rubbing, of the sweater charges your hair. Since the strands of hair have the same charge, they repel each other. That's what causes them to stick out.

◄ This machine generates enough charge to stand this student's hair on end. Doesn't she look like she has just pulled a sweater over her head?

When you walk across a carpet, some of the negative charges from the carpet move to your shoes. These negative charges travel through your body and jump to the metal doorknob when you touch it. You see a spark, and feel the moving charges as a shock. This spark and shock are the result of static electricity. Afterward, the positive and negative charges are equal again.

QUICK CHECK

LESSON 1 REVIEW

❶ What do you think would happen if a balloon with a positive charge was brought near a balloon with a negative charge?

❷ Explain why a sock and a shirt sometimes cling to each other when they are taken out of a clothes dryer.

2 CURRENT ELECTRICITY

You've seen what happens when electric charges collect in one place. You know that when the charges jump from one object to another, they make a spark. What happens if the charges are constantly moving? In this lesson, you'll have the chance to investigate moving charges.

ACTIVITY

MATERIALS
- flashlight bulb
- bulb holder
- 10 to 15 cm of bell wire (ends stripped)
- D-cell
- battery holder
- masking tape
- Teaching Resources, p. 91
- Science Log data sheet

Make It Light

What makes a bulb light? Use a bulb, some wire, and a D-cell to find out.

DO THIS

❶ Use the materials to try to make the bulb light. Do not put the wire directly from one end of the D-cell to the other. That will use up its energy quickly.

❷ Hook up your materials to match the diagrams you are given.

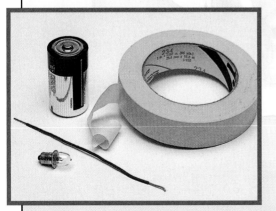

THINK AND WRITE

1. Explain why the bulb did or did not light in each of your tries.

2. What other things can you use in place of the wire? Predict which will work: a rubber band, a strip of aluminum foil, a paper clip, and a paper straw. Test each prediction and record your results.

How Do the Charges Flow?

What did you find out in the last activity?
When did the bulb light?

The bulb lighted only when you made a complete loop called a **circuit.** When the loop was complete, charges could move through the circuit. This flow of charges is called **current electricity.** It got its name because some people thought the charges flowed in the same way that water currents flow in a river.

▲ Look closely at these train tracks. What do you notice about the tracks? Will the train be able to travel all the way around on this track? This is like a *closed* electric circuit. If the circuit is closed or completed, the charges can travel through the circuit.

▲ Now look closely at this track. Will the train be able to travel all the way around it? Why or why not? This is a good model of an electric circuit that is not closed. If an electric circuit is not closed, the charges will not be able to travel through it.

THINK ABOUT IT

If you go home tonight and turn on your bedroom lamp and it lights, what do you know about the circuit it is in ?

ACTIVITY

Make a Switch

After you made the bulb light in the last activity, you had to break the circuit to turn the light bulb off. You removed the wire either from the bulb or from the D-cell. But at home, you don't have to remove a wire. You flip a switch. In this activity, you'll make a switch.

DO THIS

1 Push one thumbtack partly into the cardboard. Hook the loop of the paper clip around the thumbtack. Push the tack all the way in as shown.

2 Push the other thumbtack into the cardboard near enough to the first thumbtack so that the paper clip reaches it.

3 Slip the bare ends of one wire under each tack. Press down the tacks to be sure the wires won't slip out.

4 Make a circuit with the paper clip, the wires, the D-cell, and the light bulb.

5 Move the clip so that it touches both thumbtacks. Move the clip so that it touches only one thumbtack.

THINK AND WRITE

Write a paragraph that explains how the paper-clip switch works.

Looking Back Where do you use switches in your home? What does a switch do? In this activity, you made a switch. When the switch made a complete circuit between the D-cell and the bulb, the bulb lighted. When the switch was off, the bulb did not light. You can see that a switch is a very useful object.

A Ring of Light

In your home, more than one lamp lights at one time on one circuit. More than one appliance can run at the same time, also. There are two types of circuits that will carry electricity to more than one lamp at a time. But only one type of circuit will continue to carry electricity to other lamps if a bulb burns out in one lamp. See if you can build two kinds of circuits that will light more than one bulb at a time.

Lights in a Row

DO THIS

1 Using the materials listed, make a circuit that looks just like the one shown. The two bulbs should light.

2 Predict what will happen if you remove one of the light bulbs. Write down your prediction.

3 Remove one of the bulbs. Write what happened.

MATERIALS
- 3 bell wires (25 cm with ends stripped)
- 2 bulb holders with bulbs
- D-cell
- battery holder
- Science Log data sheet

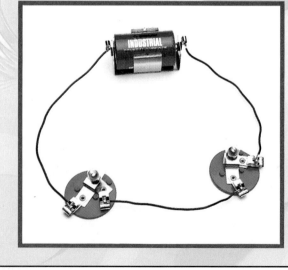

THINK AND WRITE

Why do you think you got the result that you did?

Lights Side by Side

DO THIS

1 Using the materials, make a circuit that looks like the one shown in the diagram. All the bulbs should light.

2 Predict what will happen if you remove one of the bulbs. Write your prediction.

3 Remove one of the bulbs. Record what happened.

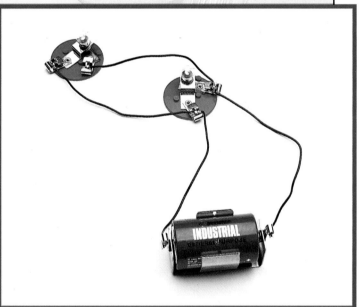

THINK AND WRITE

1. Why do you think you got the result that you did?

2. How could you add a switch to the circuit you just made so that you could turn off both bulbs at once? Draw a diagram to show how you would do it.

Types of Circuits

There is more than one type of circuit. Each type is used in a different way.

The first circuit you made in the activity is called a series circuit. A **series circuit** is a circuit that provides a single path through which electricity can flow. The electricity must flow through each part of the circuit, one after the other.

Have you heard the saying "A chain is only as strong as its weakest link"? A series circuit is like a chain. All it takes is one burned-out bulb or one loose wire to break the circuit. Electricity will stop flowing through the circuit, and none of the lights will work.

The second circuit you made is called a parallel circuit. A **parallel circuit** is a circuit that provides more than one path for electricity to flow through. Each bulb has its own loop. So if one bulb burns out, the other bulbs in the circuit are not affected.

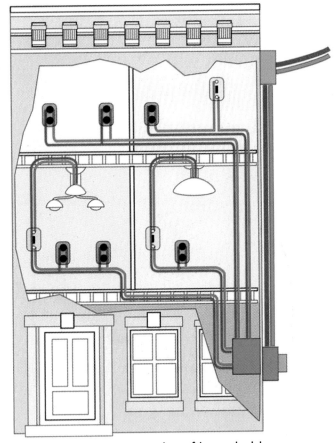

▲ Here are some examples of household circuits.

What would happen if the lights on this bridge were wired in a series? ▼

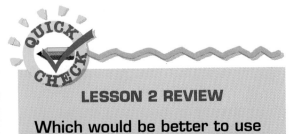

LESSON 2 REVIEW

Which would be better to use in wiring lights in a home—a series circuit or a parallel circuit? Why?

3 TELEGRAPHS

An electric circuit can be used to do much more than light a bulb. In fact, telegraphs, which are really just simple electric circuits, were used to communicate across the country even before the light bulb was invented. In this lesson, you'll read about the telegraph and have a chance to make one yourself.

Relay Race

It was April 13, 1860. The town of Sacramento, California, was decorated with banners and flags. People in the streets shouted and cheered. Bands played. Bells rang out. A holiday was declared. A new company, the Pony Express, had set a record. In just under ten days, Pony Express horseback riders had brought news and mail to Sacramento from St. Joseph, Missouri, where the rail lines from the East ended. That was less than half the time it had taken by stagecoach. People were overjoyed. Those who lived in the West no longer felt so far apart from those in the East.

▲ People celebrating the start of the Pony Express

Pony Express riders were like runners in a 2,300-kilometer (about 1,400-mile) relay race. At every 13 to 25 kilometers (10 to 20 miles) along the trail, Pony Express stations were set up. There a rider could take a two-minute break to change horses. Or, if a rider's part of the trip was complete, the saddlebag filled with the mail would be handed to a new rider. Riders and horses could rest, but the mail never stopped.

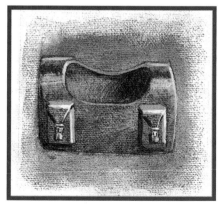

▲ A saddlebag like the ones used by Pony Express riders to carry the mail

The Pony Express riders were heroes to many people. They bravely faced many hazards along the trail. They traveled through blizzards and dust storms. They raced at top speed across deserts, along mountain paths, and through ice-cold streams. They traveled day and night. Their job was to get the mail delivered as quickly as possible.

Despite the dedication of the riders, the Pony Express would not last long. An invention that was little more than an electric circuit and a switch would quickly put it out of business.

The invention was the telegraph patented by Samuel Morse in 1837. It used electricity to send and receive messages in a code called the Morse code.

To send a message, a telegraph operator tapped a handle that worked like a switch. At the receiving end, for each tap of the handle a click would be heard or a pen would draw a dash or a dot. To produce a dot, the operator would hold the handle down for a short time, for about the count of one. To make a dash, the operator would hold it down longer, for about as long as it took to count to three. The dots and dashes of the code stood for the letters of the alphabet. In this way, words could be spelled out.

▲ One of the first messages carried by the Pony Express told of Abraham Lincoln's election as president.

Salt Lake City

▲ An early telegraph

Samuel Morse developed a code of dots and dashes that stood for letters of the alphabet. This code was used by telegraph operators. ▼

MORSE'S ALPHABET.

A · —	J — · — ·	T —	1 · — — ·
Ä · — · —	K — · —	U · · —	2 · · — · ·
B — · · ·	L ⎯	Ü · · — —	3 · · · — ·
C · · ·	M — —	V · · · —	4 · · · · —
D — · ·	N — ·	W · — —	5 — — —
E ·	O · ·	X · — · ·	6 · · · · · ·
É · · — · ·	Ö — — — ·	Y · · · ·	7 — — · ·
F · — ·	P · · · · ·	Z · · · ·	8 — · · · ·
G — — ·	Q · · — ·	Ch — — — —	9 — · · —
H · · · ·	R · · ·		0 — — — —
I · ·	S · · ·	Understood · · · — ·	

C26

In 1844 the first long-distance telegraph service was set up between Washington, D.C., and Baltimore, Maryland. The first telegraph lines were single wires that often broke.

Even when all of the lines were working, only one message at a time could go through. Bad weather weakened the signals. After a while, people worked out solutions to these problems.

On October 24, 1861, telegraph lines that stretched across the entire United States were completed. News could now travel across the country within hours. Electric wires tied the nation together. Two days later, the Pony Express company went out of business.

St. J

▲ A Pony Express rider passing workers stringing telegraph wire

THINK ABOUT IT

You have read about how the telegraph affected the Pony Express. How do you think the invention of the telephone affected the telegraph?

ACTIVITY

Make an Electromagnet

Samuel Morse's telegraph had a magnet in it, but that magnet was different from the type you use to hang things on your refrigerator. In the following activity, you'll have a chance to make the same type of magnet that was used in Morse's telegraph.

DO THIS

❶ Make a data table like the one shown. Fill it in as you work.

HOW MANY PAPER CLIPS WILL AN ELECTROMAGNET PICK UP?			
	Number of Coils		
	10	20	50
Number of Paper Clips			

❷ Wrap the wire around the nail to make 10 loops of wire, or coils.

❸ Hold the nail over a paper clip. What happens?

❹ Attach each end of the wire to the 9-volt battery to make a circuit. Hold the nail over a paper clip. What happens?

❺ Use the nail to pick up as many paper clips as you can. Record how many paper clips you can pick up.

6 Disconnect the battery and wrap 10 more loops of wire around the nail. Reconnect the battery. Record how many clips it can pick up now.

7 Repeat step 6 with 50 loops.

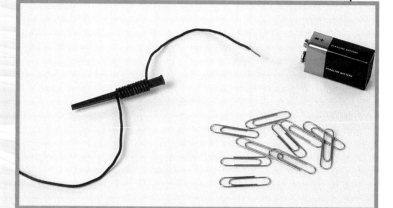

THINK AND WRITE

1. How does the number of coils affect the strength of the electromagnet?

2. Besides changing the number of coils, what else might you do to change the strength of the electromagnet? How could you test your idea?

Looking Back Telegraphs use electromagnets like the one you made in this activity. An **electromagnet** is a kind of magnet that works only when electricity flows through it. As soon as the electricity stops flowing, the magnet can no longer attract certain metals. Electromagnets are much stronger than ordinary magnets.

ACTIVITY

Send a Message

Now that you know how to make an electromagnet, you're ready to build a telegraph.

DO THIS

1 Wrap the middle of the wire around the nail 20 times to make an electromagnet. Leave both ends of the wire free.

2 Bend the tin to form a Z. Use the thumbtack to tack the bottom of the Z to the wood so that its top is almost touching the tip of the electromagnet.

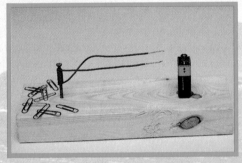

3 Test your telegraph by attaching both ends of the wire to the battery. The electromagnet should pull the tin Z down.

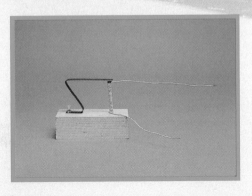

MATERIALS

- piece of wood with nail partly hammered in
- bell wire (45 cm with ends stripped)
- strip of tin (3 cm x 8 cm)
- thumbtack
- 9-volt battery
- paper-clip switch (from the activity on p. C21)
- Teaching Resources p. 92
- Science Log data sheet

4 All you need now is a switch. If you have already made a switch in an earlier activity, you can use it here. If not, the activity on page C21 shows how to make a switch.

5 Tap the paper clip against the thumbtack to send a short message in Morse code to your partner.

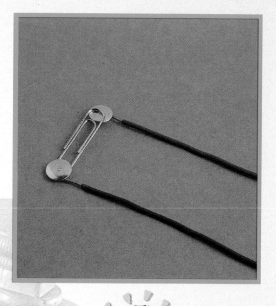

THINK AND WRITE

1. Design a plan for adding a light or bell to your telegraph. Draw a diagram of your plan.

2. **COMMUNICATING** People on the east and west coasts of the United States wanted to communicate more quickly with each other. First they used the Pony Express. Then they used the telegraph, which allowed them to send messages back and forth much more quickly. Why do you think it was important for people to get messages more quickly? Why is fast communication important to scientists?

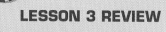

LESSON 3 REVIEW

1 What does the electromagnet do in a telegraph?

2 Would a regular magnet work as well as an electromagnet in a telegraph? Why or why not?

DOUBLE CHECK

SECTION A REVIEW

1. Why are many of the circuits in a house parallel circuits and not series circuits?

2. How is an electromagnet similar to a charged balloon? How is it different?

Section B
Light Travels

▲ Laser light show at Stone Mountain, Georgia

Have you ever tried to signal a friend by using a flashlight or a mirror? Light can be used to send signals and messages. Why can light be used in this way? How does light travel? What happens when light hits a mirror?

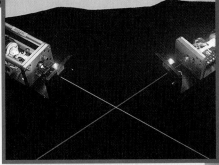

▲ Beams of laser light

   In this section, you'll have a chance to answer these and other questions about light. As you investigate, keep notes in your Science Log about your questions and the observations you make.

1 WHAT IS LIGHT LIKE?

When you shine a flashlight on an object, why doesn't the light fall on you? Have you ever looked at a wall on a sunny day and noticed a pattern of colored light? Where do the colors come from? In the following pages, you can find answers to questions like these about light.

Light It Up

LIGHT! What is it? Why is it so important to us? When you go into a dark room at night, what is the first thing you do? What would you do if no light came on when you flipped a switch? Think about how you were affected the last time the electricity went out for a few hours.

Electric lights have been used in homes and other buildings only in the last 80 years or so. Before that, people used gas or kerosene lamps.

People have long used the light of fires at night to do the things they needed to do. More than 500 years ago, the Arawak (AHR a wahk) Indians in North America used palm-tree torches. People in Polynesia hung oil-rich nuts together and lighted them. Over 700 years ago in China, people burned lumps of fat on the end of sticks.

THINK ABOUT IT

Write a paragraph about how your life would be affected if the electricity in your neighborhood was off from noon until midnight.

How Does Light Travel?

You know that light travels. Light from the sun reaches Earth. The light in your room travels to your book. How does light get from one place to another? Try this activity to find out.

DO THIS

1 Place the index cards in a stack, with the edges even. Using the hole punch, make a hole through the stack of cards.

2 Trace the shape of an index card on both ends of the shoe box. Cut the traced shape out of the ends of the box.

MATERIALS

- 4 index cards
- hole punch
- shoe box
- scissors
- sheet of black construction paper
- transparent tape
- desk
- clay
- flashlight
- ruler
- Science Log data sheet

3 Tape the construction paper to the wall. Put a small amount of clay on the desk. Stand one card on edge facing the wall, using the clay to hold the card in place.

4 Put the shoe box over the card, and shine the light through an open end of the box and toward the black paper. Record your observations.

5 Remove the shoe box. Set up another card about 5 cm from the first one, making sure the holes are in line. Shine the light again. What happens?

6 Repeat step 5 with a third and then a fourth card. Record your observations each time.

 7 Move one card to the right or left. What happens?

THINK AND WRITE

What did you observe about the light when the holes were in a straight line? What happened when one card was moved? What does this tell you about the way light travels?

Bouncing Light

A beam of light travels in a straight line
until it hits something. What happens then?
In the next activity, you'll find out.

DO THIS

1 Stand the book on edge
about 30 cm away from
a wall.

2 Place the eraser on one
side of the book as shown.
Place the ball on the other
side. The eraser and the
book should each be about
30 cm away from the wall.

3 Try to roll the ball so that it
hits the eraser after it hits
the wall.

MATERIALS

- book
- ruler
- chalkboard eraser
- tennis ball
- small mirror
- flashlight
- Science Log data sheet

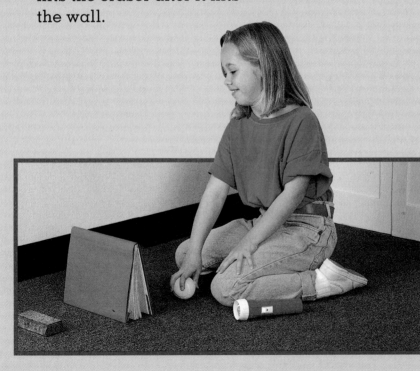

4 Place the mirror against the wall, directly in front of the book.

5 Place the flashlight where the ball used to be.

6 Shine the light on the eraser by shining the light on the mirror. You can point the flashlight in different directions, but don't pick it up and move it.

THINK AND WRITE

1. What did the ball do when it hit the wall?

2. What happened to the beam of light when it hit the mirror?

Looking Back Beams of light can be reflected. **Reflect** means "to bounce off." Reflected light is what allows you to see yourself in a bathroom mirror. The light bulb over the mirror gives off beams of light. This light bounces off your face and heads toward the mirror. Then it bounces off the mirror and goes into your eyes. That's when you see yourself.

ACTIVITY

The Colors of the Rainbow

You've discovered that light changes direction when it reflects off a mirror. What would happen to light if it passed through an object? In this activity, you'll find out.

DO THIS

1 Tape a piece of white poster board to a wall. Darken the room. Turn on the flashlight and shine it on the poster board. What do you see?

2 Have your partner hold the prism so that one flat side faces down, as shown. The prism should be between you and the poster board. Shine the flashlight on the prism. What do you see on the poster board? Record your observations.

3 Have your partner turn the prism upside down so that the flat side faces up. What happens to the order of the colors? Record your observations.

MATERIALS

- white poster board
- masking tape
- flashlight
- prism
- Science Log data sheet

THINK AND WRITE

1. How would you explain what you observed when you turned the prism upside down?

2. How is what you saw like a rainbow? How is a rainbow different? When you see a rainbow, what acts like the prism in this activity?

Looking Back There are many different colors of light. They all mix together to make white light. When white light passes through a prism, the path of the light bends. The path of some colors of light bends more than the path of others. So when a beam of white light passes through a prism, it spreads apart into bands of different colors.

Spreading Light

Have you ever seen a rainbow? Think about the activity you just did. How do you think a rainbow forms? Look for clues in the poem by David McCord.

THE RAINBOW

by **David McCord**

The rainbow arches in the sky,
But in the earth it ends;
And if you ask the reason why,
They'll tell you "That depends."

It never comes without the rain,
Nor goes without the sun;
And though you try with might
  and main,
You'll never catch me one.

Perhaps you'll see it once a year,
Perhaps you'll say: "No, twice";
But every time it does appear,
It's very clean and nice.

QUICK CHECK

LESSON 1 REVIEW

Write a paragraph explaining how light travels. Make sure you describe the observations you've made in this lesson that support your explanation.

2 EXPLORING LIGHT

You turn lights on and off every day. You've seen lighted candles many times. You know that the sun rises and sets every day. But have you ever really thought about light and some of the things it can do? Now you'll have a chance to do that.

Blocking Light

Think about light hitting a piece of construction paper, a piece of wax paper, and a piece of clear plastic. Which ones let light pass through them? How do you know?

Suppose you and a friend are playing in a room. The sunlight coming in is very bright, and it gets in your eyes. You pull down the shade. Now very little light is coming in, and it's too dark. So you put the shade back up and pull the curtains closed instead. The thin material of the curtains blocks only some of the light. You have just the amount of light you want and can go back to playing a game with your friend.

Light passes through the window glass, the curtains, and the shade in different amounts. Materials you can see through, like glass and water, allow almost all of the light to pass through. Materials that let most light pass through them are **transparent.**

Other materials permit only some light to pass through. Examples of these materials are thin fabrics and frosted glass. Materials that let only some light pass through them are **translucent.**

Light cannot pass through all materials. Some, such as brick, metal, and thick paper, can stop light completely. Since these materials block light, they make shadows. Materials that block light completely are **opaque** (oh PAYK).

THINK ABOUT IT

Look carefully at the two pictures. Why are the shadows of the children different in the pictures?

ACTIVITY

Classifying Materials

Think of objects you see every day. Which can you see through? Which let only some light through? Which can't you see through at all? Read the activity carefully. Write a hypothesis about how much light will pass through the different types of materials. Test your hypothesis by completing the activity.

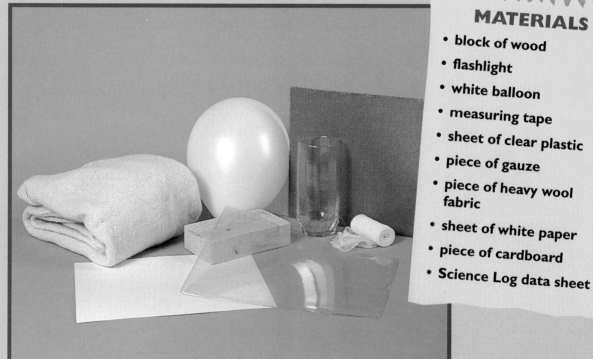

MATERIALS
- block of wood
- flashlight
- white balloon
- measuring tape
- sheet of clear plastic
- piece of gauze
- piece of heavy wool fabric
- sheet of white paper
- piece of cardboard
- Science Log data sheet

DO THIS

1 Place the wood block on a table, one meter from a wall. Point the flashlight toward the wall, and shine the light on the block. Does light pass through the block? Record your observations.

Blow up the balloon and tie it closed. Repeat step 1, using the balloon instead of the block. Record your observations.

❸ Now, repeat step 1, using the sheet of plastic. Record your observations.

❹ Shine the light on each of the other items in the same way. For each item, record what you see.

THINK AND WRITE

1. Classify the items you tested into three groups according to how much light passed through them. Make three columns, using the words *transparent, translucent,* and *opaque.*

2. **HYPOTHESIZING** You wrote a hypothesis at the beginning of this activity. Then you tested it. Was your hypothesis correct? Many scientific hypotheses are not correct, but we learn new things from them anyway. If your hypothesis wasn't correct, why wasn't it? Rewrite your hypothesis based on what you know now. Then retest your hypothesis.

LESSON 2 REVIEW

You may have noticed that many light bulbs are made with "frosted" glass. The glass is white, not clear. How do you think the frosted glass changes the light? Why might a frosted glass bulb be better to use than a clear one?

3 MAKING A PERISCOPE

When people use light to send messages, sending the message is only part of the process. Someone has to receive the message. How would you do that if you were under water in a submarine?

Up Periscope

There are many tools that allow us to use light for things other than seeing. In this lesson, you'll use what you know about light to make your own periscope.

MATERIALS

- 1-L milk carton
- ruler
- pen
- scissors
- 2 small mirrors
- Science Log data sheet

DO THIS

1. Using the ruler as a guide, draw two lines on a side of the carton as shown. The lines should be slightly longer than the width of the mirrors. Cut along each line.

2. Now draw two lines on the opposite side of the carton. Make sure the lines match the cuts you made. Then cut along each line.

❸ Insert the mirrors by sliding them through the cuts in the carton. The mirrors should be placed so that the shiny sides face each other.

❹ On the carton, draw a square across from the shiny side of the top mirror. Cut out the square.

❺ On the opposite side of the carton, draw a circle the size of a dime. The circle should be across from the shiny side of the bottom mirror. Cut out the circle.

❻ Now your periscope is ready. Use it to look over desks and around corners.

THINK AND WRITE

Draw a diagram of the periscope you made. Label the parts. Then write a paragraph explaining how a periscope works.

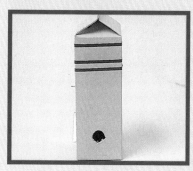

✅ DOUBLE CHECK

SECTION B REVIEW

1. Describe three things that light can do.

2. Describe ways that people use light and its properties to make useful things.

3. A clear object, such as a glass of water, allows most light to pass through it. Does it allow all light to pass through it? How do you know? How could you find out?

LESSON 3 REVIEW

What properties of light allow your periscope to work?

SECTION C
Sound

Listen. Listen to the sounds you hear every day. Sounds bring us messages. The honking horns of cars tell of a traffic jam. The sound of a siren is a warning. The sound of the telephone ringing tells us that someone wants to talk to us. The words we use to speak to one another are sounds. Many of the ways we communicate depend on sound.

In this section, you will explore sound. As you read and do the investigations, keep careful notes in your Science Log. Keeping notes will help you gain a better understanding of what sound is, how it travels, and how you hear it.

1 WHAT IS SOUND?

If a friend asked you if you knew what sound is, you would say, "Of course!" But could you describe sound? Try it. Hard, isn't it? The following activities will help you explore sound. As you do them, you will gain a better understanding of what sound is. Then you will be able to explain it.

What Do You Hear?

You will need: pencil and notebook

When we listen to sounds, we usually pay more attention to what the sounds are than to how they sound. Find a place where you can sit for a while, such as a park or the steps in front of your home or school. Sit quietly and listen to the sounds you hear. As you listen, describe the sounds in your notebook. Don't describe what makes the sound. Describe the sound itself. Is it a high whistling sound or is it low and grumbling? Is it a loud booming sound or a soft rustling sound? After you have finished describing the sounds, share your descriptions with your classmates. See if they can guess what it was you heard.

Activity

Sounds and Shakes

You probably found it hard to describe the sounds you heard. Now, look at something sound can do.

DO THIS

 1 Stretch the plastic wrap over the top of the bowl. Tape the plastic wrap to the bowl, making sure the plastic is as tight around the bowl as it can be.

2 Place the bowl on the table. Put some rice on top of the plastic wrap.

3 Hold the metal pot near the bowl. Watch the rice carefully as you hit the pot with the spoon. Record your observations.

4 Hold the pot about 1 m from the bowl. Gently tap the pot with the spoon. What happens to the rice? Record your observations.

5 Hold the pot near the bowl again, this time without the rice. Lightly rest your finger on the plastic wrap. Have your partner gently tap the pot with the spoon. Then have your partner hit the pot harder. Switch places with your partner and repeat. What did you feel when your finger was on the plastic? What, if any, difference did you feel between the gentle tap and the harder tap? Record your observations.

MATERIALS

- plastic bowl
- plastic wrap
- transparent tape
- uncooked rice
- metal pot
- wooden spoon
- Science Log data sheet

THINK AND WRITE

1. How can sounds make things move? Based on your observations in this activity, write a hypothesis to explain how sound can make things move.

2. How close to the bowl must the pot be in order to make the plastic wrap move?

3. Design another activity to test your answer to question 1.

4. **EXPERIMENTING** All experiments begin with a question. In question 1, you were asked, "How can sounds make things move?" Your answer to this question was a hypothesis that needed to be tested. The only way to test a hypothesis is to conduct an experiment in which you control the variables and collect data. What variables do you need to control in the activity you designed? How would you collect your data?

ACTIVITY

Sound Waves

In the last activity, you saw that sounds can make things shake, or vibrate. But how does sound travel? This activity will give you a chance to investigate this and other questions.

DO THIS

1 Fill the pan with water until it is $\frac{3}{4}$ full.

2 Hit one tuning fork against the rubber eraser. Observe how the tuning fork shakes and listen to the sound it makes when you hold it close to your ear. Then hit the other tuning fork against the eraser and listen to its sound. Compare the sounds of the two tuning forks.

MATERIALS

- clear plastic bowl
- water
- two tuning forks of different notes
- rubber eraser
- Science Log data sheet

3 Hit the first tuning fork against the eraser again. Quickly place the end of the tuning fork into the water at an angle. Be careful not to touch the bottom or sides of the pan. Observe the water.

Wait for the water to become still. Then repeat step 3 with the second tuning fork. Observe the water carefully. Were there any differences in the way the water moved with each tuning fork? You may want to repeat steps 3 and 4 to observe the water again.

 Record your observations.

THINK AND WRITE

1. The way the tuning fork made the water move is similar to the way it makes air move. Based on this information, draw a picture of how you think sound travels.

2. How do you think the sound of a high note differs from that of a low note? Write your conclusion.

Looking Back How did the tuning fork look after you hit it against the eraser? The tines looked like they were moving back and forth very quickly, didn't they? When you put the tines into the water, the movement produced waves. You made a good model of how sound travels. Back-and-forth vibrations of objects cause waves in the air that travel to your ear. Bones and liquid in your ear transfer the sound waves to your nerves. The nerves change the vibrations into a series of electric impulses that are sent to your brain. Then your brain interprets the sound.

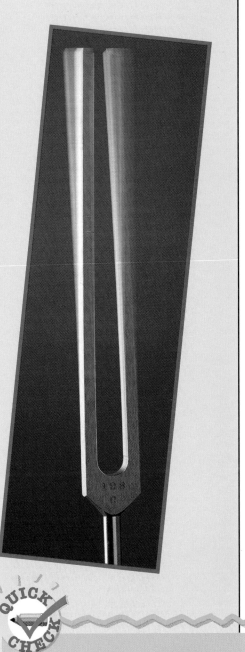

LESSON 1 REVIEW

What observations did you make in the two activities that would lead you to believe that sound travels as a wave?

2 HOW SOUND TRAVELS

Have you ever held your ear against a door to hear something on the other side? Have you ever been swimming and noticed that things sound different when your head is under water? Why do things sound different when sound waves travel through solids, liquids, and gases? In this lesson, you'll have a chance to investigate that question.

Sounds in Solids, Liquids, and Gases

Do you think sound travels best through gases (such as air), liquids (such as water), or solids (such as wood or plastic)? Record your predictions.

MATERIALS
- ruler
- tuning fork
- rubber eraser
- water-filled balloon
- Science Log data sheet

DO THIS

❶ Stand next to your partner, with your back turned. Have your partner strike the tuning fork on the eraser, and hold the tuning fork about 10 cm from your ear. Listen carefully to the sound. Switch places with your partner, and repeat this step.

Put your head down on your desk and hold your ear against the desktop. Have your partner strike the tuning fork on the eraser and touch the handle of it to the desktop about 20 cm from your ear. Listen carefully to the sound. Switch places with your partner and repeat this step.

3 **CAUTION: Do not break the balloon with the tuning fork.** Place the water-filled balloon at the edge of a table. Put your ear against the balloon. Have your partner strike the tuning fork on the eraser, and gently touch the handle of it to the balloon. Listen carefully to the sound. Switch places with your partner and repeat this step.

4 Discuss your observations with your partner. When was the sound loudest? Record your observations and conclusions.

THINK AND WRITE

1. Use your observations to write a paragraph comparing how the sounds traveled through air, wood, and water.

2. HYPOTHESIZING Based on what you discovered in this activity, form a hypothesis about where sound travels best. How could you test your hypothesis? Test it and write a paragraph about the results. Was your hypothesis supported? It's OK if it wasn't. Scientists often make hypotheses that aren't supported.

Evelyn Glennie Percussionist

If you were going to play a musical instrument, which of your senses would you use the most? Read on to see if Evelyn Glennie agrees with you.

In a large symphony hall, an orchestra fills the room with music. Clarinets, violins, flutes, cellos, basses, and drums all play together to create a wonderful sound. In the back of the orchestra, playing the drums, is Evelyn Glennie. Like the other musicians, Glennie has spent long, hard hours practicing her skills. Unlike the other musicians, Glennie is deaf.

Glennie does not hear music the way a hearing person does. She "hears" it in other ways—by reading the music from the score and by feeling it with her body.

Evelyn Glennie grew up on her family's farm in Scotland. She was born hearing, and as a young child enjoyed music. As many children do, she studied piano, clarinet, and percussion instruments. Percussion instruments include drums, maracas (muh RAH kuhz), cymbals (SIM buhlz), and other instruments that make a sound by being struck, shaken, or scraped.

As Glennie grew older, she began to lose her hearing because of an illness. Because Glennie loved music so much, she did not let her hearing loss stop her from continuing to play musical instruments.

▼ **Colorado Symphony Orchestra**

▲ **Evelyn Glennie**

She felt that her way of "hearing" music was far better than the way she had heard it as a young child. She felt that she had a unique way of experiencing music.

Glennie studied music at the Royal Academy of Music in London and graduated with honors. Since then, she has appeared in many concerts, played with the Colorado Symphony Orchestra, and made several records.

Glennie does not practice for a concert the same way other musicians do. First, she studies the music and does careful planning. "A lot of my practice is done silently, away from the instruments," she says. "I'm very, very aware of the room I'm playing in." Glennie asks questions about the room she will be playing in so she will know how sound travels in the room.

When Glennie plays music, she feels the sound vibrations through her hands, her body, and her feet. Many of these vibrations are transmitted through the floor. For this reason, Glennie often works barefoot.

For Glennie, deafness is not an obstacle. "At the end of the day, I'm just a musician," she says. "I just speak through music."

▼ **Practicing with the symphony**

QUICK CHECK

LESSON 2 REVIEW

❶ Where would it be easier for Evelyn Glennie to perform as part of an orchestra—in a room with wooden floors or in one that is carpeted? Why?

❷ Telephones allow people to communicate over long distances. Many whales can do this without using telephones. How do they communicate when they are far apart?

3 MAKING AND HEARING SOUNDS

You've seen that sound waves cause things to vibrate and that things that vibrate can produce sound waves. Sometimes it's easy to see how this happens—a guitar string vibrates when you play it, and loud music can make the glasses on a table shake. But sometimes the way sound works isn't so easy to see. For example, how can a stereo speaker sound like an entire band in concert? Also, how do we hear sound waves? In this lesson, you will have a chance to answer these questions about making and hearing sounds.

ACTIVITY

Loud and Soft

Ssh! The baby's sleeping. What can you learn about loud and soft sounds? Try this activity to find out.

MATERIALS

- safety goggles
- 5 rubber bands of different lengths and thicknesses
- shoe box
- Science Log data sheet

DO THIS

❶ **CAUTION: Use care in stretching each rubber band.** Put on the safety goggles.

❷ Wrap the widest rubber band around the shoe box as shown.

3 Pluck the rubber band lightly. What do you hear?

4 Pluck the rubber band harder. What do you notice about the noise it makes?

5 Record your observations.

6 Repeat steps 2–5 with the rest of the rubber bands.

THINK AND WRITE

1. How was the sound produced when you plucked the rubber bands?

2. How did the sound change as you plucked harder?

3. What other objects can you think of that produce sounds in the way that the rubber bands do?

4. If you wanted to form a rubber-band musical group, what would you need to do? Try out your ideas.

A C T I V I T Y

Making Sounds Louder

"Speak up. I can't hear you," said the teacher. What did the teacher want you to do? Do this activity to find out.

DO THIS

1. Strike the tuning fork on the eraser. Pay close attention to how loud a sound the tuning fork makes.

2. Strike the tuning fork again. While it is vibrating, hold it on your desktop. How loud is the sound?

3. Roll a piece of construction paper to form a cone. Then cut off the point about 4 cm from the tip. Tape the seam. Now you have a megaphone with an opening at both ends.

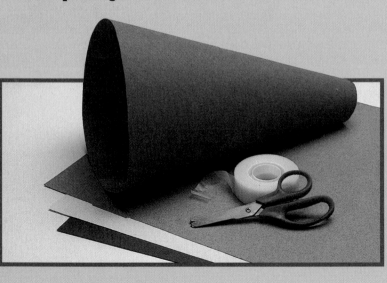

4 Stand about 1 m from your partner. Call his or her name in a normal voice. Then put the megaphone to your mouth and call him or her again. Have your partner take the cone and do the same. When was the sound louder?

5 Push the straight pin into the center of the bottom of the paper cup from the inside as shown.

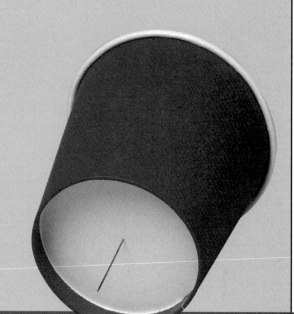

6 Put the record on the turntable. Give the turntable a push with your hand to get it spinning.

7 Hold the cup lightly in your hand. Touch the tip of the pin to the grooves of the record as it spins. Put your ear close to the open end of the cup. What do you hear? Look at the point of the pin. What happens to it as the record goes around?

THINK AND WRITE

Write a paragraph explaining what you heard in the paper cup and why. How can you make sounds louder?

How Do We Hear a Record Player?

When you held the tuning fork against your desk, the tuning fork made the desktop vibrate. Since the desktop is much larger than the tuning fork, it made the air vibrate more. The vibrating air made the sound louder.

Along the grooves of a record are tiny bumps. When the pin rode in the groove, it hit these bumps and vibrated. The cup vibrated as well. Since the cup has a larger surface than the needle, it moved more air when it vibrated. Thus, the sound was louder.

The shape of the cup also helped make the music sound louder. Sound waves bounced off the side of the cup and out the open end. The same thing happened when you called your partner while using the cone. Without the cone, the sound waves traveled in all directions. With the cone, more sound waves were directed toward your partner.

But how did your partner hear the sounds? To answer that question, you need to understand how the ear works.

Record player ▼

A close-up of record grooves ▶

C60

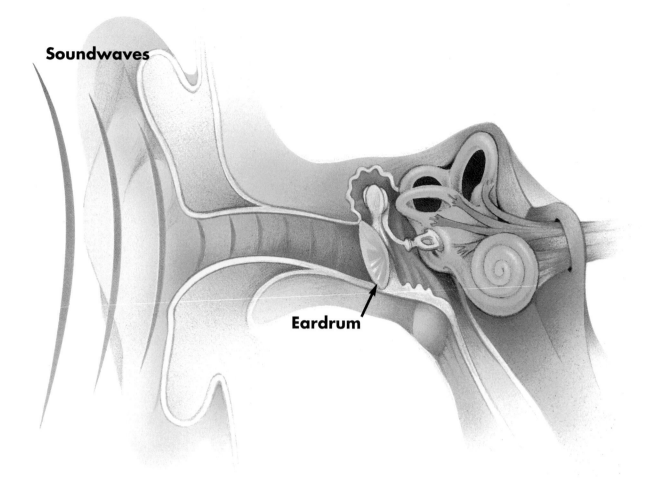

Soundwaves

Eardrum

Megaphones are usually used to make sounds louder. But you can also use them to hear better. In fact, you actually have "megaphones" on your head—your ears. Here's how the human ear works.

As sound waves move through the air, they hit the outer ear. The sound waves bounce off the outer ear. Since the outer ear has a cone-like shape, the sound waves are directed into the ear.

There, they hit a thin circle of tissue called an *eardrum*. When the sound waves hit the eardrum, it vibrates and sends signals through the nerves to the brain. The brain interprets the signals as sounds.

THINK ABOUT IT

Why do you sometimes see people put their hands behind their ears and cup their hands?

Animal Ears and Sonar

The ears of many animals are shaped differently from ours, but they work the same way ours do.

Look at the length of the jack rabbit's ears. How do its long ears help it to hear? Talk this over with your neighbor. ▼

▲ This fox can hear sounds much farther away than it can see objects. Sharp hearing is an adaptation. How is this adaptation useful for hunting prey?

A cat can move its ears around to pick up very soft sounds. Cats hunt birds, moles, and mice for food. Think about the sounds these animals make. Now you can see why cats need to have good hearing. ▼

Bats make use of sound in an unusual way. This bat is a night hunter, but it has difficulty seeing its prey. Instead, when it goes hunting, it makes quick, high-pitched squeaks. In fact, the squeaks are so high that humans can't hear them. If the sound waves of the squeaks hit an insect, they bounce back as an echo does. The bat hears where the echo is coming from and zooms in on the insect. ▶

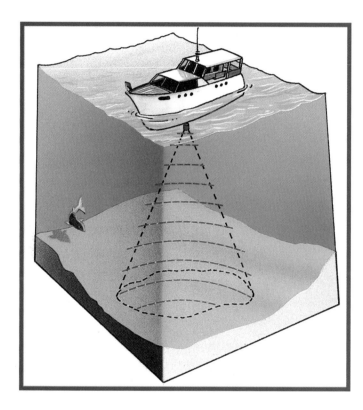

◀ Ships use sound in much the same way bats do to detect objects underwater. Their sonar equipment sends out sounds. If the sound waves hit something, an echo bounces back. The sonar equipment records these sounds, and the sonar operator can then tell from the echo where the objects are underwater.

LESSON 3 REVIEW

Describe the process that allows you to hear a person clapping.

☑ DOUBLE CHECK

SECTION C REVIEW

When Native Americans hunted buffalo for food, they needed to know if the herds were near. In order to find out, they would sometimes put their ears to the ground. Explain why they would have done this.

Modern Communication

▲ Cave painting showing a pony in the snow

▲ Cuneiform tablet

People have communicated in many ways throughout history. They have painted pictures on rocks or animal skins to tell stories. They have used drum or smoke signals as a code to warn of danger or to share news. In time, alphabets were invented so that words could be written down.

Today we communicate in many different ways, using inventions that include telephones, computers, and fax machines. You probably use at least one of these inventions every day. Have you ever wondered how they work? In this section, you will find out.

1 COMPUTERS

You can play basketball, build a house, explore new territory, or travel around the world—and never leave your chair. All of these activities can be done at a computer.

The Development of Computers

In this unit, you have read about some of the ways people communicate. Now let's look at a fairly new invention—the computer.

In the nineteenth century, Pony Express riders delivered messages over long distances, riding as fast as their horses could go. As quick as the Pony Express riders were, however, the telegraph was much quicker. The telegraph used electric current and a code to send messages to and receive them from distant places.

People continued to want to receive and process information as quickly as possible. In 1946 a breakthrough occurred—the first computer was invented. However, the first computer didn't look anything like the ones in use today.

The first computer was very large. In fact, it filled a whole room. This computer was called *ENIAC,* which stood for *E*lectronic *N*umerical *I*ntegrator *a*nd *C*omputer. What that meant was that it was a machine that processed numbers. It did much the same thing that a hand-held calculator does today. ENIAC did not have a memory, so it could not store a program. But ENIAC was fast—at least it was fast compared to paper-and-pencil calculation. It could multiply 333 ten-digit numbers a second.

▲ **ENIAC**

ENIAC worked by using electric current. But back then, large tubes and miles of wire were needed to construct the electric circuits. Before a calculation could be done, thousands of switches had to be set and many cables had to be plugged in.

There were some problems with ENIAC. The tubes that were used to build it gave off a tremendous amount of heat. Today that wouldn't be a big problem because we could just cool the room with air conditioning. In 1946, however, air conditioning wasn't in use. The room that held ENIAC was cooled by fans. Unfortunately, the fans couldn't keep the equipment cool enough, so the computer broke down frequently.

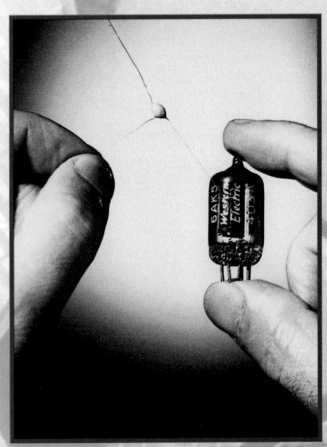

▲ **Vacuum tube**

In the 1950s, improvements were made in technology. The tubes were replaced by transistors that were smaller and did not break down as easily. This allowed computers to become smaller and easier to use. Businesses began buying computers, which were now about the size of a refrigerator. These computers had to be kept in air-conditioned rooms because they would break down if they got too hot. These computers still could only process numbers. They did not have the ability to display images on a screen.

Today you can pack a computer in a briefcase. You can find even smaller computers inside things like microwave ovens and hand-held games. Computers are much less expensive to buy, and they don't break down very often. They are also much faster than ENIAC was. As a result, there are many more computers in use today.

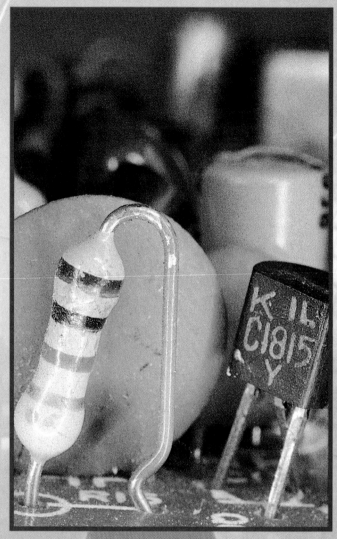

▲ **Transistor**

THINK ABOUT IT

Where and how do you use computers?

ACTIVITY

A Finger Computer

Computers can be used to calculate a huge amount of mathematical information in what seems like an instant. Have you ever wondered how computers can calculate so quickly? Do this activity to get an idea of how computers work.

MATERIALS

- 4 pieces of masking tape (2.5 cm)
- marking pen
- Science Log data sheet

DO THIS

❶ Draw a chart like the one shown.

❷ Place one piece of tape around the fingernail of your little finger on your right hand. Write the number 1 on the tape.

❸ Place the second piece of tape around the index finger of your right hand. Write the number 2 on the tape.

❹ Place the third piece of tape around the index finger of your left hand. Write the number 4 on the tape.

❺ Place the last piece of tape around the little finger of your left hand. Write the number 8 on the tape.

Number	Fingers Used
1	
2	
3	
4	
5	
6	
7	
8	
9	
10	
11	
12	
13	
14	
15	

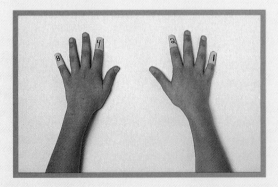

❻ Place your hands—palms down—on your desk. Curl your fingers under.

7 You will now use your fingers as a computer. To do this, remember this rule: A finger that is pointing out stands for the number marked on it. A finger that is curled under stands for zero. For example, to show zero, all four marked fingers are folded under. To show 1, the finger marked 1 is pointed out. To show 3, both the finger marked 1 and the finger marked 2 are pointed out $(2 + 1 = 3)$. The other fingers remain under.

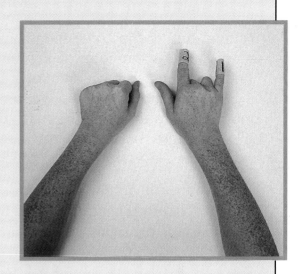

8 Now use your finger computer to show each number in your chart. You must put out fingers that add up to the number. You may not use any finger more than once for each number.

9 Record in your chart which fingers you used to make each number.

THINK AND WRITE

1. How did you show numbers in this activity?

2. COMMUNICATING When you communicate, you share information. How have computers changed the ways we communicate?

Looking Back A computer contains many electric circuits. Information travels in a computer as electric current. Just like a telegraph, a computer has parts inside it that act as switches. These switches can be turned on or off. When these switches are turned on or off, the computer can show numbers just as you did with your finger computer. As a matter of fact, by using only 20 switches, a computer can count to over one million.

Make It Smaller

Almost half of the children in the United States use a computer at home or at school. Almost 27 million American homes have computers.

How did computers become as small, fast, and inexpensive as they are? What technologies have allowed us to make computers so common and useful? As you do the activities that follow, you will find out.

Recall that the first computer was so large that it filled a room. Then when smaller parts, like the transistor, were invented, the computer became smaller. But it was still the size of a refrigerator! Now you can wear a computer on your wrist. That's right—watches that have calculators built in or that can store telephone numbers are a type of computer. This small size is made possible by the silicon (SIL uh kahn) chip. Silicon is a chemical found in sand and certain types of rocks. What is important about silicon is the way electricity can travel through it. The surface of a silicon chip can be treated so that electricity will travel very quickly through some areas and won't travel at all through other areas. This allows complicated electric circuits to be constructed on very small chips. These pictures show some inventions that have been made possible because of the silicon chip.

Hand-held video game ▶

Computer chip ▶

Digital watches can have calculators built into them. Think how handy this would be if you were in a store and wanted to calculate the sale price of an electronic game you wanted to buy. ▶

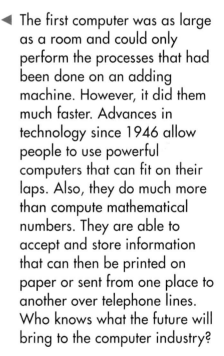

◀ The first computer was as large as a room and could only perform the processes that had been done on an adding machine. However, it did them much faster. Advances in technology since 1946 allow people to use powerful computers that can fit on their laps. Also, they do much more than compute mathematical numbers. They are able to accept and store information that can then be printed on paper or sent from one place to another over telephone lines. Who knows what the future will bring to the computer industry?

THINK ABOUT IT

1. Name two other inventions that might use silicon chips.

2. Why is it important that a computer's electric circuits be made on such a small chip? Why is speed so important?

C71

Break the Code

Early computers were invented to *compute,* that is, to do mathematical calculations. They began to take the place of instruments like the abacus (AB uh kuhs), the slide rule, and the adding machine. But is computing all they do now?

The advantage of using computers was that they could do large numbers of complicated calculations very quickly. As computers began to get smaller, it became possible to use them in more places. Because of this, people began to look for new ways to use the computer. In time, a way to process words with a computer was developed.

In order to allow the computer to process words, a new code was developed and agreed on. Look at the chart on the next page to see how the code works. Each letter of the alphabet is represented by an eight-digit code. Each digit is either a zero or a one. This is called a *binary* (BY nuhr ree) *code.* The word *binary* means "two."

Abacus ▶

▼ Old fashioned adding machine

▲ Slide rules were used to make complicated calculations.

THINK ABOUT IT

How did developing a computer that could understand letters change how computers are used?

ACTIVITY

Using a Binary Code

How do computers use the binary code to process words? Do this activity to find out.

MATERIALS
• Science Log data sheet

DO THIS

❶ Place your hands palms down on your desk. Using four fingers on each hand (do not use your thumbs), do the following: Curl your fingers under. Now all of your fingers stand for zeros. If you want a finger to stand for the digit 1, point it outward. You can now signal the code by using your fingers and the code chart. For example, the code for the letter *a* is 11100001.

❷ Find the letters for your first name on the code chart. Write down the code for your name. Use your fingers to "signal" your name.

❸ Decode the following message, and write it down. Read across the page.

a	11100001
b	11100010
c	11100011
d	11100100
e	11100101
f	11100110
g	11100111
h	11101000
i	11101001
j	11101010
k	11101011
l	11101100
m	11101101
n	11101110
o	11101111
p	11110000
q	11110001
r	11110010
s	11110011
t	11110100
u	11110101
v	11110110
w	11110111
x	11111000
y	11111001
z	11111010

11111001	11101111	11110101	11100100
11101001	11100100	11101001	11110100

THINK AND WRITE

1. How is the code you just used similar to Morse code?

2. Why do you think binary code is ideal for use with an electric switch?

3. Make up a message, and use binary code to send it to a friend.

QUICK CHECK

LESSON 1 REVIEW

How are a telegraph and a computer alike? How are they different?

2 COMMUNICATION ACROSS DISTANCES

Sound, light, and electricity are used in many inventions we use to communicate. We use these devices without thinking much about them. If the telephone rings, we answer it, speak to the caller, and then hang up. We don't give much thought to how the telephone works or to the different ways it can be used. But there are new uses of the telephone and other inventions that are very exciting. Now you'll have a chance to investigate some of these.

ACTIVITY

A Paper-Cup Telephone

You can make a simple model of a telephone that doesn't need electricity.

DO THIS

1 Use a pencil to poke a small hole in the bottom of each cup.

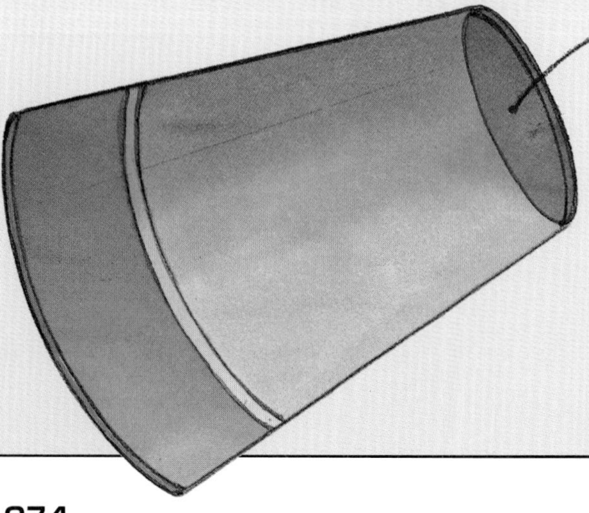

MATERIALS

- **2 large paper cups**
- **sharpened pencil**
- **string (2 m)**
- **2 toothpicks**
- **Science Log data sheet**

2 Push one end of the string through the hole in the bottom of one of the cups. Be sure to push the string from the outside to the inside.

3 Tie the free end of the string to a toothpick. You may need to break the toothpick if it is too long.

4 Repeat steps 2 and 3 with the other end of the string and the second cup.

5 Keep one end of the "telephone," and give the other to your partner. Stretch the string tight.

6 To use the telephone, one person speaks into a cup while the other person puts the other cup up to his or her ear and listens. Speak back and forth to see how well your "telephone" works.

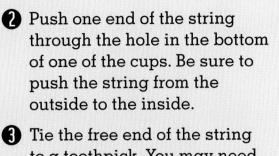

THINK AND WRITE

1. How does sound travel in your paper-cup phone?

2. **EXPERIMENTING** All experiments begin with a question. Suppose you wanted to find the answer to the question "Which material makes the best connector in a paper-cup telephone?" You would need to write a hypothesis, design a test, and carry it out. Then you would collect data, organize it, and draw a conclusion. Work with a partner to write down the steps you would follow to answer that question.

How the Telephone Works

You have just made your own paper-cup "telephone." Although it does work to send voice messages over short distances, it would not work very well over long distances. It also wouldn't be a very good system for linking large numbers of people.

In 1876 Alexander Graham Bell invented a telephone that was the model for the phones we use today. By the early 1900s, telephone use had become more common, and many wires were needed to connect the existing telephones. At first these wires were run above ground on poles. But as the telephone became more and more popular, the mass of wires became huge. Imagine what would have happened if a storm had knocked down the telephone wires for a neighborhood, a city, or even an entire state! To prevent this, many areas began to bury the wires underground in bundles called *cables.* Each cable can hold up to 2,700 pairs of wires.

▲ Old–fashioned crank telephone

▲ In some areas, telephone cables are strung on poles.

Telephone wires carry electric current. When a person speaks into the mouthpiece of the telephone, his or her voice changes the strength of the electric current traveling across the wires. When the electric current reaches the receiver at the other end, it is changed back into sound by an electromagnet. The changes in strength of the electric current coming into the electromagnet cause a part of the electromagnet to vibrate back and forth. This sends sound vibrations to the ear of the listener.

When the telephone rings, it signals that a call is coming in. When you pick up the receiver, the plunger pops up. The plunger, or *switchhook*, is really a switch. When it pops up, it completes the circuit and lets electricity pass through. When you hang up, the handset pushes the switchhook down and the circuit is broken.

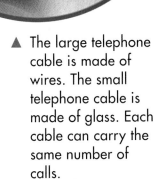

▲ The large telephone cable is made of wires. The small telephone cable is made of glass. Each cable can carry the same number of calls.

Switchhook

Receiver

THINK ABOUT IT

Why do you think a paper-cup telephone would not work well over long distances or for connecting large numbers of people?

A C T I V I T Y

Send a Fax

Telephone lines were designed to carry voice messages. But as technology improved and changed, ways to carry other types of information along telephone lines were developed.

Communicating by means of a facsimile (fak SIM uh lee), or fax, machine has become more and more common. You have seen how binary code can be used to send messages that contain words. Now find out how binary code can be used to communicate by sending pictures.

DO THIS

1. Keep one end of the paper-cup telephone and give the other to your partner.

2. Mark off a space 10 squares by 10 squares on the graph paper. Draw a simple picture by filling in some of the squares on the graph paper. Each square must be either completely filled in or completely blank.

▲ **Fax machine**

MATERIALS
- paper-cup telephone
- graph paper
- Science Log data sheet

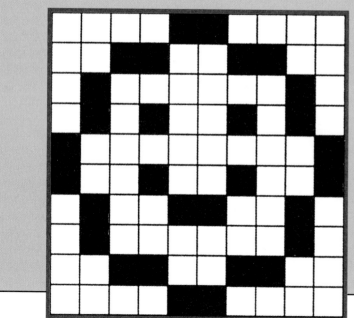

C78

3 Write the binary code for your picture. Begin with the top line of boxes on the left-hand side. If the first box is filled in, write down a 1 on the sheet of paper. If the box is not filled in, write down a zero. Repeat this step for all the other boxes in the row. Write the code for all the rows.

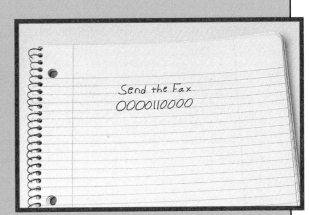

4 Now read the completed code to your partner, line by line, using the paper-cup phone. Your "receiver" should write down the code, line by line, on a piece of paper.

5 The receiver should now use the code to draw a picture on graph paper. If the first number is a 1, he or she fills in the first box on the first line. If the number is a zero, the box should be left blank.

6 Compare the receiver's drawing with the drawing you sent. In other words, compare the "faxed" copy with the original.

THINK AND WRITE

A facsimile is not an actual copy. What do you think the difference is between a facsimile and a photocopy?

Looking Back A fax machine looks at a picture as if it were made up of thousands of dots. The machine translates the dark places (dots) and light places (no dots) into binary code. This code is sent over the telephone wires to another fax machine. A printer inside the receiving fax machine prints a dot wherever the original picture is dark. The darker it is, the more dots are printed. This builds up a copy of the original picture.

Signals Without Wires

Sometimes you need to send messages, but you don't have wires. Can it be done? Read on to find out.

It is not always necessary to use a wire to send a signal. *Radio waves* are bursts of energy created by electromagnets. These bursts can be sent from one antenna to another through the air. Radio waves are used to send signals that bring you the music and news you listen to on your radio at home or in your car. Radio waves are also used to carry signals between cellular phones. This is why we can have portable telephones as well as telephones in cars and on airplanes. These telephones are not connected to telephone cables.

Car phones are fairly common these days. ▼

▲ Making phone calls from the backyard—no problem.

◄ You can even call home from an airplane.

Some telephone signals are transmitted by microwaves. These bursts of energy are similar to the ones used in a microwave oven, but not as powerful. For communications, microwave signals are sent from tower to tower across long distances.

Microwave transmission towers transfer signals that enable us to make phone calls without wires. ▶

Each microwave tower has a dish-shaped antenna to catch the signal and pass it on to the next tower. Each tower is about 50 kilometers (30 miles) from the next. Tens of thousands of these towers are located all over the United States. But microwave towers cannot be built over oceans. So how are signals sent across the ocean? They used to be sent along cables under the water. But today they are sent to a satellite in space! The satellite then bounces the signal back to Earth on the other side of the ocean.

▲ Satellites relay signals all over the world.

▲ Satellite dishes receive the signals relayed by satellites.

QUICK CHECK

LESSON 2 REVIEW

❶ Why do you think microwave towers are located about 50 kilometers (30 miles) apart rather than about 500 kilometers (300 miles)?

❷ Why would using satellites to transmit signals be better than using underwater cables?

3 THE FUTURE OF COMMUNICATION

As you have read, many improvements have been made in communication since the days of the Pony Express. What lies ahead? What new inventions are being worked on? What will communication be like in the next century? Read the following article for a peek at the future.

VIRTUAL REALITY

Computers Create Lifelike Worlds You Can Step Into

by Brianna Politzer

from *3-2-1 Contact*

LITERATURE

You're sitting in your living room, playing a video game. You pull the joystick to the left, and the plane you're flying swoops over a river valley.

Suddenly—zap!!—you blink your eyes and you're no longer in the room, but sitting inside the cockpit of the plane. You see the dark purple mountains on either side of you, the river below, the clouds above. You hear the wind rushing over the wings, the hum of the engine. You no longer need the joystick. To fly higher, you look upward. By simply moving your head, you send the plane left or right.

Sounds like a science-fiction movie, right? Wrong!

New computer technology makes it possible to experience flying a plane, traveling through space or even visiting imaginary worlds—without ever leaving the room. Scientists call it virtual reality,

Autodesk's virtual racquetball is a whole new ballgame. Players swing a real racquet to hit a computer ball.

because it feels so close to being real.

With virtual reality (or artificial reality, as it's sometimes known), the user wears a special glove called a data glove and a pair of goggles. Inside the glove and goggles are tiny electronic sensors. When you move your head or your hand, the sensors tell the computer to respond. (This is how you controlled the plane's movements.)

The computer interprets your movements as commands. In a virtual world, you reach your hand toward an object and close your fingers. The computer understands the motion as a command to pick up the object.

The goggles make virtual reality

Jaron Lanier, founder of VPL, thinks virtual reality allows people to interact better. Some critics think it will keep people apart and in their own worlds.

more…real. In each eyepiece of the goggles is a tiny computer screen that displays a computer image. The image on each screen is slightly different. When you see both screens at the same time, the image looks three-dimensional. It's so lifelike, it's almost like being there.

Is It Live or…?

"It feels like you're inside a cartoon," says Jaron Lanier. A pioneer in artificial reality, Lanier is the head of a company called VPL in Redwood City, California. VPL makes gloves and goggles for virtual reality programs. "Everything feels real, although it doesn't quite seem natural."

In one project Lanier is working on, you put on gloves and goggles and step into a world where there are strange vines and bushes growing everywhere. "When you pick up the plants, they change shape and make music," Lanier says.

In another virtual world, created by scientists at a company called Autodesk in Sausalito, California, you sit on a real bicycle, put on goggles and begin to pedal. As you pedal faster, something incredible happens: It seems as if the bicycle is rising into the air. Soon, you feel you're flying above the Earth, just like the kids in *E.T.*

"It's like being in a dream, a vivid dream," says Randal Walser, a scientist at Autodesk. "You feel as if your entire self is in another place."

Autodesk has also developed a virtual reality racquetball game. Two people play together. Both see the imaginary ball and their imaginary racquets. They control their racquets by the motion of their gloved hands. They even hear a "thwack!" as the racquet hits the ball.

Sometimes artificial reality can be produced without gloves and goggles. This happens at an exhibit called "Videoplace" at the Connecticut State Museum of Natural History. Visitors stand in front of a screen. Below the screen is a video camera. Walk in front of the camera and your shadow appears on the screen.

As you face the shadow, a strange green, insect-like creature darts onto the screen and dances on the shadow's head. Hold out your hands and the creature crawls onto the shadow's fingers. Capture the creature between the shadow hands and it explodes!

In another game at Videoplace (games are changed by walking away from the camera, then walking back in front of it), a person's finger leaves different-colored trails on the screen.

At Videoplace, visitors can light up the skyline just by pointing a finger.

When all five fingers are spread out, the trails disappear, as if a chalkboard had been erased.

These and other games at Videoplace are made possible by 14 separate computers. Each computer is connected to the video camera, explains Myron Krueger, the exhibit's inventor.

"The computers analyze your silhouette 30 times every second," says Krueger. "It can tell what part of your body is where on the screen. If you hold up one finger, the computer knows that it's one finger. If you hold up all five fingers, the computer also knows that."

Inside the Body

But virtual reality isn't all fun and games. The technology has serious uses, too.

Scientists are now making virtual reality programs that allow a surgeon to travel inside an enlarged, three-dimensional computer image of a patient's body. The graphics are made from very detailed pictures similar to X-rays. If a patient had a cancerous tumor, for example, a surgeon could travel inside a picture of his body to get a better view of how to operate.

Architects are even strolling through virtual reality buildings. If they don't like the way things are laid out, they can change the building *before* it's actually built.

And in Japan, a company uses virtual reality to sell its kitchens. Before ordering a real kitchen, customers walk through a virtual version, opening virtual cabinets and checking out virtual appliances. They can even pick up virtual dishes— carefully. If dropped, they'll "virtually" break!

Future air traffic controllers may direct planes with the movement of a gloved hand.

The Power Glove brings virtual reality to video games.

Perhaps the most exciting use of virtual reality is to get a bird's-eye view of planets and galaxies. Users of a virtual reality project at NASA—the U.S. space agency—can "fly" through outer space.

Spaced Out

Michael McNeill, a scientist at the University of Illinois, is helping NASA with this project. "You really feel like you're floating in space," he says. "You move around, in and out, just by moving your head. It's much different from just looking into a computer screen. It's like you're there. Space is all around you."

One current program lets you zoom through the Valles Marineris, one of the longest canyons on Mars. This wild ride is based on real photos taken by *Viking* spacecraft. Also, NASA scientists hope that, one day, astronauts will see a planet's surface through the eyes of a roving robot. They will use goggles and data gloves to command the robot from the safety of a space ship or home base.

C87

Virtual reality may sound like a thing of the future, but some kids are already experiencing a version of it. The Power Glove is similar to expensive data gloves. With the Power Glove, you don't actually enter the video game world. But it does let you move things around the screen by pointing instead of using a joystick.

And recently, Meredith Bricken, a scientist at the University of Washington, taught kids at local schools how to program their own virtual worlds. She gave the kids software that allowed them to create 3-D drawings on the computer. Some of their projects included a pool you could dive into, a space station on the moon and a mountain that could be explored from the inside out.

"Virtual reality brings out your sense of adventure," Bricken says. "Adults have mapped the real world pretty thoroughly. But now there are new worlds to explore."

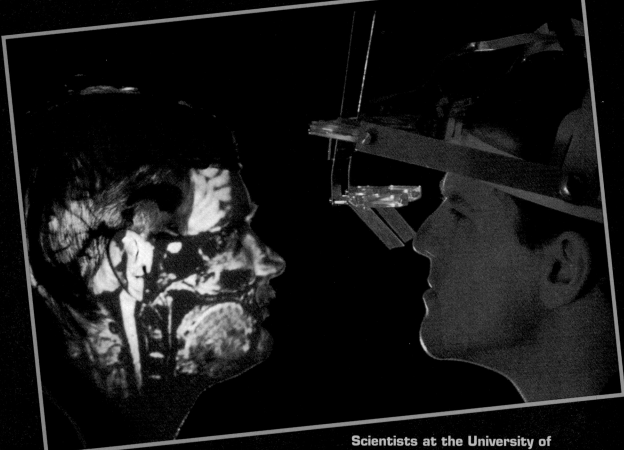

Scientists at the University of North Carolina peer into a virtual head. They hope to someday treat sick patients this way.

By "pushing" one virtual molecule against another, scientists can see how different chemicals react to each other.

QUICK CHECK

LESSON 3 REVIEW

The technology that allows the development of virtual reality has been used to build games and museum exhibits. What other uses can virtual reality programs have? How could virtual reality help you to learn science?

DOUBLE CHECK

SECTION D REVIEW

1. How would your life be different if electric current had not been discovered?

2. How has the invention of binary code changed communications?

3. List two ways computers could be used in the future. Explain how these uses would change your life.

I REFLECT

It's time to think about the ideas you have discovered during your investigations. Think, too, about your many accomplishments.

SUMMARIZE

Answer the following in your Science Log.

1. What **I Wonder** questions have you answered in your investigations? What new questions have you asked?

2. What have you discovered about electricity, light, and sound? How have your ideas changed?

3. Did any of your discoveries surprise you? Explain.

Series Circuit

In a series circuit, the electricity has to go through each object in the circuit. If one object doesn't work, electricity won't go through any part of the circuit.

▲ Earmuffs keep your ears warm, but they can also make it more difficult to hear sounds.

▲ Some types of ear coverings are used to protect a person's ears from harmful loud noises.

CONNECT IDEAS

1. Think about what would have happened if you had tried using a rubber band instead of a paper clip when you built your switch. Why do you think wires usually are covered with rubber?

2. Rainbows are formed because sunlight splits into colors. Explain how you think a rainbow is formed in the sky. Why do rainbows appear after a rainstorm?

3. How do you think programs are transmitted to your television set? Write a paragraph using what you've learned about telephones and fax machines.

4. Why does covering your ears make it more difficult to hear sounds around you?

SCIENCE PORTFOLIO

❶ Complete your Science Experiences Record.

❷ Choose a few samples of your best work from each section to include in your Science Portfolio.

❸ On A Guide to My Science Portfolio, tell why you chose each sample.

I SHARE

Scientists share their discoveries and ideas and learn from one another. How can you share what you've learned?

Decide

► what you want to say.

► what the best way is to get your message across.

Share

► what you did and why.

► what worked and what didn't work.

► what conclusions you have drawn.

► what else you'd like to find out.

Find Out

► what classmates like about what you shared—and why.

► what questions your classmates have.

Connect these items to make a parallel circuit.

I ACT

Science is more than discoveries— it is also what you do with your discoveries. How might you use what you have learned about electricity, light, sound, and communication?

▶ Invent a flashlight that can send its beam around a corner. Demonstrate it for your class.

▶ Set up a musical instrument demonstration in your classroom to show how different sounds are produced.

▶ Draw a poster that compares parallel and series circuits, and use it to explain the difference to your family.

▶ Make a display that shows how communication has improved from the time of the Pony Express until today. Put the display someplace in your school where other classes can view it.

▶ Write a short play about the invention of the telegraph. Put on the play for other classes.

THE LANGUAGE OF SCIENCE

The language of science helps people communicate clearly. Here are some vocabulary words you can use when you talk about electricity, light, sound, and communication with friends, family, and others.

binary code—a code used in computers and other electronic communication devices. This code has only two signals, which are produced by switching electric current on or off. Many combinations of *on* or *off* signals are used for letters, pictures, and numbers. **(C72)**

circuit—a path that electricity follows from one point to another. Series circuits and parallel circuits are two kinds of circuits. **(C20)**

compute—to do mathematical calculations. **(C72)**

current electricity—a type of electricity in which the electric charges are in motion and can be made to flow through wires or other conductors. **(C20)**

▲ Electricity is transmitted through wires.

electric charges—these are a part of every object, but they are too small to be seen. Charges are either positive or negative. Negative charges can be rubbed off one object and built up on another object. When an object has more positive charges than negative charges, it is positively charged. When an object has more negative charges than positive charges, it is negatively charged. **(C14)**

▲ Static electricity

electromagnet—a type of magnet that requires electricity in order to work. If the electricity is shut off, the magnet will not function. These magnets can be very powerful. Their power is increased by increasing the amount of electricity flowing through them or the number of turns of wire in their coils. **(C29)**

▲ Electromagnet

ENIAC—stands for *Electronic Numerical Integrator and Computer*. It was the first computer and only processed numbers, but it worked very rapidly. **(C66)**

fax machine—short for *facsimile machine*. Translates print or pictures into binary code. The code is sent over telephone wires to another fax machine, which translates the code back into print or a picture. **(C78)**

Morse code—Samuel Morse was credited with the invention of the telegraph. He developed a code of dots and dashes that matched the letters of the alphabet. Telegraph operators could send messages over wires using the code. **(C26)**

opaque materials—materials that do not allow any light to pass through them. Opaque materials cause shadows to form. Examples include solid objects such as a brick, a piece of cardboard, or a building. **(C41)**

parallel circuit—an electric circuit that has more than one path for the electric current to flow through. This means that if one item connected to the circuit goes out, the other items in the circuit will continue to receive current, so they will continue to work. **(C24)**

▲ Parallel circuit

prism—a triangular piece of glass or plastic. When white light passes through a prism, its waves are bent and spread apart into different colors. Water droplets can act as prisms. That is the way a rainbow forms. **(C38)**

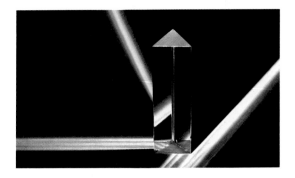

reflect—to bounce back. Mirrors reflect light, and satellites can reflect radio waves and microwaves. **(C37)**

series circuit—an electric circuit that has only one path for the electric current to flow through. The current must flow through each item before passing to the next. This means that if one item connected to the circuit goes out, the other items in the circuit will not continue to receive current, so they will not continue to work. **(C24)**

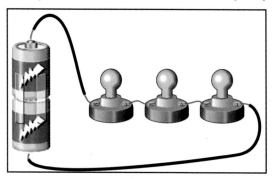

▲ Series circuit

silicon—a chemical found in sand that is important because electricity can travel through it. Used in microchips, it has allowed the development of smaller computers such as the laptop and those that can be put into watches. **(C70)**

▲ Silicon chips on a wafer

sound waves—back and forth movements in solids, liquids, or gases caused by vibrations. Sound waves are interpreted by the brain. **(C50)**

switch—an object that is used to complete or interrupt a circuit through which electricity flows. A switch must be made of a material through which electricity can flow, such as metal. **(C21)**

telegraph—a device that uses electricity to send messages. By switching electric current on and off, a series of "dots" and "dashes" could be sent across electric wires to distant places. These dots and dashes made up a code, called Morse code, which stand for the letters of the alphabet. **(C25)**

translucent materials—materials that allow some but not all light to pass through them. Examples include frosted glass and some thin fabrics. **(C41)**

transparent materials—materials that allow almost all light to pass through them. Examples include clear glass and clear plastic. **(C41)**

virtual reality—recent computer development that allows game players to feel as if they are inside the game. It is also being developed for use by doctors, air traffic controllers, scientists, and salespeople. **(C82)**

MOUNTAINS AND MOLEHILLS

Mountains and Molehills

Rocks, Minerals, and Landforms

I WONDER

Science begins with wondering. What do you wonder about when you see land like that shown?

Work with a partner to make a list of questions you may have about land. Be ready to share your list with the rest of the class.

► Canyonlands National Park, Utah

▼ Grand Tetons National Park, Wyoming

I PLAN

You may have asked questions such as these as you wondered about the land in pictures or the land around you. Scientists also ask questions. Then they plan ways to find answers to their questions. Now you and your classmates can plan how you will investigate Earth's landforms.

My Science Log

- How do different kinds of rocks form?

- Why does the land look a certain way in one place and very different in another place?

- Where do fossils come from?

- How do we use rocks and minerals in everyday life?

With Your Class

Plan how your class will use the activities and readings from the **I Investigate** part of this unit.

On Your Own

There are many ways to learn about Earth and its landforms. Following are some things you can do to explore Earth's landforms by yourself or with some classmates. Some explorations may take longer than others. Look over the suggestions and choose...

- **Projects to Do**
- **People to Contact**
- **Books to Read**

PROJECTS TO DO

ROCK COLLECTING

Rocks can tell you a lot about the history of the land. You just have to know how to "read" them. What can the rocks in your area tell you? Start a classroom rock collection. Everyone in your class should bring a few rocks to school. Use the appearance of the rocks to put them into different groups. Then use a book on rocks and minerals to find out the kinds of rocks you have. What kinds of rocks are common where you live? What do the rocks tell you about where you live?

FINDING YOUR WAY

How much do you notice about the land around you each day? Test yourself. Draw a map that shows how to get from your school to another place in town. Everyone in class should show how to get to the same place. On the map, you may show when to go straight ahead, left, or right. But don't show street names or addresses. Show landforms or natural objects (such as a hill or a big oak tree) or objects people have made (a white fence or a bus shelter). See how much you can remember about the landscape. When you finish, share your map and compare it with your classmates' maps.

PEOPLE TO CONTACT

IN PERSON

How has the land in your area changed over the years? To find out, talk to someone who has lived in your area a long time. The person can be a relative, a friend, or a neighbor. How was the land different when he or she was your age? Were there woods or swamps that no longer exist? Did your school or house exist? If not, what was on the land? Record your interview for the class.

- Friends of the Earth
- National Audubon Society
- National Park Service
- Sierra Club
- U.S. Environmental Protection Agency
- U.S. Geological Survey

BY TELEPHONE

The land is an important resource. Many government agencies and private groups work to preserve the land so that people can enjoy its beauty. They also work to make sure that plants and animals that live on the land are protected. You can call some of these agencies and groups for information. Some of them will send you materials in the mail.

BY COMPUTER

Use a computer with a modem to connect to on-line services or bulletin boards. You can look for environmental news from around the world. You can also "talk" with others to find out what the land is like where they live.

BOOKS TO READ

The Rock

**by Peter Parnall (Macmillan, 1991),
Outstanding Science Trade Book.** The rock was huge and gave shelter to many plants and animals. Trees grew there. Animals came to eat, to hide, and to hunt. There was a pond where animals came to drink. When the fire came, the rock changed. At first it was bare except for ashes. But nature restored it so the plants and animals returned. For centuries the rock stood firm. The book explains how nature continues.

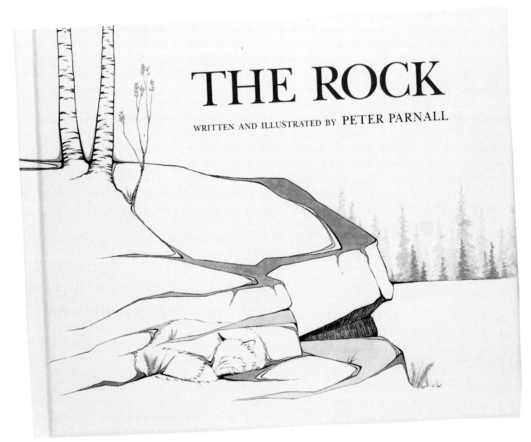

Earth Alive!

by Sandra Markle (Lothrop, Lee & Shepard, 1991). In this book, you will see how Earth is always changing. It boils, melts, and crumbles. It is moved by air and water, so it slides, flies, and explodes. Some changes take place suddenly, and some take millions of years. Look around and think about it. The Earth is exciting, dangerous, and beautiful.

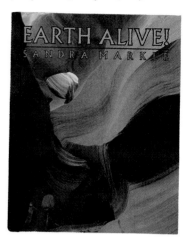

More Books to Read

The Big Rock

by Bruce Hiscock (Atheneum, 1988), Outstanding Science Trade Book. The rock in the mountains will last a long time. It has been part of Earth's crust for billions of years. This book will show you how the rock began. There were ancient seas, and then earthquakes that formed mountains. The mountains eroded. The glaciers came, and the force of the ice carried the rock away and left it where it is now.

Rocks and Soil

by Joy Richardson (Franklin Watts, 1992). The large, color photographs in this book help explain the world beneath your feet. You'll learn about Earth's crust, soil, minerals, rocks, and crystals. How do we use the treasures of the Earth? How do we find out about the past? It's all told in this book.

The Sun, the Wind and the Rain

by Lisa Westberg Peters (Henry Holt, 1988), Outstanding Science Trade Book. On the beach, Elizabeth builds a mountain out of sand. Read this book to find out how the wind and rain wear it away, just like a real mountain. The ocean washes away another one she builds, just as the cliff she walks on is being washed slowly away, too.

The Village of Round and Square Houses

by Ann Grifalconi (Little, Brown, 1986), Caldecott Honor Book. This story is based on something that really happened in a village in central Africa. In this village, some people live in one square house while others live in one round house. It was not always this way. Before the volcano erupted, life was different. This story will tell you why it changed.

INVESTIGATE

To find answers to their questions, scientists read, think, talk to others, and do experiments. Their investigations often lead to new questions. In this unit, you will have many chances to think and work like a scientist. How will you find answers to questions you asked?

▶ **RECOGNIZING TIME/SPACE RELATIONSHIPS**
Time relationships tell you the order of events. Space relationships tell you about locations of objects. Understanding these relationships can help you make accurate models.

▶ **INTERPRETING DATA** Data is information given to you or information that you gather during activities. When you interpret data, you decide what it means.

▶ **CLASSIFYING/ORDERING** When you classify objects, you put them into groups according to how they are alike. Ordering is putting things in an order. For example, you might order things from first to last, smallest to largest, or lightest to heaviest.

Are you ready to begin?

SECTIONS

Rocks and Minerals

▲ **Gold ore**

If you were walking through the woods, you probably wouldn't look twice at most rocks. Many are dull gray or brown. But what would you do if you thought there was gold, silver, or diamonds hidden inside a rock? You'd be sure to pick it up and take it home, wouldn't you?

Are there really valuable things in rocks? How can you identify these things? How can people use rocks? In this section, you'll discover some things about rocks. Keep a record in your Science Log of what you find out.

1 EXPLORING ROCKS AND MINERALS

Have you ever collected rocks? Or have you seen someone else's collection? What makes rocks different from one another? In this lesson, you'll investigate rocks. You'll see how different kinds of rocks form. You'll see how rocks can change. You'll also investigate some materials that make up rocks.

▼ Granite

Kinds of Rocks

If rocks could talk, each one would tell a different story. Let's take a hike into the Grand Canyon to learn the stories of some rocks.

Igneous Rocks

You're at the bottom of the Grand Canyon. The canyon is deep enough to swallow a building with 500 floors. The water of the Colorado River smashes against hard rocks. The rocks are extremely old—almost half as old as Earth itself!

These rocks are granite. You see that they have many sparkling flakes in them. But if you could have seen the rocks millions of years ago, you wouldn't have recognized them. At that time, they were red-hot and melted. Over a long time, they slowly cooled and became granite.

Rocks that start out as red-hot liquids are called **igneous** (IHG nee uhs) **rocks.** *Igneous* is a word that means "fire." So you can think of igneous rocks as "fire rocks."

Granite may form cliffs and mountains, such as these being enjoyed by a rock climber. ▶

D13

Sedimentary Rocks

Millions of years ago, there was no Grand Canyon. At that time, an ocean covered the land. Rivers that ran into the ocean carried sand and other bits of rock. These materials, called *sediments* (SED uh muhnts), settled on the ocean floor. So did the remains of sea creatures. As time passed, more and more sediments piled up, in layer upon layer. The weight of the layers squeezed the sediments. Chemicals in the sediments cemented them together. Eventually, the squeezing and the cementing hardened the sediments into layers of rock.

As you climb upward in the Grand Canyon, you see the layers of rock. One of them is a reddish brown. It's called *sandstone.* Sandstone belongs to a second type of rock, called sedimentary (sed uh MEN tuhr ee) rocks. Sedimentary rocks are formed when sediments harden.

▲ Sandstone can also form cliffs and mountains. Sandstone can be shaped by water, such as the Colorado River.

Sandstone is a sedimentary rock. ▶

D14

Metamorphic Rocks

Sometimes rocks that have already formed get buried deep within the Earth. Forces within the Earth squeeze the rocks from many directions. At the same time, heat from deep inside the Earth makes these rocks very hot, but it does not melt them. The squeezing and the heat change these rocks from one kind into another.

At the bottom of the Grand Canyon, you might see dark gray rocks called *slate*. Slate is one type of metamorphic (met uh MAWR fik) rock. *Metamorphic* means "changed." All metamorphic rocks form from other rocks. Slate is a metamorphic rock because it formed from a rock called *shale*. Igneous, sedimentary, and even other metamorphic rocks can be changed by heat and squeezing to form new metamorphic rocks.

▲ Shale is a sedimentary rock.

Slate is the metamorphic rock formed from shale. ▼

THINK ABOUT IT

How could a metamorphic rock become an igneous rock?

The Rock Cycle

As you explore the Grand Canyon, you find all sorts of rocks. Some are soft and crumble between your fingers. Others are hard and have sharp edges. Some look as if they're made up of small rocks glued together. Others seem to be made of a single substance.

No matter what the rocks look like today, you can be sure that at one time they looked different. That's because rocks change as time passes.

A cycle is a group of changes that take place over and over again. This diagram of the rock cycle shows how materials that make up rocks are used again and again.

You've read about three different types of rocks—igneous, sedimentary, and metamorphic. You can see in the diagram of the rock cycle how these types of rocks are related.

In the diagram, find the arrows with the words *heat and pressure* on them. The heat comes from inside the Earth. The pressure comes from the weight of rocks pressing on other rocks. All types of rocks can be changed by heat and pressure. What kinds of rocks shown in the diagram can become metamorphic rocks?

Next, find the arrows with *wearing away by water and wind* written on them. This process forms sediments. When pressure is applied to sediments, sedimentary rocks form. What kinds of rocks can become sedimentary rocks?

Now, find the three arrows with *melting* written on them. When heat causes rocks to melt, the substances in them may change and recombine. What kinds of rocks shown in the diagram can become red-hot melted rock?

The rock cycle shows that Earth recycles its rock materials. They just keep changing from one kind of rock into another.

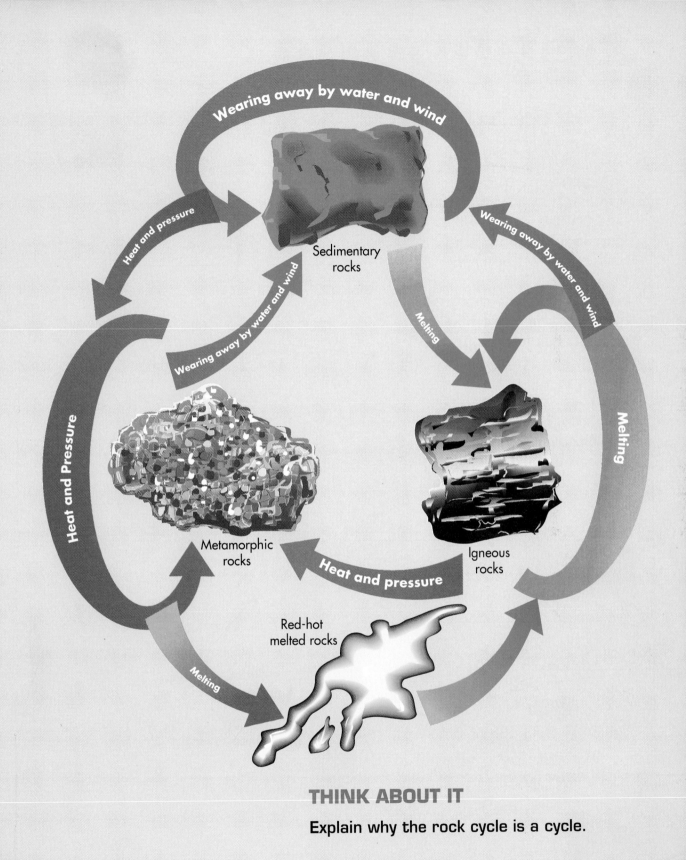

Wearing away by water and wind

Heat and pressure

Sedimentary rocks

Wearing away by water and wind

Wearing away by water and wind

Melting

Heat and Pressure

Metamorphic rocks

Heat and pressure

Igneous rocks

Melting

Melting

Red-hot melted rocks

THINK ABOUT IT

Explain why the rock cycle is a cycle.

ACTIVITY

Stories in Rocks

The rocks around you tell a story. They tell what the land around you was like long ago. The land may have been very different from what it is now. Maybe it was under an ocean. Maybe a volcano once poured hot, melted rock on the land. Maybe the rocks you playfully kick today were once deep inside the Earth. See if you can discover the story of the land around you.

DO THIS

1. Look at the three labeled rocks. Observe them with and without the hand lens. Each rock has a letter on it. *M* stands for *metamorphic*, *S* for *sedimentary*, and *I* for *igneous*.

2. Examine each of the mystery rocks. Compare them with the labeled rocks.

MATERIALS
- 3 labeled rocks
- 3 numbered mystery rocks
- hand lens
- Science Log data sheet

❸ Record the number of each mystery rock. Next to the number, write the letter of the labeled rock that the mystery rock is most like.

THINK AND WRITE

1. What do the mystery rocks seem to tell you about the land they came from? What events might have formed these rocks?

2. **CLASSIFYING/ORDERING** Sometimes putting things in order or classifying them helps you learn about them or find them for later observations. In this investigation, you classified mystery rocks by comparing them with rocks you knew about. Did this help you gather data about the rocks? Why or why not?

ACTIVITY

Identifying Minerals

What are rocks made of? All rocks are made of one or more minerals. A diamond is a mineral. A chunk of quartz, which is like a big piece of hardened sand, is also a mineral. A diamond and a chunk of quartz look very similar. How could you tell them apart? You could do it if you tested their hardness. That's because every mineral has a specific hardness. How can you find out the hardness of a mineral? Do the following activity to find out.

▲ Which is the diamond? ▲

MATERIALS
- chalk
- copper wire
- iron nail
- other materials of varying hardness
- mineral kit
- Science Log data sheet

DO THIS

❶ Make a chart like the one shown.

SCRATCH–TEST RESULTS		
Material to Be Tested	**Materials It Scratches**	**Materials That Scratch It**
Chalk		
Copper Wire		
Iron Nail		

2 Try to scratch the chalk, wire, and nail with your fingernail.

3 Try to scratch all the materials with each other.

4 Choose three other materials to test for hardness. Add them to your chart.

5 On your chart, record which materials scratched which.

6 List the materials from the hardest to the softest. This will create a hardness scale.

7 Test each material, and decide where it fits in the hardness scale.

THINK AND WRITE

1. Which material was the hardest? What evidence do you have for your answer?

2. Which material was the softest? What evidence do you have for your answer?

3. How would your hardness scale help you classify rocks and minerals?

4. **INTERPRETING DATA** You collected data in this activity. You also interpreted the data. What senses did you use? How did you interpret the data you collected?

LESSON 1 REVIEW

1 Some islands are volcanoes that rise from the bottom of the ocean. What kinds of rocks would you find on the islands when they first form?

2 If you found a piece of sedimentary rock on a mountain, what would this tell you about the land?

3 Only another diamond can scratch a diamond. So what can you say about diamonds?

2 USING ROCKS AND MINERALS

Many of Earth's rocks are treasure chests. Within them, you might find the materials to make a brass trumpet, a sports car, or a jet airplane.

You Use Rocks Every Day

Some rocks contain metals, such as aluminum, iron, and nickel. These metals can be separated from the rocks. Then they can be used to make trumpets, sports cars, jet airplanes, and a lot of other things. You might be surprised at how many ways you use rocks. In fact, your life would be very different without them.

Copper comes from rocks. The pennies in your pocket have copper in them. Without copper, you wouldn't have electric lights in your home or be able to watch TV, because copper is used to make the wires that carry electricity. Copper can be combined with zinc, another metal, to form brass. Brass is used to make some instruments. ▶

Calcopyrite, shown here, contains copper. ▶

Aluminum comes from a type of mineral called *bauxite* (BAWKS yt). Aluminum is used to make cans, pots and pans, airplanes, rockets, and lightweight ladders. ▶

Bauxite ▶

◀ What does a sports car have to do with rocks? Many of the parts of cars are made of steel, and iron is used to make steel. Iron comes from a type of rock called *hematite* (HEM uh tyt).

Hematite ▶

Sometimes rocks are used pretty much as they are. Buildings may be made of blocks of rock, such as granite. Some of the world's greatest statues are made of the rock called *marble*. Gemstones need only to be cut and polished to make beautiful jewelry. ▶

THINK ABOUT IT

Explain three ways you use rocks.

ACTIVITY

Rock Hunt

Lots of things in and around your home, school, and community are made from rocks and minerals. Let's see how many of these things you can find and classify.

MATERIALS
• clipboard
• Science Log data sheet

DO THIS

1 Make a chart like this one to record your findings. Put the chart on the clipboard.

ROCK HUNT			
Object	Where I Saw It	Use	Classification

2 Look around your home, school, or community for objects made from rocks or from materials that came from rocks.

3 When you see an object that you think was made from rocks or a rock material, write its name under the word *Object*. In the next two columns, write where you saw the object and what it's used for.

④ Classify each object. You can classify things by how they are used. For example, one group might be jewelry. Another group might be things used in construction. Still another group could be things used in transportation. Or you can make up your own groups.

THINK AND WRITE

1. Which objects are made from things taken out of rocks?

2. Which objects are made of things that still look like rocks?

3. Look over your chart. Which group has the most objects in it? Explain why the objects in this group are important to you.

4. **CLASSIFYING/ORDERING** In this investigation, you classified some objects made from rocks. The groups were based on the uses of things made from rocks. In what other ways might you have classified these objects?

Stone Art

If you want a message to last a long time, carve it in stone. What kinds of messages might these be? Imagine taking trips to three places to find out.

Mount Rushmore

You're a tourist visiting Mount Rushmore, a hill of granite in the Black Hills of South Dakota. You see an awesome sight—four huge faces carved in the mountain side. The faces are those of four American presidents—Washington, Jefferson, Lincoln, and Theodore Roosevelt.

Suppose you came from a time far in the future. When you looked at the faces on Mount Rushmore, what would you think? What message would you get?

The Maya

A team of scientists walks through a thick forest in Guatemala. Suddenly, the trees thin out. There is a clearing ahead. As the scientists enter the clearing, they see a huge building made of rock. And they know they have found the lost city of Tikal.

Tikal was one of many cities built by a people called the *Maya*. Most Maya lived in what is now Guatemala and Mexico. Their cities are at least a thousand years old.

The Maya were very good at science and engineering. They used limestone, a sedimentary rock, to make buildings called *pyramids*. The pyramid at Tikal is as tall as a 15-floor apartment house. The Maya used the pyramids for religious ceremonies.

Near the pyramids, the scientists find a piece of stone about the size of a person. The Maya carved all sorts of pictures in the stone. The pictures form a kind of calendar and diary. The scientists will try to figure out what stories the pictures tell. What kinds of things do you think the stories might be about?

Homes of Rock

The two cowboys shivered. An icy wind blew through the red-sandstone canyon in Colorado. The month was December. The year was 1888.

Snow covered most of the sandstone around the cowboys. But every now and then, a gust of wind would sweep the snow off the rocks. All of a sudden, one gust cleared a large area. Then the cowboys saw something they had never seen before. They stared at the ruins of houses that seemed to climb up the steep cliffs.

Thousands of people once lived in these houses. These early Americans are known as the *Anasazi* (an ah SAHZ ee). But between 600 and 700 years ago, the Anasazi left their homes. Why? Scientists suggest two reasons. Maybe the land became too dry for crops, such as corn, to grow. Or maybe other Native American people attacked the Anasazi and forced them to leave.

Today many tourists visit these cities in the cliffs. Scientists also go there to try to solve the mysteries of the Anasazi.

THINK ABOUT IT

What are three ways people in the Americas have left records of history in stone? What kinds of stone records do you think people today leave?

Maria Martinez
She Turned Rocks into Art

You have learned that you use rocks in many ways. Other people use rocks in ways you may not have thought of. Read about Maria Martinez, a Navaho potter, who used rocks in a very interesting manner.

If you were to look at the ground near the town of San Ildefonso (SAHN eel day FAHN soh) in New Mexico, you might see brown chunks of clay. In another place, you might see some dark ash that fell from a volcano long ago. You might think that both the clay and the ash were good for nothing. But to Maria Martinez, these pieces of rock were the stuff from which fine works of art could be made.

Maria Martinez was one of the great Native American makers of pottery. She made beautiful jars, bowls, and pitchers.

Pottery is made from clay, water, and materials like ash from volcanoes. When the mixture is soft and wet, it can be made into many different shapes. It is then dried, painted, and put in an oven to harden.

Maria Martinez's people had made pottery for hundreds of years. During her long life, Maria Martinez learned how to make pottery as her people had done in the past. But she also used her imagination to make new and beautiful designs.

QUICK CHECK

LESSON 2 REVIEW

❶ What are some ways you use rocks or things made from rocks in your everyday life?

❷ Name three ways that rocks and things made from rocks make your life better.

DOUBLE CHECK

SECTION A REVIEW

1. People use steel tools to carve statues. If you had a choice of carving a statue from chalk or diamond, which would you choose? Why?

2. Why are some rocks better than wood for building houses?

SECTION B
Shaping the Earth

In the western part of the United States, the jagged tops of the Rocky Mountains may be covered with snow all year round. As you travel east, the land changes. The Great Plains of the Midwest are as flat as a tabletop. The mountains of the South and East are covered with trees and other plants.

This is what the land of the United States looks like today. But it didn't always look like this, and in the future, it will look different than it does today. The land is constantly changing. What makes it change? How can a mountain grow old? How does a valley form? How can huge blocks of rocks become dusty sand? As you explore this section, you will find some answers. In your Science Log, keep a record of what you discover.

1 LANDFORMS AND MAPS

Do you have a globe in your classroom? Do some of the land parts feel rough and bumpy? What do you think these bumpy places are supposed to be? You know that land looks different in different places. Why is this so? Parts of land are high, like hills and mountains. Some parts of the Earth are very flat, like the plains found in the middle of the United States. How do mountains form? Why does Earth's surface vary so much? The following pages will give you a clue.

Earth's Landforms

To understand differences in the land, you need to look at the structure of the Earth. Let's look at that structure.

Earth is made up of layers. The outer layer of Earth, the *crust*, is only a few kilometers thick. Below the crust is a layer called the *mantle*. Below the mantle are two more layers. The *outer core* is a layer of liquid metal, and the *inner core* is a solid ball of iron and nickel.

Crust

Mantle

Inner Core

Outer Core

Earth's **landforms** are features that can be seen on Earth's crust. *Mountains* are landforms that rise very high above the land around them. The low areas between the mountains are called *valleys.* Rivers are often found at the bottom of valleys. These rivers form valleys as rain flows downward from steep mountain slopes.

▲ These mountains at Glacier National Park are so high that they're covered with snow most of the year. The valley below is green with plants.

Wide, flat areas of land are called *plains.* Soil in the plains is usually good enough for crops to be grown there. A *plateau* is also a flat area, but it rises above the land around it. It looks like a mountain with the top cut off.

Compare the types of landforms shown here. How are they like the landforms where you live? How are they different?

▲ The land of the Colorado Plateau is like a tabletop.

▲ The Great Plains of the Midwest are flat and ideal for growing crops. This is where most of the country's farmland is located.

THINK ABOUT IT

Not many crops are grown on plateaus. Why not?

ACTIVITY

Folds in Earth's Crust

Heat and pressure from below Earth's crust can affect surface landforms. To see this for yourself, try this activity.

MATERIALS

• **4 paper towels (single sheets)**
• **water**
• **Science Log data sheet**

DO THIS

❶ Stack the four paper towels on a table. Fold the stack in half.

❷ Carefully dampen the paper towels with water.

❸ Put your hands on the edges of the damp paper. Very slowly push the edges of the wet paper towels toward the center.

THINK AND WRITE

1. What happened as you pushed the damp paper towels?

2. Compare the area of the paper towels before you pushed them and after you pushed them.

3. Compare the height of the paper towels before you pushed them and after you pushed them.

Looking Back In this activity, the layers of paper towels stood for layers of rock that make up part of Earth's crust. When you pushed the edges of the paper towels together, the layers bent and folded. Part of the "crust" became higher than the "land" around it. This is similar to what has happened in some places on Earth. Some mountains have formed over a very long period of time as pieces of crust and mantle collided with other pieces of crust and mantle. Areas of folded rock formed the Appalachian Mountains. Other mountains formed when forces on rock layers caused them to break and one part was pushed up. Still other mountains formed because of volcanoes.

A Slice of Rock

To learn more about different landforms, you can look at a map. Many of the maps that you've seen show highways and roads. But there are also maps that show the structures of landforms.

One type of map is called a *cross-section map*. This map shows the rock layers inside a landform. It is similar to what you would see if you sliced into a layer cake and looked inside. If the rock layers have been folded, the folding will show on this kind of map. Cross-section maps, like all other maps, have a scale. A scale shows how the distance on a map compares to the real distance on Earth.

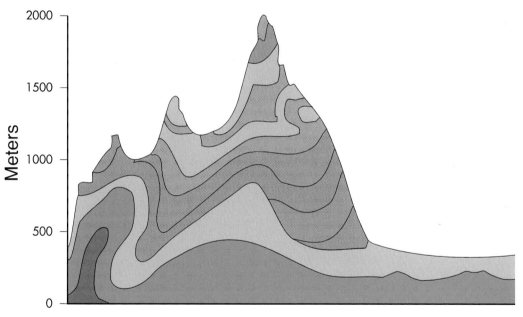

A cross-section map also shows the elevation of a landform. *Elevation,* or the height of the land, is measured from a beginning point called sea level. **Sea level** is the average level of the sea where it meets the land. Suppose a mountain has an elevation of 4,200 meters (13,779 feet). This means it rises 4,200 meters above sea level.

THINK ABOUT IT

Look at the cross-section map. What is the elevation of the mountain?

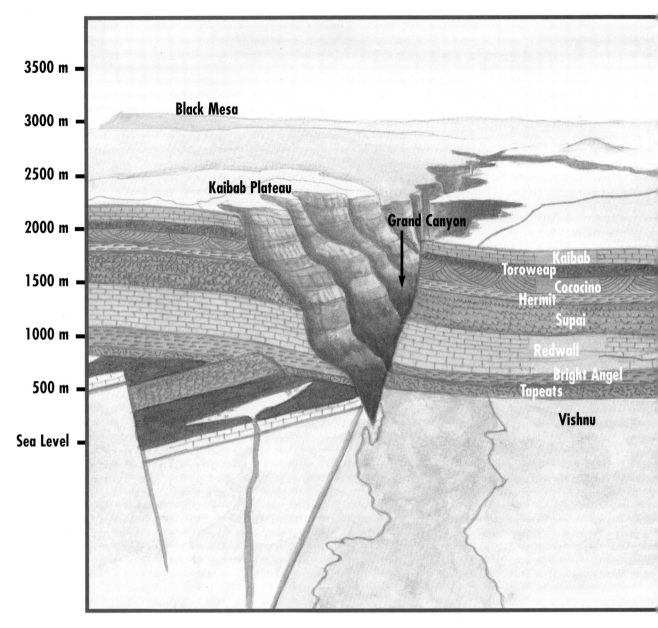

Labels in figure (top to bottom / left to right):
3500 m
3000 m — Black Mesa
2500 m
2000 m — Kaibab Plateau — Grand Canyon
1500 m — Kaibab / Toroweap / Cococino / Hermit
1000 m — Supai / Redwall
500 m — Bright Angel / Tapeats
Sea Level — Vishnu

A Slice of the Grand Canyon

Now let's take a look at a cross-section map of a famous landform—the Grand Canyon. The Grand Canyon is a beautiful landform located in Arizona. A canyon is actually a very deep, steep-sided valley formed by a river. Try to answer the questions as you look at the cross-section map of the Grand Canyon.

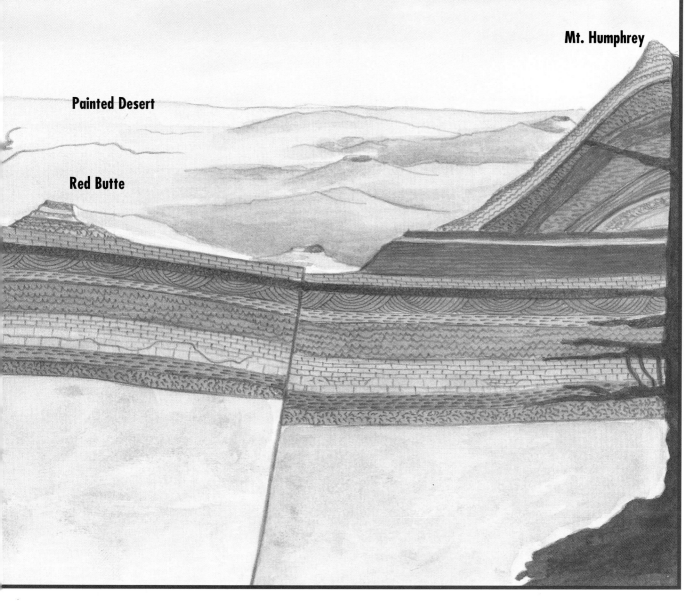

Painted Desert

Red Butte

Mt. Humphrey

THINK ABOUT IT

1. The bottom of the Grand Canyon cuts deep into the ground. But it is still above sea level. What is the elevation of the bottom of the Grand Canyon?

2. What is the elevation of Mount Humphrey?

3. Your car stops near Red Butte, and you decide to climb it. You want the climb to be as easy as possible. Which side of Red Butte do you climb? Why?

Visiting the Grand Canyon

Another useful map is an elevation map. This type of map shows how high or low the land is—it shows *elevation.* However, because the map is flat, different elevations are shown in different colors. Which color shows high elevation?

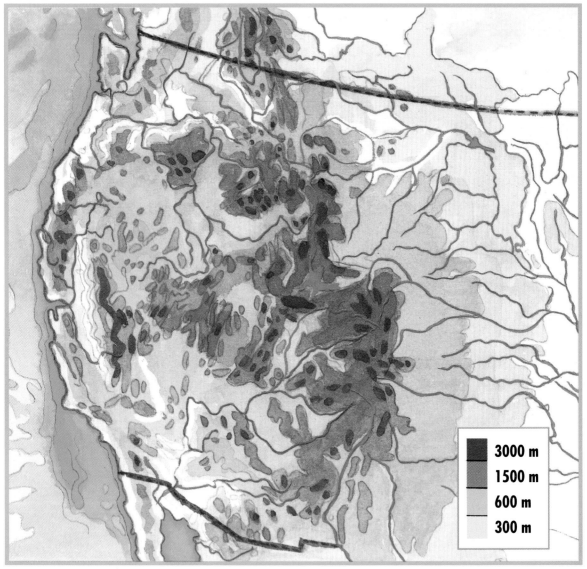

■	3000 m
■	1500 m
	600 m
	300 m

Suppose you and your family arrive at the Visitor Center at the Grand Canyon National Park. A park ranger gives you a map that shows the elevation of areas in and around the canyon. You begin to plan a trip through the canyon. As you think about your trip, some questions pop into your mind. You study the map in search of the answers.

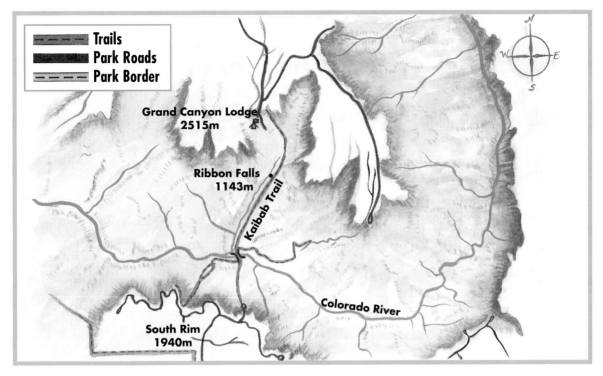

Trails
Park Roads
Park Border

Grand Canyon Lodge
2515m

Ribbon Falls
1143m

Kaibab Trail

Colorado River

South Rim
1940m

You decide to take a helicopter ride across the Grand Canyon from south to north, following the Kaibab Trail. Will the elevation be the same where you land as where you take off? How do you know?

Down the trail, you see the Phantom Ranch suspension bridge. What does the bridge cross?

You get to Ribbon Falls and have a picnic lunch. After lunch, you start a hike that will end at the Grand Canyon Lodge. Will you be walking downhill, uphill, or on flat land? How do you know?

When you get to the Colorado River, you change your mind about crossing the Grand Canyon. Instead, you decide to hop on a raft. In which direction will the river carry you? How do you know?

QUICK CHECK

LESSON 1 REVIEW

❶ What kind of map would you use if you wanted to see the rock layers inside a mountain?

❷ When would you rather have an elevation map—when traveling across mountains or when traveling across a plain? Explain your answer.

❸ Name four landforms and draw a diagram of each one. Tell how they are alike and how they are different.

2 WEATHERING

Look at the cliff in the photograph. Notice all the broken rock at the cliff's base. Where do you think the rock came from? In this lesson, you'll find some answers.

Physical Weathering

You've already read about landforms. You've probably realized that landforms are made from rock. You've also read that landforms change over time. Since landforms change over time, it makes sense that the rocks that help make up the landforms also change. You learned some ways rocks change when you studied the rock cycle in the last section. In what other ways do you think rocks change?

Any process that causes rocks to break down is called **weathering.** Weathering is caused by water, wind, ice, plants, and other factors.

When the weather is warm, water seeps into the cracks in rocks. If the temperature gets cold enough, the water turns to ice. Ice takes up more space than water does. That means that water expands when it freezes. When water expands in the cracks of rocks, it breaks the rocks apart.

Water can freeze in the cracks of rocks and break the rocks apart. ▶

Plant roots can break large rocks into small pieces. ▼

Can you break apart a rock with your bare hands? Probably not, but many plants can break rocks when their roots grow into the cracks in the rocks. As the roots grow thicker, they push against the sides of the cracks. They push so hard that they break the rock open. This is another way that big rocks get smaller. The breaking up of rocks by water, ice, and plants is called **physical weathering.**

THINK ABOUT IT

How can water change rocks?

D41

Sand at Work

Rocks are weathered by water, ice, and plants. Do the following activity to discover another material that causes weathering of rocks.

DO THIS

1 Measure and record the mass of the rocks. Then measure and record the mass of the jar and the sand together.

2 Put the rocks in the jar with the sand, and fasten the lid tightly.

MATERIALS

- balance with masses
- sandstone pieces
- plastic jar with lid
- sand
- Science Log data sheet

3 Each day for a week, shake the jar for 30 minutes.

4 After a week, measure and record the mass of the rocks. Also measure and record the mass of the sand and the jar.

THINK AND WRITE

1. Describe what the sandstone looked like at the beginning of the experiment. Describe what the sand looked like.

2. After a week, what happened to the sandstone? What happened to the sand? Explain your observations.

3. Compare the masses of sand and rock from steps 1 and 4.

4. **INTERPRETING DATA** Use your interpretation of the data in this activity to infer what happened at a red-sand beach. Above the beach is a red-rock cliff. The beach is completely covered with red sand. Where do you think the sand came from?

Looking Back In this activity, you observed that sand particles can wear away rock. This also happens in nature, with the help of the wind. Sand particles blown by the wind are like the particles in sandpaper. The wind blows the sand particles against rock. The rock is worn away in the same way that wood is worn away by sandpaper. This process is called *abrasion*.

Chemical Weathering

If you've ever visited a large underground cave, you might have seen what looked like stone icicles hanging from the cave's ceiling or rising from its floor. What are those odd-looking stone shapes? How and why did they form?

Chemical weathering is a process that takes place when certain chemicals act on rocks. The process that formed these stone icicles began when water dissolved the minerals in certain types of rocks. The water flowed into underground caves and dripped from the ceilings. As the water dripped, it left behind tiny bits of minerals that built up to form the pointed stone.

THINK ABOUT IT

Inside a cave, what kind of rock has weathered? What kind of chemical did the weathering?

MATERIALS
- **6 clear jars or plastic cups**
- **wax pencil**
- **limestone rock chips**
- **sandstone rock chips**
- **quartzite rock chips**
- **water**
- **vinegar**
- **Science Log data sheet**

Dissolving Rocks

Chemical weathering can take place inside a jar just as it does outside. Try the activity to find out more.

DO THIS

1 Use the pencil to write the word *limestone* on two of the jars. On two other jars, write *sandstone*, and on the last two jars, write *quartzite*.

2 Put a few limestone chips in the jars labeled *limestone*. Put a few sandstone chips in the jars labeled *sandstone*. Put a few quartzite chips in the jars labeled *quartzite*.

3 Fill one jar of each pair with water. Fill the other jar of each pair with vinegar. (Vinegar is a mild acid.)

4 Observe and record what happens in each jar. Repeat the observation 20 minutes later and then again the next day.

THINK AND WRITE

1. Which kind of rock changed?

2. What caused the rock to change? How do you know?

3. Look at the photograph of the cave. It has stone icicles on the floor and the ceiling. What kind of rock do you think the cave is made of? Explain your answer.

4. **INTERPRETING DATA** You had to use the data you collected in the activity to help you answer the question about the stone icicles in the cave. What was the data? How did you interpret the data and apply it to the cave?

▲ **Elephant rock**

Looking Back Chemical weathering can also occur in other ways. The rocks in the picture are part of the Valley of Fire in Nevada. Notice that part of the rock formation is a reddish brown while some is a lighter color. The rocks didn't always look like this. Once, all the rock was the same light color. What turned part of it darker? Oxygen in the air combined with iron in the hill to make rust. Rust is soft and flaky, and it easily turns to dust.

Unusual Rock Shapes

These shapes are the results of the actions of wind, water, and ice. It took millions of years for these unusual shapes to form.

◄ Ship Rock in New Mexico is all that is left of the inside of an old volcano. It is made of a dark igneous rock called *basalt*.

This unusual shape formed when soft, easily weathered rock underneath harder rock was worn away. ▶

◄ In Death Valley, California, Mushroom Rock formed because of the wind blowing sand against the rock.

These rocks in the Black Hills of South Dakota are called *Needles,* because of their sharp points. The rocks formed when weathering occurred. ▶

◀ Soft layers of rock are worn away faster than hard layers. That's how these unusual "creatures," called *rock goblins,* formed.

LESSON 2 REVIEW

❶ Explain how desert sandstorms can weather rock.

❷ Some factories send chemicals into the air that mix with rain and form an acid. If you were building a stone house nearby, what kind of rock would you *not* use? What kinds of rock might you use? Give examples and explain.

3 EROSION

Many people have seen the Grand Canyon. They have described the stacked layers of rock as looking like pages in a book. They have told about the pink rattlesnakes that hide among the rocks. They have heard mountain lions roaring in the night. And they have seen eagles soaring through the air.

An 11-year-old Native American boy named Andrew Jones wrote a poem about his experience in the Grand Canyon. These are his words.

Canyons, Echoing
going away—coming back
repeating my voice

Andrew's voice echoed because of the steep walls of the canyon. How could such walls form?

What Is Erosion?

The process by which running water formed the Grand Canyon is called *erosion*. Look at some examples of erosion.

Erosion is the process by which weathered rock and soil are moved from one place to another. Water moving over the land and in rivers is the most effective agent of erosion. An *agent* is any force that erodes rock or soil. Other agents of erosion are waves, gravity, wind, and huge, moving sheets of ice called *glaciers*.

During erosion, weathering continues. Moving rocks bump each other and break up more. The moving rocks also wear away the rock over which they move.

▲ Waves can carry rocks and sand along a coast. The waves also pick up and smash rocks against the rocks of the shore, causing erosion.

▲ Glaciers pick up soil, rocks, and even boulders like this one and can carry them hundreds of kilometers from where they started.

Wind can move large amounts of sand from one area to another. ▼

◄ Gravity pulls weathered rock and soil down hills. Erosion by gravity can cause landslides or rockslides.

THINK ABOUT IT

How do weathering and erosion work together to change landforms?

ACTIVITY

How Does Moving Water Change Land?

Of all the forces that change the land, one of the most powerful is moving water. The carrying away of weathered rock by running water is one type of erosion. Scientists have found evidence that the Colorado River carved the Grand Canyon in this way in only five million years. That means its rushing water wore away and carried off enough rock to make a canyon 2,000 meters (about 6,560 feet) deep. Not all rivers are as powerful as the Colorado. What makes one river a better carver than another? Let's find out.

MATERIALS

- large tray
- sand
- books
- pitcher
- water
- Science Log data sheet

DO THIS

1. Make a layer of sand in one half of the tray. Put one book under the end of the tray that holds the sand.

2. Slowly pour water onto the sand.

3. After a few seconds, stop pouring. Observe what happened to the sand. Draw a diagram to show what happened.

4. Repeat steps 1–3, but this time pour the water faster.

5. Repeat steps 1–3, but this time tilt the tray more by putting more books under it.

THINK AND WRITE

1. In this activity, what did the sand and the water stand for? How did the changes you made affect the flow of the water?

2. What increased the cutting power of your "river" the most?

D50

Roads of Water

Rivers have been used by travelers all over the world. On these pages, you will learn how these roads of water form.

▲ The Colorado River moves swiftly through the Grand Canyon.

▲ The Yukon River moves slowly through Alaska and Canada.

▲ In the spring, snow begins to melt high in the mountains. Drops of water splash from rock to rock. The drops come together to make little trickles of water that run downhill. A rain shower adds more water, and the trickles become a stream.

Mountains stretch over many states. But the waters that flow down them end up in just a few great rivers. In the United States there are three mountain areas that each feed a great river. Because these areas drain water off the land, they are called *drainage basins*.

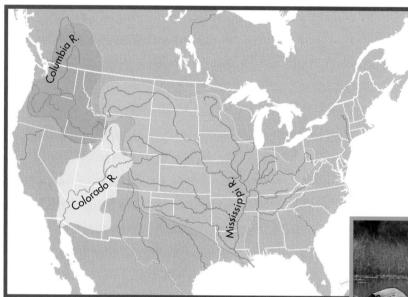

▲ Drainage basins of the Colorado, Columbia, and Mississippi rivers

The map on this page shows the drainage basins for the Colorado, Columbia, and Mississippi rivers. In some places, such as the Grand Canyon, the rivers plunge steeply downward. In other places, such as the southern part of the Mississippi, the rivers run toward the ocean over land that is almost flat.

No matter how these rivers flow, they always do the same things. They wear away parts of the land. They carry worn-away bits of rock, sand, soil, and clay wherever they go.

THINK ABOUT IT

How can water carve a valley?

▲ The source of the mighty Mississippi River is so shallow you can walk across it.

As the Mississippi moves toward the Gulf of Mexico, it becomes wider and deeper. ▼

The End of the River Road

You have seen why rivers are important agents of erosion. Now see what happens to the materials they carry away.

When rivers reach the sea, their waters slow down. They can no longer hold the bits of rock, sand, soil, and clay they have been carrying. So they begin to drop these materials.

In some places, the dumped materials pile up to make new land. This new land at a river's mouth is called a *delta*. One of the largest deltas in the world lies at the mouth of the Mississippi River, where it empties into the Gulf of Mexico. This delta looks like a huge fan. It's a fan that is 60 kilometers (37 miles) across!

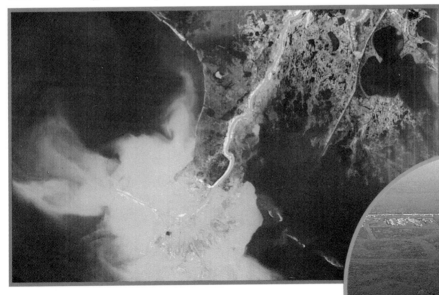

◀ The Mississippi delta as it looks from space

The Mississippi delta has rich soil. ▼

Rivers don't just wear away the land. Sometimes they build up the land. The soil in deltas is very rich in nutrients. Plants that grow in the delta grow in soil that came from mountains and land hundreds of kilometers to the north.

THINK ABOUT IT

Why are rivers important to the land and to people?

Glaciers—What Are They?

Glaciers aren't things most people can see in their neighborhood. However, there have been times in Earth's history when glaciers covered much more of Earth than they do today. Read the next article to find out what glaciers are and what they do.

HUGE RIVERS of ICE

from *National Geographic World*

LITERATURE Listen. All is quiet as you gaze across the mountains. Below you a giant ribbon of ice winds among the rocky peaks. The ice looks firm and still—but it's on the move. How do you know? Once in a while the ground shakes slightly, and a rumble like distant thunder breaks the quiet. The ribbon of ice is actually a *river* of ice. It's a glacier. Glaciers form in parts of the world where snow piles up faster than it melts—in mountains or in other areas that stay cold most of the year. Over time, the snow crystals change to ice. When the ice is thick enough, its own weight causes it to move. Only then is it a glacier. The build-up may take a few years or hundreds of years. Once in motion, the ice creeps down a slope, perhaps traveling only an inch a day.

In Greenland and in Antarctica, glaciers called ice sheets cover thousands of square miles. Most glaciers are smaller and form on high mountains such as Alaska's Mount McKinley.

Different parts of the same glacier move at different speeds. The sides and bottom of the moving ice grind against mountain walls. These parts move more slowly than does the ice in the center. Gradually the sections pull apart and the ice cracks, forming deep canyons, or crevasses (krih VASS uhz).

A river of ice inches down a valley in the Austrian Alps. This moving ice is called a glacier. It formed over many years, as snow collected near the peaks and the crystals turned to ice. As more snow fell, the ice grew so thick that it began to move under its own weight. A glacier wears away mountainsides as it moves.

Master Mountain Carvers

A glacier changes the land. It digs out rocks and boulders, gradually carving a huge, bowl-shaped hollow called a cirque (SUHRK). As it creeps downhill, the glacier scrapes the valley floor and the mountain walls.

Continuing its slide, the glacier and the rock material along its edge grind against the mountainsides. This forms a deep, U-shaped valley that will remain long after the glacier has melted.

Icescapes

White areas on the map show glaciers around the world. Such ice spreads across one-tenth of Earth's land. It occurs on mainlands and on islands. The largest glaciers, called ice sheets, lie in polar regions—in Greenland and in Antarctica. They are about two miles thick in places.

QUICK CHECK

LESSON 3 REVIEW

1 Why might one river change land differently from the way another river changes land?

2 When a river overflows its banks, what kind of damage occurs?

3 How are the actions of a river and a glacier alike? How are they different?

DOUBLE CHECK

SECTION B REVIEW

1. How do maps help people understand different landforms?

2. Tell how weathering and erosion are alike. Tell how they are different.

Earth's History

▲ **Uncovering dinosaur fossils**

▲ **Dinosaur footprint**

Using a small brush, you slowly move away soil clinging to a large, flat rock. As you brush, you see that the rock isn't flat all over. There are dents in it. A few more strokes of the brush, and the dents take on a shape. You finally realize that you are looking at the footprint of a dinosaur!

Now that you've discovered the footprint, questions race through your mind. What kind of dinosaur made the prints? What did it look like? How long ago did it live? In this section, you will learn how studying rocks and the remains of once-living things can help answer questions such as these.

1 ROCK LAYERS AND THE FOSSIL RECORD

Suppose you are looking into a bedroom with no one in it. What can you tell about whose room it is? There are many clues in the room that can give you answers. In this lesson, you'll learn that many clues found below Earth's surface can tell you about Earth's past. You've already read about how sediments can become rock over millions of years. The rock layers contain many clues that tell what the land was like when the layers were formed.

Rock Layers

Scientists gather data from Earth's surface and from beneath it. Read on to get an idea of how that happens.

To understand how people gather information from layers of rock, think how you might investigate a garbage dump. Suppose you've been asked to find out how old the garbage dump is. You've taken on the messy job of digging through the dump from top to bottom.

You use the newspapers you find in each layer of the dump to determine the age of the garbage around it. At first, you are digging through a layer of newly dumped garbage. As you dig farther down, you find a layer of garbage a year old. Even farther down is a layer that's two years old, and so on, until you reach a layer of ten-year-old garbage. The next sample is soil with no garbage. You now know that the garbage dump is ten years old.

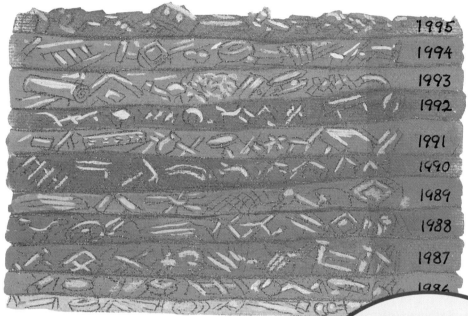

1995
1994
1993
1992
1991
1990
1989
1988
1987
1986

The rock layers of Earth's crust are laid down in much the same way as the layers of garbage in a garbage dump. Rocks are often found with one layer resting on top of another. And, like the top garbage layers, the rock layers on the top are the newest. The layers of rock get older the farther down you go.

▲ This roadbed was cut through a hill containing layers and layers of rock.

Scientists use the order of rock layers to decide how old the rock layers are. Finding the age of rocks helps scientists find out the history of plants and animals on Earth. How are rocks related to plants and animals? Fossils may be found in some rocks. A **fossil** is the preserved trace or remains of a once-living thing, usually a plant or an animal. When scientists figure out how old the rocks are, they can also figure out how long ago these organisms lived.

Sometimes scientists do just the opposite. If they know the time in history when a plant or an animal lived, that tells them how old the rock layer is.

This fossil is of an ammonite, a very old kind of shellfish. ▼

▲ This is a fossil of one of the first birds on Earth.

Plants can form fossils, also, as you can see from these fossil leaves. ▶

THINK ABOUT IT

How are the newspapers in a garbage dump like the fossils in rock layers? How are they different?

A C T I V I T Y

The Age of Fossils

In this activity, you and your classmates will make your own model rock layers and fossils. Then you will see if you can find out how old your classmates' fossils are.

MATERIALS

- modeling clay (5 colors)
- shoe box with lid
- seashells (5 kinds)
- wax pencil
- wax paper
- Science Log data sheet

DO THIS

1 Make a chart like the one shown.

"ROCK" LAYERS AND "FOSSILS"		
Layer	Clay Color	Shell Number
1		
2		
3		
4		
5		

2 Use clay of one color to make a layer on the bottom of the shoe box. Press one of the seashells into the clay to make a print. Remove the shell and mark it with a code number. Don't use code numbers that are in order, such as 1, 2, 3, 4, 5. Record the color of the clay layer and the code number of the shell used to make the print.

3 Put a sheet of wax paper over the clay layer. Also place a sheet of wax paper in the box lid.

D60

4 In the box lid, make a new layer out of another color of clay. Press a different shell into the top of this layer. Mark this shell with a different code number. Record the clay's color and the shell's code number.

5 Carefully put this layer over the first layer. Put a sheet of wax paper over the new layer.

6 Repeat steps 4 and 5, using all the colors of clay to make more layers and shell prints. When you finish, put your shells in the box lid.

7 Exchange your clay layers and shells with those of another group. Make a chart like the one you made at the beginning of the activity. Then remove and examine each layer of clay. Do not mix up the order of the layers. Match each shell to its print. Use your chart to record the color of the clay and the code number of the shell that made the print.

THINK AND WRITE

1. The layers of clay are model rock layers, and the shell prints are model fossils. Use what you know about rock layers to write the numbers of the shells in order from oldest to newest. Explain how you figured out the order.

2. RECOGNIZING TIME/SPACE RELATIONSHIPS Time relationships tell you the order of events. Space relationships tell you about locations of objects. How did you use both the time relationships of the rock layers and the space relationships of the fossils in this activity?

LESSON 1 REVIEW

How are rock layers and fossils related?

2 FOSSILS

Think back to the photo of the dinosaur footprint at the beginning of this section. Think about how the print was made. The rock it is in began as mud. The dinosaur's feet left their marks in the mud wherever the dinosaur stepped. The mud was slowly covered over. After a very, very long time, the mud was changed by heat and pressure into rock. Over time, the soil and rock above the footprint were worn away. The rock that used to be mud was exposed, revealing the print.

Kinds of Fossils

Fossils can be formed in several ways. Read on to find out more.

Imprints

As you have probably realized by now, the dinosaur's footprint is a fossil. It is the trace of a once-living animal. Fossils such as trails, burrows, and wormholes were formed in the same way as the footprints. They were originally made in soft dirt or mud that was later changed into rock.

Fossil worm burrow ▼

These fish all died at once. Something happened to all of them, and they ended up on the bottom. The shape of their bones was pressed into the soft bottom that, over time, hardened into rock. This formed an almost flat fossil called an imprint. Common imprints are of fish, leaves, feathers, and, of course, footprints. ▶

Molds and Casts

The animal that lived in this shell died a long time ago. The shell fell to the bottom of the ocean. Mud quickly covered the shell. Over a very long time, the mud changed into rock around the shell. Water seeping through the rock dissolved the shell. Left behind in the rock layer was a space that had the shape of the shell. A space left behind in hardened material is a kind of fossil called a *mold*. But the process did not stop. Sometimes a mold fills with minerals that harden. The minerals take the shape of the living thing or the part of a living thing that was buried. A filled-in mold is a kind of fossil called a *cast*. The photograph shows the cast of a sea animal called a *trilobite* (TRY loh byt).

▲ This shellfish fossil looks just like the outside of the real thing!

▲ This trilobite fossil is a cast.

D63

Dinosaurs lived on Earth more than 65 million years ago. But scientists know a lot about these animals because they have found their bones. Bones of once-living things, such as dinosaurs, are usually casts, although they can form in the same way as petrified (PEH trih fyd) wood. You'll learn about that later.

Scientists put together the fossil bones to make a skeleton. From the skeleton, scientists can make a model of a whole dinosaur. Digging up the bones is very delicate work. Each bone must be dug up separately, cleaned, and preserved. Then the bones can be put together.

◄ Scientists unearthing the bones of a dinosaur in Wyoming.

This dinosaur skeleton ▶ was found in the same area as the dig in the picture above.

Wood Fossils

This is a "forest" of stone trees called a petrified forest. *Petrify* means "turn to stone." The real trees died long ago. Water, containing minerals from rocks, seeped into the wood. As the wood slowly rotted away, the minerals took its place. The minerals hardened into stone in the shape of the wood they replaced. ▼

Preserved in Sap, Ice, or Tar

This insect is millions of years old. It got stuck in the sap of a tree. The sap hardened into a fossil called *amber*. The whole insect was preserved inside. You can even see its wings. ▶

Whole animals can also be preserved in ice. Woolly mammoths lived thousands of years ago where the land was covered with ice. When some of these animals died, their bodies were trapped in the ice and frozen. People have found the frozen animals with their skin and fur preserved. ▼

In some areas of Earth, there are deep holes filled with tar. When an animal or a plant falls into the tar, it is preserved. The saber-toothed cat skull shown here was preserved in a tar pit. ▼

THINK ABOUT IT

1. How are the fossils that are found in amber, in tar, and in ice alike?

2. How are molds and imprints the same? How are they different?

Fossils: Clues to the Past

Scientists and teachers may use many words to explain how fossils help you understand Earth's history. A poet often uses far fewer words to tell you the same thing. Read this poem to learn more about fossils.

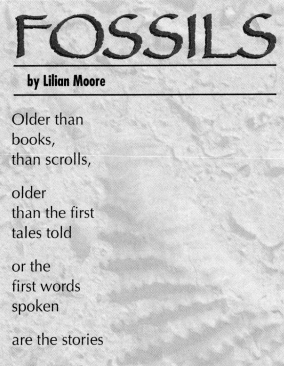

FOSSILS

by Lilian Moore

Older than
books,
than scrolls,

older
than the first
tales told

or the
first words
spoken

are the stories

in forests that
turned to
stone

in ice walls
that trapped the
mammoth

in the long
bones of
dinosaurs—

the fossil
stories that begin
Once upon a time

THINK ABOUT IT

What does the poem tell you about fossils?

Riddle of the Grand Canyon

You've discovered that by studying rock layers, you can solve riddles about what the land was like a long time ago. In a similar way, fossils can help scientists solve riddles about things that lived a long time ago.

The drawing shows layers of rock found in the Grand Canyon and fossils found in the layers. Both the rocks and the fossils are clues to the history of the Grand Canyon. Look at the drawing and read the captions. Then answer the questions to find out how good a scientific detective you are.

1. What is the oldest layer of rock?

2. What is the youngest layer of rock?

3. What do the kinds of fossils found in the Toroweap Formation and Kaibab Limestone tell you about the history of the Grand Canyon?

4. Which animals probably lived on Earth first, sharks or brachiopods? What evidence supports your answer?

Kaibab limestone
Fossils of sharks, sponges, and sea lilies

Toroweap formation
Fossils of corals and animals called *brachiopods* that looked like clams

Coconino sandstone
Fossils of reptiles and scorpions
Rocks that look like hardened sand dunes

Hermit shale
Fossil of a large amphibian that lived in swamps
Fossils of ferns and insects

Supai formation
Fossils of plants and primitive reptiles that lived in swamps

Redwall limestone
Fossils of brachiopods found here as well as in the Toroweap formation

Bright angel shale
Fossils of small sea animals found here

Tapeats sandstone
Fossil algae

Vishnu schist
No fossils here
Igneous rocks cut through this layer.

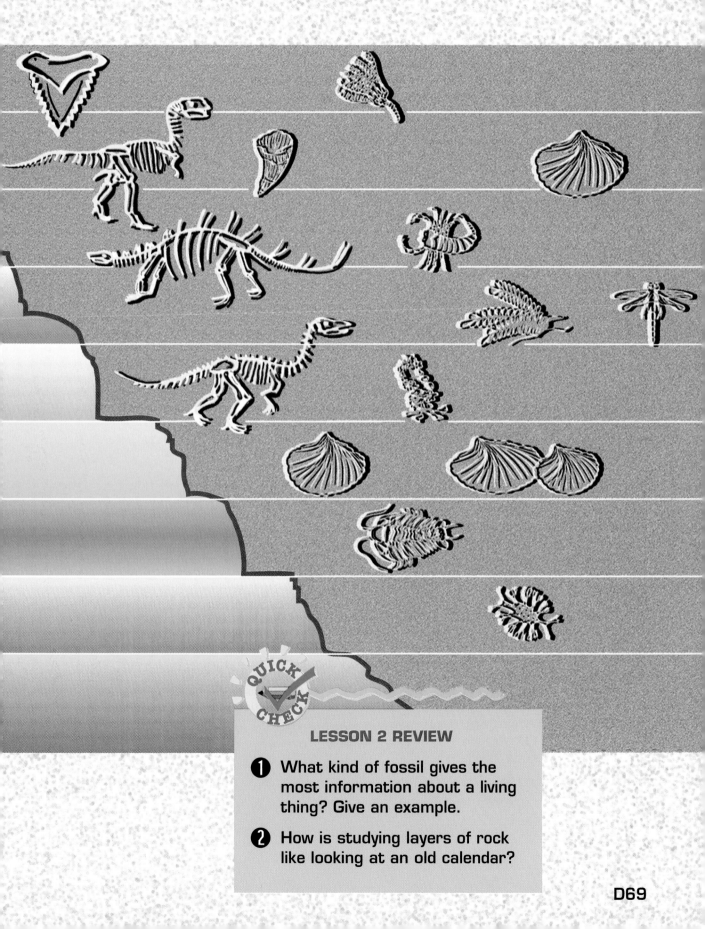

LESSON 2 REVIEW

❶ What kind of fossil gives the most information about a living thing? Give an example.

❷ How is studying layers of rock like looking at an old calendar?

3 GEOLOGIC TIME

How long is a long time ago? To your grandfather, a long time ago is when he was in fourth grade. To a fourth-grade student, a long time ago is when he or she was in first grade. To a dinosaur expert, a long time ago is when dinosaurs still lived on Earth. In this lesson, you will learn about Earth's history. It describes what has happened since the Earth formed a very, very, very long time ago.

Cryptozoic Eon	Phanerozoic Eon					
	Paleozoic Era					
Precambrian or Hadean, Archean, and Proterozoic Eras	Cambrian Period 570-505 million years ago	Ordovician Period 505-438 million years ago	Silurian Period 438-408 million years ago	Devonian Period 408-360 million years ago	Carboniferous Period 360-286 million years ago	
Beginning of Earth Seas form Mountains start to form Life begins in the sea Jellyfish appear	Continents partly covered with seas Trilobites, sponges, brachiopods evolve	Volcanoes very active Mountains grow First fish evolve	First land plants evolve Coral reefs form	New York's Acadian Mountains rise First forests evolve First insects, sharks and amphibians evolve	Appalachian Mountains rise Ice Age comes First reptiles, mosses, and insects that fly	
	Early / Middle / Late	Early / Late		Early / Middle / Late	Mississippian / Pennsylvanian	

Once upon a Time . . .

About 140 million years ago, a strange animal had appeared on Earth. It had wings with claws on them and sharp teeth in its jaws. It had a long tail and looked very much like a small, flying dinosaur. You can see a picture of its fossil on page D59.

But when scientists examined the animal's fossil, they found evidence of something else—feathers! Had they discovered the first bird? That question is still under debate. How did they know it was 140 million years old? They knew because the fossil was found in rock that was 140 million years old.

The chart shows a calendar of Earth's history and some of the living things that first appeared during different parts of Earth's history.

Because Earth's history is so long, its parts are not divided into days, weeks, months, or years. The largest parts of Earth's history are divided into eras. Eras are divided into periods.

		Mesozoic Era		Cenozoic Era	
Permian Period 286-245 million years ago	**Triassic Period 245-208 million years ago**	**Jurassic Period 208-144 million years ago**	**Cretaceous Period 144-66 million years ago**	**Tertiary Period 66-2 million years ago**	**Quaternary Period less than 2 million years ago**
First cone-bearing plants evolve	New Jersey palisades form First dinosaurs and mammals evolve	Rocky Mountains rise First birds evolve Age of dinosaurs begins	First flowering plants evolve Dinosaurs mysteriously die out	Alps in Europe, Andes South America, and Himalayan Mountains in Asia rise First horses	Ice ages come Large parts of North America and Europe covered with ice Modern humans evolve
Early / Late	Early / Middle / Late	Early / Middle / Late	Early / Late	Paleocene / Eocene / Oligocene / Miocene / Pliocene	Pleistocene / Holocene

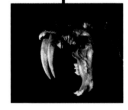

THINK ABOUT IT

Which era is the oldest?
Which is the youngest?

Making a Geologic Time Line

Compared with all of Earth's history, how long have fish been on Earth? During what portion of Earth's history did dinosaurs live? An easy way to answer these questions is to make a time line. In this way, you can actually *see* periods of time. Here's how you can make a chart that helps you see time.

DO THIS

MATERIALS
- roll of colored paper
- tape measure
- scissors
- adding machine tape
- white glue
- marker
- Science Log data sheet

❶ Measure and cut 460 cm of colored paper. Then measure and cut 460 cm of adding machine tape. Glue the adding machine tape across the top of the colored paper.

❷ At the left end of the tape, draw a line and write below it *Formation of Earth—4.6 billion years ago.*

❸ Measure 330 cm from the right side of the paper. Draw a line across the tape and label it *First organisms—3.3 billion years ago.*

4 Add the labels for *a–i* on the right. Each measurement should be made from the right side of the paper. Make drawings to illustrate your time line.

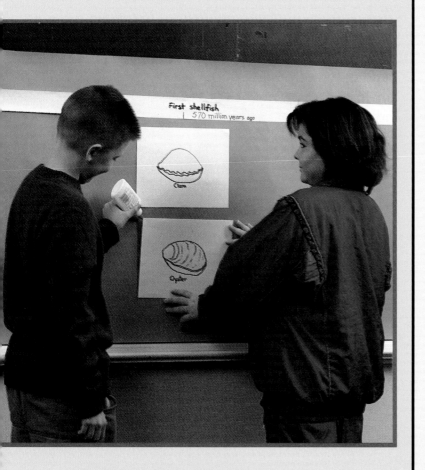

a. 57 cm: First shellfish (early animals that were like clams, oysters, and mussels)—570 million years ago

b. 47 cm: First fish—470 million years ago

c. 35 cm: First amphibians (early animals that were like frogs, toads, and salamanders)—350 million years ago

d. 31 cm: First reptiles (early animals that were like dinosaurs, lizards, and snakes)—310 million years ago

e. 22.5 cm: First dinosaurs, first mammals—225 million years ago

f. 14 cm: First birds—140 million years ago

g. 6.5 cm: Last dinosaurs—65 million years ago

h. 2 mm: First humans—2 million years ago

i. 0 mm: Today

THINK AND WRITE

1. Describe in words, not numbers, how long dinosaurs lived on Earth compared with the whole history of Earth. Do the same for fish.

2. **RECOGNIZING TIME/SPACE RELATIONSHIPS** The history of Earth is measured in time. But your time line is measured in distance. Explain how time and distance are related on your time line.

The Fossil History of the Horse

From doing the last activity, you know that it takes a very long time for animals and plants to change. Scientists use fossils they have found to trace the history of some plants and animals.

By digging up fossil bones and teeth, scientists have learned a lot about how horses have changed over time. Scientists know that horses looked much different 50 million years ago from the way they look today. The fossils of horses provide a record of how they have changed over time.

The first ancestor of the horse evolved about 50 million years ago. It was about as big as a medium-size dog. It had four toes on its feet instead of hoofs. Look at the drawing to see how the horse's hoofs evolved.

The shape of the teeth show that the earliest horses ate leaves and other soft plant parts. Slowly, the teeth changed and became flatter. These changes made the teeth better for grinding tough plants like grasses. Today's horses eat this kind of tough plant food.

◀ **Evolution of the horse**

QUICK CHECK

LESSON 3 REVIEW

Suppose you picked up a rock and found a fish fossil. By studying your time line, what could you say about the age of the rock?

✔ **DOUBLE CHECK**

SECTION C REVIEW

1. What are the types of fossils? How does each type form?

2. How do scientists know that organisms change over time?

SECTION D
National Treasures

The land and water of our country are national treasures. The land is the source of many minerals. Minerals are needed to produce such things as electricity and steel. Some parts of the country have fantastic works of nature, like the coral reefs off the coast of Florida and Death Valley National Monument in California.

You can use and enjoy these treasures today. But many of them may be in danger. As you read on, you will find out why. You will also discover how you can help save these treasures.

1 USING RESOURCES WISELY

You switch on an electric light. A lump of coal was probably burned to generate the electricity. You throw an empty can in the garbage. There goes another bit of aluminum. Well, Earth has plenty more coal and aluminum, doesn't it? Yes, but what happens when all the coal and aluminum are used up?

Running Out of Resources

What are resources? How do we use them? Where do they come from?

Coal and aluminum are examples of natural resources. A **natural resource** is any useful material that comes from Earth. Earth has two kinds of resources.

Renewable resources can be replaced during an average human lifetime (about 75 years). Resources that come from living things, such as wood from trees, are renewable.

Either **nonrenewable resources** can't be replaced once they are used or it would take a very, very long time for them to be replaced. Oil and minerals must be used carefully because they are nonrenewable resources. Usually, soil is also considered a nonrenewable resource, since it takes a very long time to form soil that is good for growing things.

▲ Soil like this takes hundreds of years to form.

▲ Oil, a nonrenewable resource, is removed from the Earth using wells like these.

THINK ABOUT IT

Write three ways that you could use nonrenewable resources wisely.

ACTIVITY

Resources for the Future

Resources are being used up at a faster rate than ever before. How is this happening? You can find out by doing this activity.

MATERIALS

- popcorn
- 4 bowls
- 14 index cards
- 15 small lunch bags
- Science Log data sheet

DO THIS

1. Fill the bowls with popcorn.
2. Fourteen students should each draw an index card out of a paper bag. The cards have these labels:

   2 cards — You

   4 cards — Child

   8 cards — Grandchild
3. Each student should take a lunch bag.
4. The students who drew the You cards should go to the bowls and fill their lunch bags with popcorn. Record the amount of popcorn taken and the amount left—for example, $\frac{1}{2}$ bowl taken, $3\frac{1}{2}$ bowls left.

5 Now the students with the Child cards should fill their bags with popcorn. Record the amount of popcorn taken and the amount left.

6 Finally, the students with the Grandchild cards should divide the popcorn that is left and put it in their bags. How much popcorn did each "grandchild" get?

THINK AND WRITE

1. The popcorn in this activity was a model for a resource. How would you describe the way the resource was used?

2. Suppose there is a fourth group of 16 students called Great-grandchildren. You are instructed to be sure that each "great-grandchild" gets at least $\frac{1}{2}$ bag of popcorn. What would you need to do to be sure enough popcorn is left for them?

3. **CLASSIFYING/ORDERING**   When you classify objects, you put them into a group of things that are like them. In this activity, what type of resource did the popcorn represent? Why did you classify the popcorn as this type of resource?

Looking Back   You may have noticed that the number of people increased from You to Children to Grandchildren. This increase represents the way the world's population has been growing for at least the last 400 years.

The more people there are on Earth, the more resources that are needed to support them all. The increase in the number of people is part of the reason our natural resources are being used up. It is also an important reason for being careful with our resources.

Destroying the Land to Get Resources

Resources that come from the land have to be removed from the land. These resources may be rocks, such as coal, marble, and granite. Or the resources may be minerals within the rocks. These useful minerals are called *ores*.

In some places, the resources are hidden deep in the ground. To get at these resources, mines with deep shafts and tunnels are built. Often the tunnels are not high enough for the miners to stand up. ▶

◀ In other places, the resources are near the surface of the land. Then they're easier and less expensive to remove. But to remove them, miners must strip away the soil and rock on the surface and dig deep pits. This kind of mining is called *strip mining*. The Kennecot copper mine, shown here, is the largest strip mine in the world. Look carefully at the picture to see the cranes parked in the mine.

In strip mining, a bulldozer or other earth-moving machine is used to cut large pieces of Earth's surface into strips. These strips are removed and taken to factories where the ore is separated from the rock.

But what's left behind? A gigantic hole in the ground. All the fertile topsoil needed by plants is gone.

▶

◀ Can the land be restored or returned to its original condition? One way to do this is to save and store the topsoil. Then, after the coal, aluminum, or copper is taken from the ground, the topsoil can be put back. Young trees can be planted. In recent years, laws have been passed to make mining companies restore the land after it is mined.

This picture shows a strip mine that was restored. Now it is a lake with a park around it.

THINK ABOUT IT

How are rock and mineral resources removed from the land?

Recycle It!

There's another way to save resources and land. Don't throw away anything made of a nonrenewable resource. What should you do with an aluminum can when it's empty? Recycle it by sending it to a collecting station! Then it will be sent to a factory where it can be melted down and made into new products. How much of a nonrenewable resource can one person save? Here's a way to find out.

DO THIS

❶ Collect all the aluminum cans and other aluminum products you and your family use in a week. Rinse them out and put them in a trash bag.

MATERIALS

- **aluminum used by your family in one week**
- **large plastic trash bag**
- **bathroom scale**
- **graph paper**
- **Science Log data sheet**

❷ Weigh the bag of aluminum and record the weight. You can do this by first weighing just yourself and then weighing yourself while you're holding the bag. Subtract your weight from the weight of you and the bag together. That will give you the weight of the bag.

3 Share your data with your classmates. Record the weights of their bags, too.

4 Make a bar graph showing all the weights. You can use the graph below as a model.

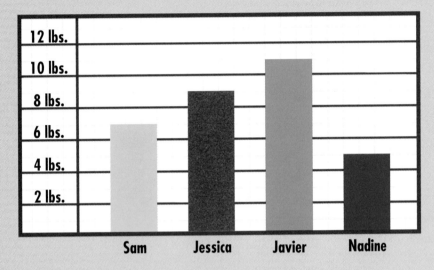

Sam	Jessica	Javier	Nadine

THINK AND WRITE

1. What was the greatest weight of aluminum collected? What was the least weight collected?

2. What was the total weight collected by the class?

3. What might explain the difference between the greatest and least weights collected?

4. Suppose that for every week in the year, you collect the same amount of aluminum as you did in this activity. How much would you recycle in a year? If the whole class recycles, how much aluminum would be recycled in a year?

LESSON 1 REVIEW

Think about the resources you use each week. Make a list of them. Divide the list into renewable and nonrenewable resources. How can you reduce the uses of each resource?

2 SAVING OUR NATIONAL PARKS

As the population of the United States has grown, more and more land has been needed for farms and factories. To protect the natural beauty of our country, a national park system was created. But now many parks are in danger because of the huge numbers of people that visit them. What kinds of dangers do the national parks face? In this lesson, you will find out.

Tour Our National Parks

There are 50 national parks in the United States. These are places where people go to see some of the natural wonders of our country.

▲ Hawai'i Volcanoes National Park is famous for its fiery mountains.

◄ Redwood National Park in California has the tallest trees on Earth.

◄ Yellowstone National Park covers parts of Wyoming, Idaho, and Montana. Many people come to see its geysers. Geysers are springs that send up fountains of hot water from inside the Earth. Yellowstone has more geysers than any other place in the world.

Visitors can walk beside an underground river in Mammoth Cave, Kentucky. Inside the cave, they can also see columns made of stone hanging from rocky ceilings or rising from rocky floors. ►

People also enjoy visiting Everglades National Park. Here they can see interesting birds and a wide variety of plants, including some of the most unusual orchids in the world.

Millions of people every year come to national parks in cars, vans, campers, buses, and, in some cases, boats. That is where the problem begins.

Hikers come to see the unspoiled beauty of a national park. But they often trample trailside flowers and plants. Some thoughtless visitors litter the woods with garbage. ▶

Some people like to let others know that they've been somewhere. So they may be tempted to carve their names on a tree or spray paint them on a rock or building. But carving may injure or kill the tree. And paint is ugly compared with mountain flowers or a sparkling granite boulder. The natural beauty is no longer natural and untouched. ▶

The people who visit national parks need places to sleep, to eat, and to shop. Their gas tanks must be filled. Some areas in national parks look more like shopping centers than parks. As these areas grow, they take over the living space of plants and animals. The natural area shrinks. ▼

Park rangers try to make sure that people obey park rules. But the number of people visiting parks is increasing faster than the number of rangers. So other ways have to be found to protect national parks. ▼

Here are some suggestions that have been made to protect national parks. Read them carefully before you do the activity that follows.

- **Limit the number of people who can visit a national park at any one time.**
- **Make people park their cars outside the park. Have buses or other large vehicles move people into and around the park. This would reduce traffic and air pollution.**
- **Reduce the number of restaurants, snack bars, shops, and gas stations in the park.**
- **Limit activities that harm living things in the park, such as hiking away from the trails.**
- **Provide more money to study how to preserve national parks.**
- **Provide money to educate people about the value of national parks and the ways to keep them healthy.**

▲ Park shuttle buses, such as these in Glacier National Park in Montana, reduce the number of vehicles in the parks.

THINK ABOUT IT

How do people harm our national parks?

How Can We Save Our National Parks?

Different people have different answers for this question. For example, a souvenir-shop owner might have a very different opinion than a park ranger has. In this activity, you and your classmates will investigate the opinions of different people. Then you will decide what you think should be done to save our national parks.

MATERIALS
- yarn
- 7 index cards
- tape recorder or video camera
- Science Log data sheet

DO THIS

1 Work with six other students. The members of your group should play the roles of the following people:

> 10-year-old park visitor
> adult park visitor
> park ranger
> souvenir-shop owner
> scientist who studies park plants
> local member of Congress
> reporter

Make a name tag for each member of the group. Make them like the ones shown in the picture.

 Your group will discuss the suggestions listed on page D87 from the points of view of the people you are playing. Which of the suggestions do you recommend? Which are you against? Why?

❹ Use a tape recorder or video camera to record the discussion. Then review the tape and make notes about each person's ideas.

THINK AND WRITE

Based on the discussion, suggest one or more ways to save our national parks that would be acceptable to all the people in the group. This might require some or all of the people to give up something they want.

QUICK CHECK

LESSON 2 REVIEW

❶ What is the main reason many national parks are in danger?

❷ "Leave only footprints. Take only memories." This is a rule for visiting parks. Explain what it means.

✅ DOUBLE CHECK

SECTION D REVIEW

1. What is the difference between a renewable resource and a nonrenewable resource? Give examples.

2. When might a renewable resource become nonrenewable?

3. How might the discovery of copper in a national park affect the park?

I REFLECT

It's time to think about the ideas you have discovered during your investigations. Think, too, about your many accomplishments.

SUMMARIZE

Answer the following in your Science Log.

1. What **I Wonder** questions have you answered in your investigations? What new questions have you asked?

2. What have you discovered about rocks, minerals, Earth's history, and Earth's resources? How have your ideas changed?

3. Did any of your discoveries surprise you? Explain.

What I Learned About Earths Rocks and Resources

I learned that there are different kinds of rocks. Rocks are made of minerals. Some rocks have fossils in them.

I found out that the land changes all the time and that weathering and erosion cause the changes.

I discovered that the Grand Canyon has many layers of rock and that each layer is older than the one on top of it. I learned that people have to be careful with resources because many of them can't be renewed.

CONNECT IDEAS

1. Explain how a sedimentary rock can become a metamorphic rock.

2. How did the Grand Canyon form?

3. How is a cast fossil different from a mold fossil?

4. How have scientists determined that plants and animals have changed over time?

5. What are natural resources, and how do we use them?

SCIENCE PORTFOLIO

❶ Complete your Science Experiences Record.

❷ Choose one or two samples of your best work from each section to include in your Science Portfolio.

❸ On A Guide to My Science Portfolio, tell why you chose each sample.

I SHARE

Scientists share their discoveries and ideas and learn from one another. How can you share what you've learned?

Decide

▶ what you want to say.

▶ what the best way is to get your message across.

Share

▶ what you did and why.

▶ what worked and what didn't work.

▶ what conclusions you have drawn.

▶ what else you'd like to find out.

Find Out

▶ what classmates liked about what you shared—and why.

▶ what questions your classmates have.

I ACT

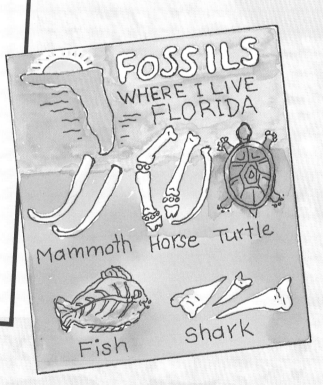

Science is more than discoveries
—it is also what you do with
those discoveries. How might you
use what you have learned about
the land?

▶ Tell people why it's important
not to throw away metal products
like those made of aluminum
and copper.

▶ Collect rocks and set up a rock
collection to show other students
about the rocks in your area.

▶ Make a poster showing the fossils
that can be found in your area. Use
the poster to teach your family and
friends about fossils.

▶ Set up a recycling program in your
community or school.

▶ Join a group that is helping preserve
national, state, or local parks.

FOSSILS
WHERE I LIVE
FLORIDA

Mammoth   Horse   Turtle

Fish   Shark

THE LANGUAGE OF SCIENCE

The language of science helps people communicate clearly when they talk about nature. Here are some vocabulary words you can use when you talk about rocks, the land, and the history of the Earth with friends, family, and others.

erosion—the carrying away of weathered material by water, wind, or glaciers. Erosion of the Grand Canyon was caused, in part, by the Colorado River. **(D49)**

fossil—the preserved trace or remains of a once-living thing. Examples are an imprint, a mold, and a cast. Fossils are also found in glacial ice, amber, and tar pits. **(D59)**

igneous rock—rock that forms from red-hot liquid rock. Volcanoes produce igneous rocks. **(D13)**

Obsidian is an igneous rock. ▶

chemical weathering—the breaking down of rocks by the action of chemicals. Limestone is chemically weathered when it is dissolved by water. **(D44)**

crust—the outer layer of the Earth. **(D31)**

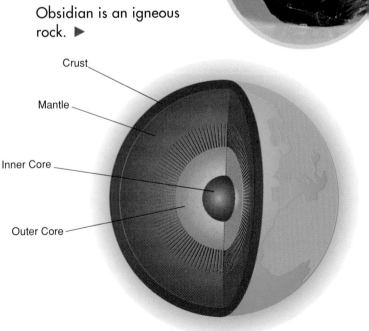

Crust

Mantle

Inner Core

Outer Core

landforms—features of Earth's crust, such as mountains, valleys, and plains. **(D32)**

metamorphic rock—rock that forms from rocks when they are heated and squeezed in the Earth. **(D15)**

minerals—the materials that make up rocks. **(D20)**

natural resource—any useful material that comes from the Earth. **(D77)**

nonrenewable resource—either a resource that cannot be replaced once it is used up or a resource that would take a very, very long time to be replaced. The formation of new coal, for example, would take millions of years. **(D77)**

physical weathering—the breaking apart of rocks by wind, water, ice, and plants. The roots of plants can grow in the cracks in rocks and break the rocks apart. **(D41)**

▲ Roots of plants can cause weathering.

renewable resource—a resource that can be replaced in a reasonable amount of time. Wood is a renewable resource because new trees can grow to replace those cut down. **(D77)**

▲ Wood is a renewable resource.

sea level—the average level of the sea where it meets the land. **(D35)**

sedimentary rock—rock that forms from sediments that harden under conditions of extreme heat and pressure. Limestone is a sedimentary rock. **(D14)**

weathering—the breaking down of rocks by water, plants, ice, wind, and chemicals. **(D40)**

A WALK IN THE FOREST

A Walk in the Forest

Comparing Ecosystems

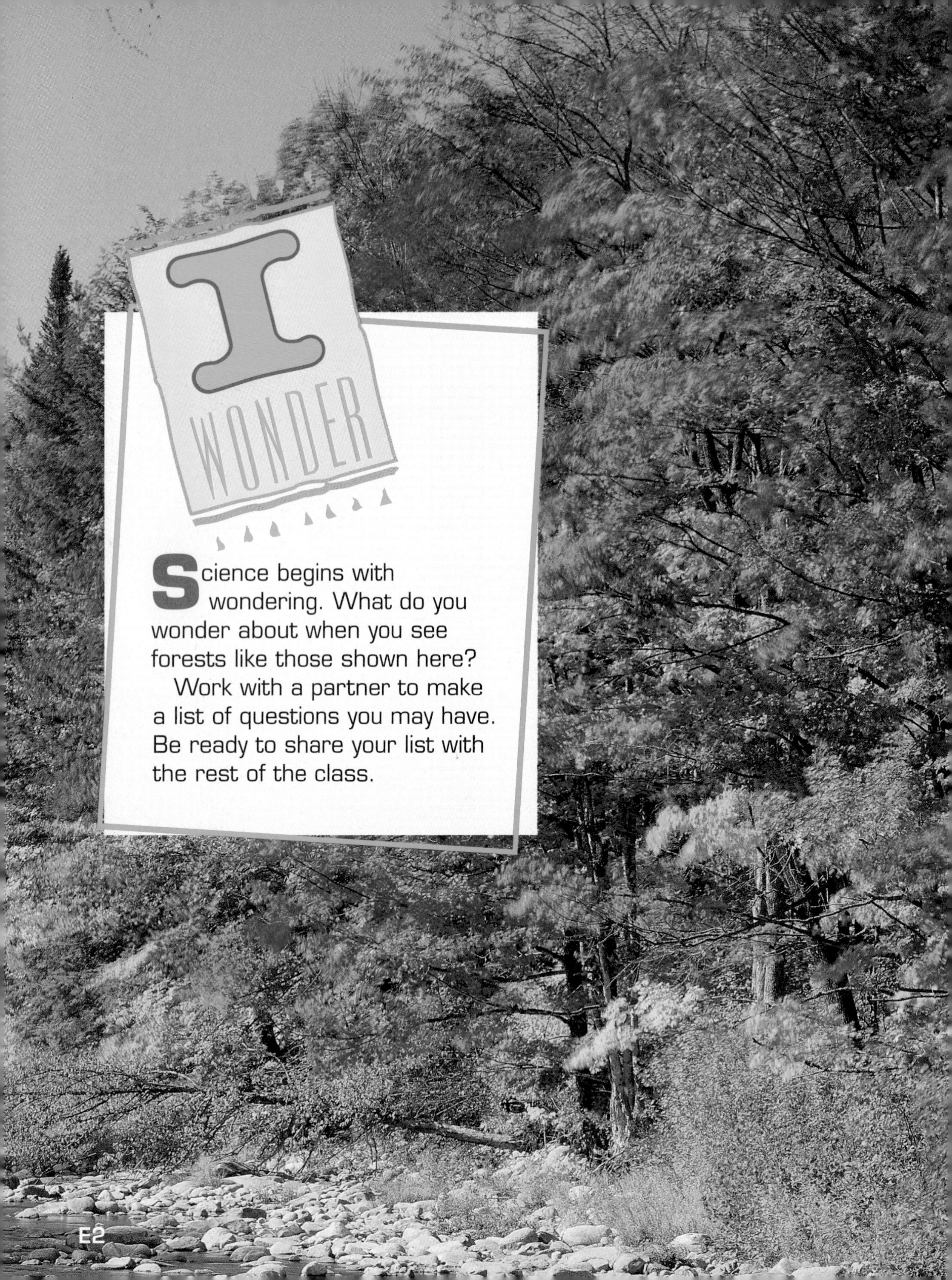

I WONDER

Science begins with wondering. What do you wonder about when you see forests like those shown here?

Work with a partner to make a list of questions you may have. Be ready to share your list with the rest of the class.

◄ **A forest in the White Mountain National Forest, New Hampshire**

▼ **A rain forest in Puerto Rico**

I PLAN

You may have asked questions such as these as you wondered about forests. Scientists also ask questions. Then they plan ways to help them find answers to their questions. Now you and your classmates can plan how you will investigate forests.

My Science Log

- Where do forests grow?

- What are some different kinds of forests?

- Where does soil come from?

- What are the parts of a plant?

With Your Class

Plan how your class will use the activities and readings from the **I Investigate** part of this unit.

On Your Own

There are many ways to learn about forests. Following are some things you can do to explore forests by yourself or with some classmates. Some explorations may take longer to do than others. Look over the suggestions and choose . . .

- **Projects to Do**
- **People to Contact**
- **Books to Read**

PROJECTS TO DO

SCIENCE FAIR PROJECT

Review the **I Wonder** questions you and your partner asked. One way to find answers to these questions is through a science fair project. Choose one of your questions. Plan a project that would help you answer the question. Discuss your plan with your teacher. With his or her approval, begin work by collecting materials and resources. Then carry out your plan.

TIMELY OBSERVATIONS

Choose a tree that is growing outdoors nearby. Study it in all four seasons of the year. Measure the shade that the tree provides at the same time of day in each of the different seasons. Measure the distance around the trunk. Look at the shape of the tree. Compare its shape with the shapes of other trees close by. Study its leaves, needles, flowers, fruit, cones, and bark. You may want to make rubbings of the bark located on its trunk and on one of its branches. How are the patterns in the bark on your tree different from the bark patterns of other trees?

START A COLLECTION

You can start a leaf collection from trees in your area. Gather leaves that have fallen to the ground. Study them with a hand lens, and write descriptions about them. Put the leaves between two paper towels, and press the covered leaves in a book. After five days, remove the pressed leaves and tape or glue them to pages in a booklet. Write a caption for each leaf. Tell where you found it and something else about the leaf. Share the booklet with your classmates.

PEOPLE TO CONTACT

BY TELEPHONE

To learn about forests in your area, talk to a ranger at a national park. Find out what forest workers do to keep forests alive and healthy. Ask the ranger what kinds of trees, other plants, and animals live in the forest. Record the answers to your questions. Then use your notes to write a magazine article about your interview with the forest ranger.

IN PERSON

With an adult, visit an arboretum (ahr buh REET uhm) or a botanical garden near you. Arboretums and botanical gardens are places where trees and other plants are grown by scientists. As you talk to the guide, take notes and make drawings of what you see. Then design a guidebook for other students.

BY MAIL

There are many organizations that are interested in forests. Here is a list of groups you might contact. After you have received information, share it with your classmates. With them, come up with ideas for how people your age can conserve resources, such as forests, soil, and water.

- American Forestry Association
- Friends of the Earth
- Rainforest Alliance
- Sierra Club
- Soil and Water Conservation Society

BOOKS TO READ

....
The Great Kapok Tree

by Lynne Cherry (Harcourt Brace, 1990), Outstanding Science Trade Book. Is one tree in the forest important? In this book, a man with an ax does not think it is. When he falls asleep, the animals who live in the forest tell him why each tree should be spared. Each tree is a part of the living rain forest that provides for many. When he wakes up, will the man remember what the animals have said?

A Tree in a Forest

by Jan Thornhill (Simon & Schuster, 1992). Read about a maple tree that for 200 years has been part of the forest community. It shelters animals. It provides maple syrup for people. As the tree grows old, it cannot withstand the hardships of weather and pollution. One day it falls over. It crumbles and decays. But that's not the end! Find out how new life begins after the tree falls.

More Books to Read

The Singing Fir Tree

by Marti Stone (G. P. Putnam's Sons, 1992). This book is about a woodcarver named Pierre, who wants to carve a masterpiece. To do this, he must cut down the beautiful singing fir tree that is loved by the villagers. What will Pierre do?

The Forest

by Ron Hirschi (Bantam Books, 1991). Can you guess from the picture clues in this book the animals that live in the forest? The animals live beneath the ground, in the water, and in trees. Some eat plants but must run and hide when the meat eaters hunt. The forest is a busy place.

Crinkleroot's Guide to Knowing the Trees

by Jim Arnosky (Bradbury, 1992), Outstanding Science Trade Book. In this book, Old Crinkleroot takes you on a walk through the forest and introduces you to the trees. Can you identify the trees? What does a tree need to grow? Crinkleroot will make you feel at home in the woods.

The Hidden Life of the Forest

by David Schwartz (Crown, 1988). A bear and her cub snuggle in their winter cave. This book gives you a close look at other animals that are "hidden" in the forest.

INVESTIGATE

To find answers to their questions, scientists read, think, talk to others, and do experiments. Their investigations lead to new questions.

In this unit, you have many chances to think and work like a scientist. How will you find answers to questions you asked?

▶ OBSERVING   You use your senses of sight, hearing, smell, and touch to observe the world around you. Sometimes you use instruments to extend your senses.

▶ INTERPRETING DATA   Data is information given to you or information that you gather during activities. When you interpret data, you decide what it means.

▶ HYPOTHESIZING   You form a hypothesis when you want to explain how or why something happens. Your hypothesis is an explanation based on what you already know. A hypothesis should be tested in an experiment.

Are you ready to begin?

SECTIONS

SECTION A
Exploring Forests

There are many kinds of forests. Some kinds grow where it is hot in the summer and cold in the winter. Other kinds grow where it is hot all the time. Still other kinds of forests grow in cool, moist areas. The trees of some forests are leafy and green only in the summer. The trees of other forests have green leaves all year.

When you think about a forest, what comes to mind? What kinds of plants and animals do you think live there?

In this section, you'll find out where on Earth forests grow. You'll explore how three kinds of forests are different from each other. In your Science Log, write about what you discover.

1 WHERE ARE FORESTS FOUND?

In the winter, what's it like where you live? Is it cold and rainy, or is it snowy? Or is your winter warm and sunny? Is your summer usually wet or dry? The amount of precipitation in an area is important to the people, animals, and plants that live there.

▲ **Birch and hardwood trees near Marvindale, Pennsylvania**

ACTIVITY

Forests and Rainfall

Forests in different areas of the world get different amounts of rain. How does the amount of rain affect forests?

MATERIALS
- 2 world maps (Rainfall and Forests)
- green and yellow markers or crayons
- scissors
- Science Log data sheet

DO THIS

❶ On the Rainfall map, color the areas marked with this symbol (*) green. These areas of the world receive between 50 cm and 400 cm of rain each year.

❷ On the Forests map, color the areas marked with this symbol (*) yellow. These areas have forests.

THINK AND WRITE

1. Study the two maps. How do the areas colored green compare with the areas colored yellow? Record your observations.

2. To compare the colored areas on the two maps more directly, try this. Cut out the colored part of the Rainfall map. Place this cutout on the Forests map. What do you observe?

Looking Back Like all living things, plants need water. Tall trees in a forest need a lot of water, usually much more than low-growing plants covering the same amount of land. Rain is the main source of water for trees. So it's not surprising that most forests can grow only where there's enough rain for their needs.

Forests and Temperature

You've seen that forests grow only in parts of the world where there is enough rain to meet their needs. There is also a relationship between forests and temperature.

As you can see on the map, Earth has different temperature zones. In the areas of Earth near the equator, it is always hot. It's like summer all the time. These areas are called the **tropical zones.**

Other areas of Earth have seasons with different ranges of temperature. These areas have cold or mild winters and hot or warm summers. These are the **temperate zones.**

Still other areas of Earth have long, very cold winters. The summers are short and may be mild or cool. These areas are near the poles, so they are called the **polar zones.**

Now look at the forest areas on the map. Which temperature zones have the fewest forests? How would you explain your findings?

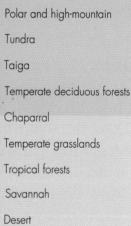

☐ Polar and high-mountain

☐ Tundra

☐ Taiga

☐ Temperate deciduous forests

☐ Chaparral

☐ Temperate grasslands

☐ Tropical forests

☐ Savannah

☐ Desert

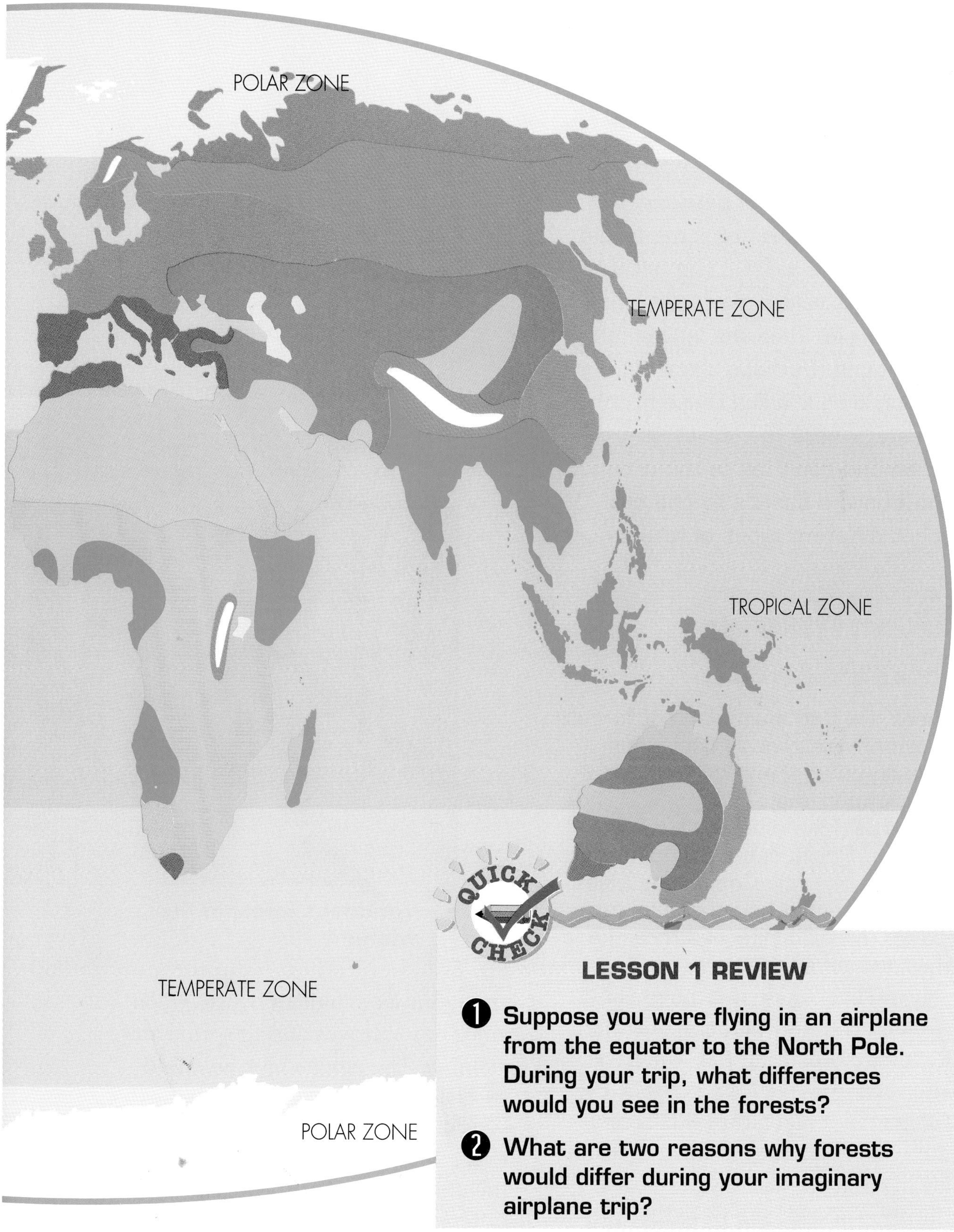

POLAR ZONE

TEMPERATE ZONE

TROPICAL ZONE

TEMPERATE ZONE

POLAR ZONE

QUICK CHECK

LESSON 1 REVIEW

1 Suppose you were flying in an airplane from the equator to the North Pole. During your trip, what differences would you see in the forests?

2 What are two reasons why forests would differ during your imaginary airplane trip?

2 KINDS OF FORESTS

In places where the seasons change, the leaves of some forest trees change color in the fall. They turn bright yellow, fiery red, and deep purple. Then the leaves fall to the ground. Perhaps the trees in your area are like those of other forests, where the leaves stay green and don't fall to the ground. You'll have a chance to find out about different types of forests.

▲ **Deciduous forest in the summer**

Deciduous Forests

There are two main kinds of forests in temperate zones—deciduous (dee SIJ oo uhs) and coniferous (koh NIF uhr uhs). They are named after the main types of trees they contain. Deciduous trees lose their leaves in the fall. Coniferous trees bear cones and have needles for leaves. Most coniferous trees keep their leaves all year.

▲ **Deciduous forest in the winter**

If you live where there are many deciduous trees, you know that their leaves are broad and flat. You have also seen how the leaves change every fall. As the temperature gets cooler, the color of the leaves changes from green to shades of yellow, red, and purple. These colors were there all along but were hidden by the green color of the leaves during spring and summer. The green color is caused by **chlorophyll** (KLAWR uh fil), a substance that plants need to make food. When the weather turns cooler, the chlorophyll disappears and the other colors show through.

THERE ARE FOUR LAYERS OF PLANTS IN A DECIDUOUS FOREST.

The most common trees form the top layer, called the **canopy** (KAN uh pee) **layer.**

Below the canopy are shorter trees and shrubs, which make up the layer called the **understory layer.**

Short woody plants form the **shrub layer.**

The lowest layer is the **herb layer,** which is made up of plants that grow close to the ground.

THINK ABOUT IT

Describe an animal that might live in each layer of the deciduous forest.

Coniferous Forests

Like deciduous forests, coniferous forests also grow in temperate zones. But coniferous forests are found in areas where the climate is cooler, and they can grow in areas where there is less rainfall.

The leaves of most coniferous trees are shaped like needles and have a waxy covering. Both the shape and the covering help keep water in the leaves. It's easy to recognize these trees because they have cones. In addition, most conifers display leaves that remain green all year.

Trees in a coniferous forest grow close together. In fact, the branches of the *canopy layer* are so close together that very little sunlight reaches the ground.

Only ferns and mosses grow on the *forest-floor layer* underneath the trees. So a coniferous forest has only two layers—the canopy layer and the forest-floor layer.

▲ Coniferous forest near Whitefish, Montana

▲ Needles from a Monterey pine tree

▲ Cones from a blue spruce tree

THINK ABOUT IT

Explain why a coniferous forest has just two layers.

E21

A Forest in the Class

Now it's time for you to try constructing a forest. Remember all you have studied. Keep adding to your forest as you continue through this unit.

DO THIS

❶ Your teacher will tell you which kind of forest you'll be studying. Use books to find out about this kind of forest. What plants live there? What animals live there? What nonliving things are in the forest?

❷ List your forest plants and animals on the chalkboard.

❸ Look in books to see the colors and shapes of the living things in your forest.

❹ Draw and paint different living things and nonliving things in the forest.

❺ **CAUTION: Be careful when you use scissors.** Cut out your pictures. Attach the pictures of trees and other plants to the walls of your classroom first. Add your pictures of insects and other animals in and around the trees. Then add the nonliving things such as rocks and soil.

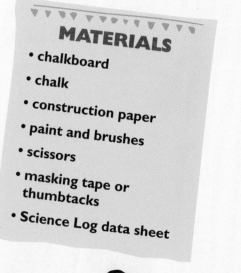

MATERIALS
- chalkboard
- chalk
- construction paper
- paint and brushes
- scissors
- masking tape or thumbtacks
- Science Log data sheet

THINK AND WRITE

1. Which kind of forest is nearest to where you live? What plants and animals live there? What nonliving things are there?

2. How are other kinds of forests different from the kind in your area?

Looking Ahead If you live in a temperate region, the nearby forests may be deciduous or coniferous. Another major kind of forest grows in tropical areas, where the weather is warm all year. How is this kind of forest different from the two kinds you just studied? Turn the page to find out more.

ACTIVITY

Making a Rain Forest Model

One way to find out about a rain forest is to build a model. Try the next activity.

MATERIALS
- terrarium
- ruler
- small pebbles
- charcoal
- graduated cylinder, 250 mL
- potting soil
- water
- tropical plants, such as ferns or African violets
- moss
- Science Log data sheet

DO THIS

1 Make rain forest "soil." Put a layer of pebbles, then a layer of charcoal, and then a layer of potting soil into the terrarium. Each layer should be 3 cm deep.

2 Add 120 mL of water to the soil.

3 Place your plants on the soil. Then cover their roots with 3 cm of moss.

4 Place the lid on the terrarium.

5 Put the terrarium in a bright place, but not in direct sunlight.

6 Observe your rain forest for two weeks. Record your observations.

THINK AND WRITE

1. How was your rain forest model like a real forest?

2. **OBSERVING** For investigations that go on for days or weeks, there are likely to be changes in what you observe. Observe the plants in the terrarium once a week for six weeks, and draw a picture of them. Note how the plants change.

A C T I V I T Y

Variety in Forests

Some kinds of forests have a greater variety of living things than other kinds of forests. In this activity, you can see what that means.

DO THIS

1 Make a data table like the one shown.

2 Write the number 1 on one card. Write the number 2 on the other.

3 Each kind of bean stands for a different kind of tree. Tape the first card to the 15-bean-soup tray. This is the rain forest. Tape the second card to the other tray. This is the deciduous forest.

MATERIALS
- 2 small index cards
- marker
- transparent tape
- tray of "15-bean-soup" beans
- tray of black, red, and white beans
- 2 paper cups
- Science Log data sheet

VARIETY OF BEANS

Tray 1		Tray 2	
Kind of Bean	Number of Beans	Kind of Bean	Number of Beans

4️⃣ Scoop one cup of beans as a sample from each tray. One person should work with the sample from tray 1. Another person should work with the sample from tray 2.

5️⃣ Pour each cup of beans carefully into a pile. From each of these piles, sort each kind of bean into a different, smaller pile.

6️⃣ Count the number of beans in each small pile. Record the numbers on the data table. Remember that each kind of bean stands for one kind of tree in the forest.

THINK AND WRITE

1. How many kinds of trees were in each kind of forest?

2. Which kind of forest had the most trees of one kind?

3. Suppose a plant disease killed all trees represented by the black beans. Which kind of forest would be affected more? Why?

4. **INTERPRETING DATA** If the 15-bean tray represents the rain forest and the 3-bean tray represents the deciduous forest, what does the data you collected tell you about the types of trees in each type of forest? Look at your answers to questions 1–3. How did you interpret data in order to answer the questions?

The Layers of the Rain Forest

You've already made a model of a rain forest and discovered that there is great variety in it. Most tropical rain forests are warm and moist throughout the year. In this environment, many different kinds of plants and animals live in the layers of the rain forest. In fact, scientists haven't yet recorded the names of all the plants and animals that live there. Look at the art. You'll see a variety of plants and animals just about everywhere!

Hawk

Chameleon

Hummingbird

Peace Lily

Opossum

Croton

Jaguar

Armadillo

Emergent Layer The very tallest trees make up the emergent layer. These trees tower over all other layers of the rain forest. Camouflaged among the branches, birds such as eagles and hawks look down and watch for prey.

Canopy Layer Underneath the emergent layer, the branches of tall trees spread out and form a canopy over the lower layers. More animals live here than in any other layer of the rain forest. Animals live near the top of the trees, in the canopy, where there is sunlight, warmth, and food. You find parrots, monkeys, and lizards living in the canopy layer.

Understory Layer Below the canopy layer, you will find the shorter trees and plants that make up the understory layer. The understory receives less light than the canopy layer, so it is darker and cooler. Because this layer is shady, you must look closely to see the spiders, insects, and frogs that live among the plants in the understory.

Forest-Floor Layer At ground level, there are few flowering plants or shrubs. The emergent layer and canopy layer receive most of the sunlight, so only plants that are able to grow in the shade grow on the forest-floor layer. Large animals such as jaguars, armadillos, and wild pigs live on the forest floor.

QUICK CHECK

LESSON 2 REVIEW

❶ How do the plants of deciduous forests, coniferous forests, and rain forests differ? How are they the same?

❷ Do you think a deciduous forest has a greater variety of plants than a coniferous forest? Why or why not?

❸ How might the rainfall and temperature of a coniferous forest be different from those of a rain forest?

3 A FOREST COMMUNITY

The community you live in includes the people, buildings, and natural surroundings where you live. In your community, people depend on each other to meet their basic needs, such as food, clothing, and shelter. A forest is also a community, because living things in the forest depend on each other to meet their basic needs.

All the organisms that live in a forest are members of the community. In this lesson, you will read about a deciduous forest community. Think about the different kinds of living things described. Notice how the plants and animals depend on each other.

▲ **Jim Thorpe, Pennsylvania**

THE FOREST

by **David Bellamy**
from *Our Changing World: The Forest*

The oak is very old and is like a world in itself.

 It's a fine spring day and the forest is home to many animals and birds. In some areas, foresters are working: cutting trees and planting new ones to provide paper, timber, and firewood for the world outside. Here, some visitors have found a beautiful place for a picnic under a huge oak tree.

The oak is very old and is like a world in itself. High on its branches, the crows feed their young. A woodpecker drills into a dead branch to find grubs to eat, and a squirrel, who was busy eating the leaf buds, chases away a small bird. Even the yellow fungus is feeding on the dead wood.

Every year the old tree grows new bark, wood, and leaves. These provide food for many different insects like caterpillars and leaf miners. It's a good thing that the birds like to eat these insects or there would be far too many and they could kill the trees.

Some caterpillars hide from the birds by wrapping themselves up in the leaves while they turn into moths. Some insects lay their eggs in the softer parts of the buds, leaves, and twigs. The tree then grows a lump around the eggs, which protects them till they hatch. Leafy trees like the oak are the only place in which many of these creatures can make their home.

More small creatures live among the mosses and lichens (LY kuhnz) on the oak tree's trunk. Millions of tiny green plants cover the side of the trunk where the rainwater runs down, and the tree creeper climbs up hunting for insects. On the other side, the lace-web spider sits by her trap waiting for something to drop in. The peppered moth is nearly invisible against the bark.

The bark protects the trunk and branches and makes a firm foothold for all the mosses and lichens, while ferns and other plants root in the cracks. As the tree grows taller and broader, the old bark splits and new layers grow to fill the cracks.

It's nearly midsummer and the oak has grown many juicy
new leaves. The old leaves have been eaten by so many
insects that they are in tatters.

Under the trees it is cool and shady, even in midsummer.
A young deer comes to graze on the fresh green grass. Most
of the plants already bear fruits and seeds. They flowered in
spring before the leaves shut out the sunlight.

Last year's fallen leaves have almost disappeared. Pulled underground and eaten by earthworms, the leaves enrich the soil. The acorns have gone, too, all except one which has taken root beneath an oak tree. At first the seedling fed on the fat acorn. Now, its new leaves make their own food from the sunlight that filters down. The young tree grows very slowly, but one day, if it survives, it could take the place of one of the giant old forest oaks, blown down by a storm. Not all acorns grow up into trees: if they did there would soon be no room in the forest.

At night, when the forest is dark and mysterious to us, wood mice are out looking for fallen acorns to store away for winter. One is just about to nibble the top off the oak seedling, but the hungry owl, with its enormous eyes that allow it to see so well in the dark, has spotted the mouse and is swooping down. The forest can be a dangerous place for mice as well as seedlings.

THINK ABOUT IT

How do the birds, insects, and trees depend on each other in the forest?

A Forest Food Chain

You have seen how animals depend on one another for food. All living things need food for energy to carry on the activities of life.

All the plants, animals, and other organisms in an area make up a **community.** Living things of a community interact and depend on one another for food. A community and the area's nonliving things make up an *ecosystem.* In a forest ecosystem, all living things depend on each other for energy. You have read about how living things in a forest ecosystem get food. Food provides energy for all living things. A *food chain* shows how one living thing provides energy for another.

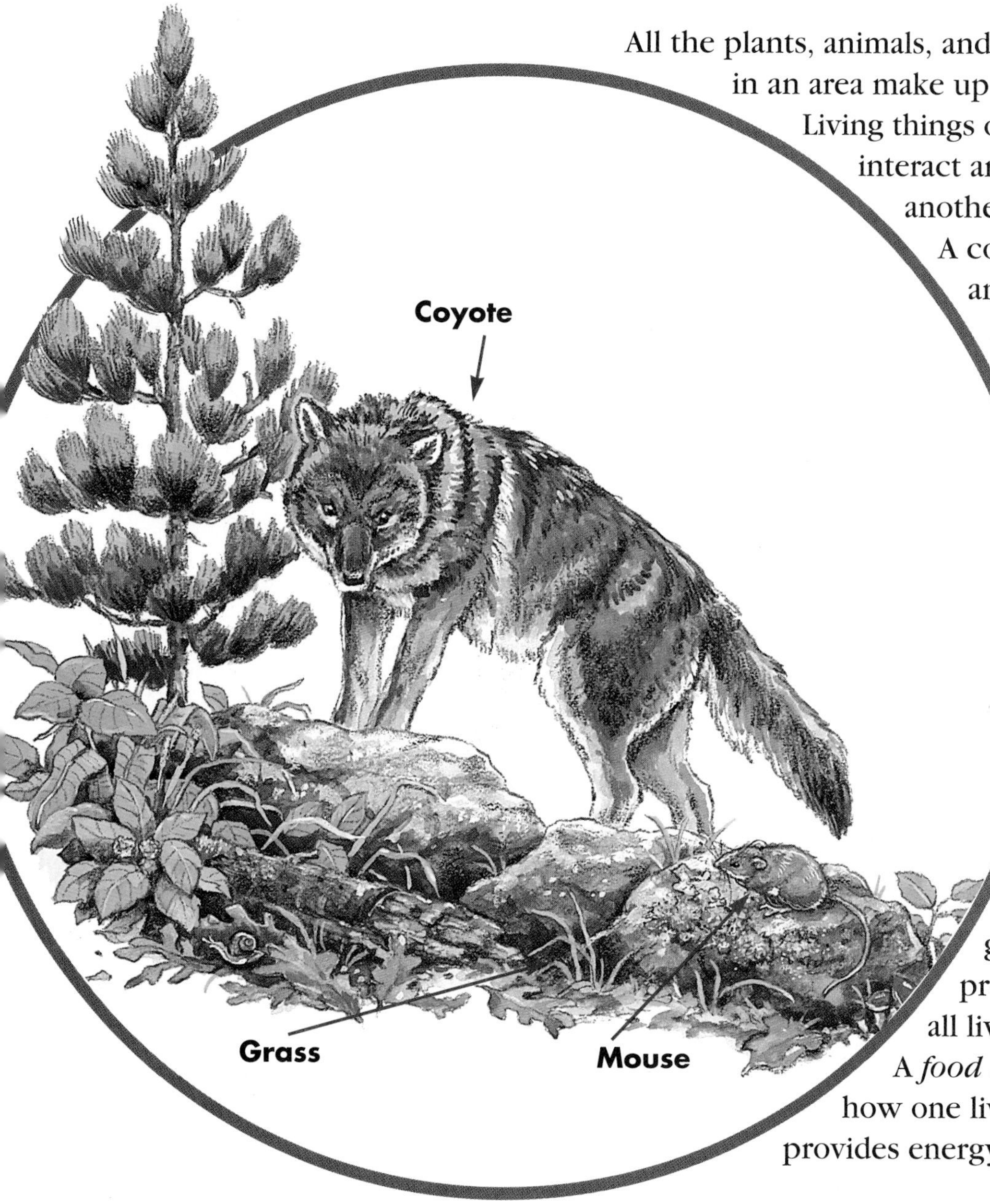

Coyote

Grass

Mouse

▲ **A forest food chain**

THINK ABOUT IT

How are a community and an ecosystem alike? How are they different?

A C T I V I T Y

A Chain in Class

In this activity, you will see how living things depend on each other for energy in the form of food.

MATERIALS
- ball of yarn
- scissors
- index card
- hole punch
- marker
- Science Log data sheet

DO THIS

1. **CAUTION: Be careful when you use scissors.** Cut a piece of yarn long enough for a necklace. Then punch a hole in the index card.

2. Put the yarn through the hole. Hold your card, and stand in a circle with your classmates.

3. Everyone in the circle should name a living thing in a forest ecosystem.

4. When you name an organism, write its name on the card you are holding. Then tie the card around your neck. You are now that part of the ecosystem.

5. To start, a person who has the name of a plant on his or her card should hold the end of the ball of yarn. The "plant" should name an animal that eats it and should pass the ball of yarn to that person. The first "animal" should name another animal, one that eats the first, and should pass the ball of yarn on. For example, an "acorn" passes the yarn to a "squirrel." The "squirrel" passes the yarn to a "fox."

6. Keep going until you come to the top of a food chain. Then start a new food chain. Continue until everyone in class is in a food chain. Draw the food chain you were in.

THINK AND WRITE

1. How is your chain like a forest ecosystem?

2. Suppose you removed one thing from the chain. What would happen to other things in the chain that depend on it?

3. **HYPOTHESIZING** A hypothesis is a statement that tells what you think will happen in a certain situation. Suppose this is a food chain in a forest.

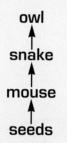

owl

↑

snake

↑

mouse

↑

seeds

Write a hypothesis about what will happen if all the snakes in the forest die. How could you test your hypothesis?

QUICK CHECK

LESSON 3 REVIEW

❶ Why is the survival of each type of plant and animal in a forest ecosystem important?

❷ Sometimes one type of living thing in a forest ecosystem is destroyed. It might be killed by people, by disease, or by pollution. What might the loss of that living thing mean for the forest?

DOUBLE CHECK

SECTION A REVIEW

1. How do you think weather affects forest ecosystems?

2. Suppose a planet is discovered that has water, air, and soil like Earth's. The warmest parts of this planet have temperatures and rainfall like those in Earth's temperate zones. What kinds of forests would you expect to find on this planet? Why?

The Soil Under Your Feet

Yesterday you came home with mud all over your shoes. As you came into the house, someone called out, "Take off those shoes! Don't bring that dirt in here!"

Dirt. It's everywhere. But what you think of as dirt is usually *soil*. And without it, your life would be very different indeed.

You walk on soil in a forest or in a park. It squishes under your feet when it's wet and muddy. You can kick it into clouds of dust when it's dry.

As you read through this section and do the activities, you'll be investigating soil. You'll discover what soil is and how it forms. You'll also discover how soil helps forest plants grow. Record your discoveries in your Science Log.

1 WHAT IS SOIL?

You probably don't think much about soil—until you want to plant something. Plants need soil to grow.

A C T I V I T Y

A Close-Up Look at Soil

Why do you think soil is so important to plants? What is soil made of? You're about to discover some things about soil that may surprise you.

DO THIS

1. Your teacher will give you soil for this activity. Put a spoonful of soil on your paper plate. Use the toothpick to spread it out as much as you can.

2. Use your hand lens to look at the soil carefully. Look for particles that came from animals, plants, or rocks.

3. Rub a little of the soil between your fingers to find out how it feels.

4. Draw what you observe, and write about it.

THINK AND WRITE

1. What kinds of things did you find in the soil?

2. Based on what you observed, how do you think new soil forms?

3. **OBSERVING** When you do an experiment, you observe things that happen. Observing usually means looking, but you can also observe with other senses—such as touch, hearing, and smell. In what different ways did you observe the soil in the activity?

ACTIVITY

Layers of Soil

One way to study soil is to look for particles that came from animals, plants, or rock. Another way is to observe what happens when you mix soil with water. Try these methods in this activity.

DO THIS

1 Your teacher will give you soil for this activity. Use a spoon to fill a jar halfway with the soil.

2 Add water to the jar. The water level should be 3 cm above the top of the soil.

MATERIALS
- soil sample
- spoon
- clear plastic jar with lid
- water
- ruler
- Science Log data sheet

3 Place the lid tightly on the jar. Shake the jar for 30 seconds, and then put it on a table. Observe what happens inside the jar.

4 Wait until all the material in the jar has settled. Then draw what you see.

THINK AND WRITE

1. What did you find floating on the surface of the water?

2. How did the material in the jar look after it settled? Why do you think the material settled in this way?

Looking Back Before you started to study soil, it may have seemed simple—just dirt. Now you know that soil is a mixture of many things.

Some parts of soil come from rock, and other parts come from once-living plants and animals. The amounts of these materials are not always the same.

Soils that have different amounts of these materials often look and feel different. Different types of soil may also come from different types of rock.

One easy way to observe the differences between soils is by their color. Look for different soils in the photographs.

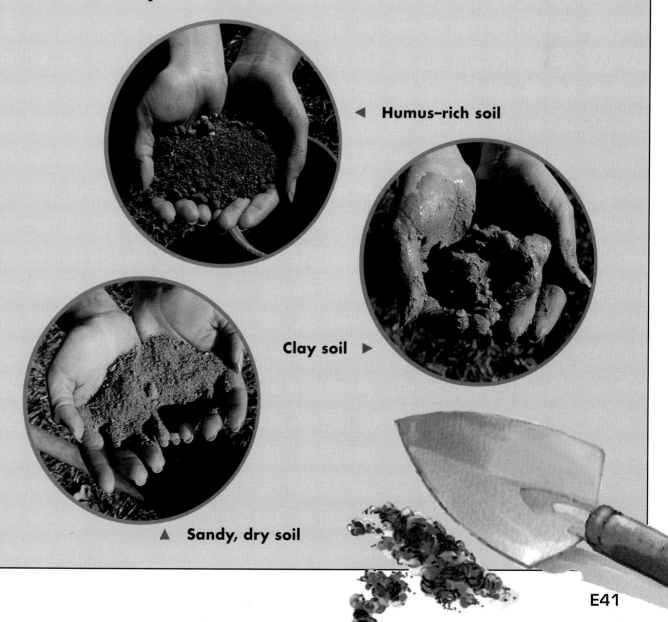

◀ **Humus–rich soil**

Clay soil ▶

▲ **Sandy, dry soil**

Where Does Soil Come From?

All soil has one thing in common. It is mainly tiny pieces of rock. Where do the rock pieces come from?

Look at the pebbles and soil at the base of this cliff. As this picture was taken, soil was being made. Most of the material in the soil at the bottom of the cliff came from pieces of rock that had broken off the cliff. How was the rock that fell to the ground broken into smaller pieces?

Water has many ways of wearing down rock. Falling or running water—from rain, waves, waterfalls, and rivers—breaks up big pieces of rock into very small pieces.

Freezing can break up rock, too. Small amounts of water run into cracks and holes in the rock. When the water gets cold enough, it freezes and expands. This makes the cracks even bigger. When this happens many times, the rock breaks into small pieces.

Have you ever been on the beach on a windy day? Sometimes the wind is so strong that it picks up sand and blows it around. If you're standing up, this blowing sand hits your body. The tiny particles sting as they strike you. The same thing happens to rock when the wind blows. But the rock doesn't feel the sting. Instead, tiny pieces of it are chipped away. Plants can also break up rock into small pieces. Tree roots often grow into small cracks in rock. As the roots get bigger, so do the

▲ Rocky cliff at Zion National Park, Springdale, Utah

cracks. Some plants, such as lichens, give off chemicals that break up the rock they grow on.

Pieces of rock aren't the only things in soil. It also contains decayed bits of plants and animals.

The once-living bits of plant and animal matter in soil are called **humus** (HYOO muhs). Tiny organisms that live in soil break down dead organisms. Some of the humus-making organisms are **bacteria** (bak TIR ee uh). Bacteria are very tiny. They're so small that you can't see them without a microscope.

Besides bacteria, living things such as worms, insects, and fungi (FUHN jy) break down dead organisms. **Fungi** look like plants but are not green and can't make their own food. They get their food by breaking down dead plants and animals.

The best soils for growing most plants have a lot of humus. You can tell if soil is rich in humus by the dark color of the soil.

Maybe forming soil is more complicated than you thought. Most changes that turn rock and once-living matter into soil happen very, very slowly. It can take thousands of years to make a layer of soil only as thick as your finger.

THINK ABOUT IT

Explain how both living and dead trees help form soil.

Granite peak broken by freezing of water and ice in cracks. ▼

▲ Lichen–covered rock

Plant Matter into Soil

People often mix plant matter into soil. They do this to add humus to the soil. How does this work? What happens to plant matter that is put into soil?

MATERIALS
- clear plastic jar
- paper cup
- soil with humus mixed in
- water
- apple peel
- banana slices
- dry cereal
- plastic wrap
- masking tape
- Science Log data sheet

DO THIS

❶ Spread a cup of soil on the bottom of the jar. Sprinkle water on the soil to moisten it.

❷ Put the apple peel, banana slices, and dry cereal on top of the soil. Place them so they touch the sides of the jar.

❸ Spread another cup of soil on top of the plant parts. You should be able to see the plant parts after you have covered them.

❹ Cover the jar with the plastic wrap. Use the tape to hold the wrap in place and to seal the jar. Put the jar in a warm place out of direct sunlight.

❺ Check the jar once a week for 4 weeks. Record your findings.

THINK AND WRITE

1. If you were to observe the jar every week for the next 8 weeks, what changes do you think you would see? Explain your answer.

2. **HYPOTHESIZING**   After the changes take place, you may want to add a plant to your jar to see if it grows well. Write a hypothesis about the way a plant would grow in the soil you are making. How could you test your hypothesis?

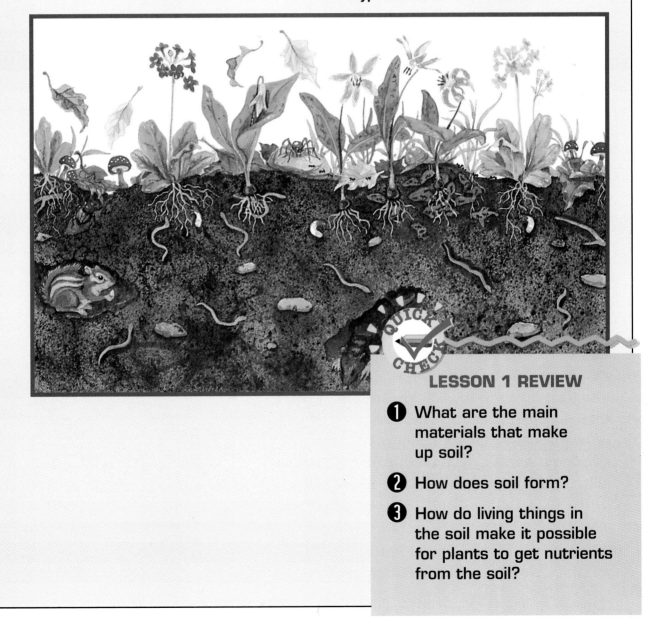

QUICK CHECK

LESSON 1 REVIEW

❶ What are the main materials that make up soil?

❷ How does soil form?

❸ How do living things in the soil make it possible for plants to get nutrients from the soil?

2 COMPARING SOILS

All soils have the same basic parts, including bits of
rock and animal and plant matter. Still, soils are not all
alike. Where are different soils found, and how do they
affect plants? As you read, you'll find out about the
soils of temperate forests and tropical rain forests. How
are their soils alike and different?

Soils of Coniferous and Deciduous Forests

Two main types of forests in
temperate regions are coniferous and
deciduous forests. You may recall that
coniferous forests contain evergreen
trees, most of which have needles for
leaves. Evergreen trees do not lose
their needles all at once. New needles
replace the old ones all year round.
Deciduous forests contain trees that
lose their leaves in the fall. The soils of
these forests are similar. They are
often thick and rich with humus. In
deciduous forests, the leaves that have
fallen to the ground decay. They add
nutrients, materials plants need to live
and grow, to the soil.

   Most of the eastern United States
was once covered with coniferous and

▲ Small animals, such as spiders,
earthworms, and centipedes, live among
or under the fallen leaves on the
forest floor.

E46

deciduous forests. As people settled in these areas, they cut down the trees to build houses and to clear farmland. When the trees were cut down, a rich soil was left behind. But over the years, farming removes the nutrients from the soil.

Look at the diagram. It's a drawing of soil under a deciduous forest. What is each layer of soil like?

The top layer of soil is called *topsoil*. It contains most of the humus that is found in the soil. Plants get most of the nutrients they need from this soil layer.

The middle layer of soil, called *subsoil*, contains less humus than the topsoil. This layer stores much of the water that seeps down from above. It also collects nutrients washed out of the topsoil by rain.

The next layer of soil, called *parent material*, contains large particles of rock. These rock particles continue to break up and become smaller.

The lowest layer is called *bedrock*. Much of the mineral content of soil comes from this layer.

THINK ABOUT IT

Suppose the layer of topsoil blew away. How would that affect the growing of plants?

▲ **Farmer plowing field near Posen, Michigan**

Topsoil

Subsoil

Parent material

Bedrock

Soil layers under a deciduous forest

Soils of Tropical Rain Forests

Tropical rain forests are both rich and poor. They are rich in plant life but poor in soil.

Two-thirds of all the different kinds of plants and animals in the world live in tropical rain forests. One tree in a rain forest might have 100 different kinds of plants wrapped around it or hanging from its branches.

Yet the soils in tropical rain forests are poor in nutrients. In fact, they have fewer nutrients than some soils in temperate coniferous and deciduous forests.

To understand why rain-forest soils are poor, think about where nutrients are found in different kinds of forests. In deciduous or coniferous forests, the topsoil contains most of the humus. Remember that most of the nutrients are found in the humus.

In a rain forest, leaves or branches of trees and other plants fall to the ground. Unless animals carry off or eat these plant parts, they break down quickly into nutrients. But the frequent rains wash the nutrients right out of the soil.

There is another source of nutrients for the plants in a rain forest. Falling leaves and vines are often caught in the branches of rain-forest trees. They never get down to the ground.

Instead, the dead plant matter decays on the tree branches. Some plants may even grow in this decayed material. Humus-forming organisms live in this material, also. Bacteria, fungi, and worms make their homes in the branches of the trees.

People who live near rain forests sometimes cut them down to clear the land for growing food. They also cut down some of the trees for their valuable wood. Once a rain forest is destroyed, most of the nutrients are removed from the area. The nutrient-poor soil cannot even be used to grow crops for very long.

▲ **Slash and burn of a rain forest in Honduras**

When the nutrients in the soil have been used up and crops will no longer grow, the people leave the area. The soil is left bare. With no tree roots or crops to hold the soil in place, it often washes or blows away. The people may then clear new parts of the rain forest, causing more damage to the rain-forest soil.

Water, minerals, and nutrients all pass through the tree. Because of the warmth and moisture in a tropical rain forest, nutrients are recycled from the soil through the tree in the canopy very quickly. This means that the soil is poor in nutrients and crops do not grow well in this soil. ▶

Photosynthesis occurs in the leaves.

The nutrients help the tree to grow.

Dead leaves and animals fall to the ground.

The tree takes up the nutrients through its roots.

Bacteria and fungi break down dead materials in the soil to form nutrients.

QUICK CHECK

LESSON 2 REVIEW

❶ Where are nutrients found in a temperate forest and in a tropical rain forest?

❷ Why is soil in tropical rain forests poor in nutrients?

DOUBLE CHECK

SECTION B REVIEW

1. Plants in temperate forests are anchored in the soil by their roots. In what other ways is soil important to these plants?

2. When a rain forest is cleared, this means the trees are cut down. You've read how this may affect the soil. How might cutting down the trees affect other plants and animals that live in the rain forest? Write a paragraph that describes how cutting down trees in the rain forest affects more than just soil.

SECTION C
Plants

Imagine taking a walk in a cool, green forest. Huge trees tower over you. Their branches meet high above your head. Rays of sunlight filter through the spaces between the leaves. Small patches of sunlight make patterns on the forest floor. What plants, other than trees, do you see in the forest? How are all of these plants alike? How are they different?

In this section, you will explore plants. You will compare the leaves, roots, and stems of different plants. You will discover how plants take in water and how seeds travel from place to place. You'll also meet someone who works in a forest. Keep a record of your discoveries in your Science Log.

1 LEAVES, ROOTS, AND STEMS

Look around you. Look up, too. Can you see any plants? You might notice a houseplant such as a geranium. Maybe you see an elodea or other water plant in an aquarium. Can you see an oak tree or another kind of tree outside the window? The plants you see every day may look very different. Yet most of them have the same basic parts. What are the three main parts of most plants, and what do they do?

▲ **Flowers in a windowbox**

Leaves

You may wonder why leaves are an important plant part. They are important because they make food. Plants make their own food through the process called *photosynthesis* (foht uh SIN thuh sis). Most food-making takes place in the leaves of plants.

Perhaps you've seen cows or deer grazing on grass. Animals cannot make their own food. Some of them depend on leaves for their supply of food. In turn, humans may eat the animals that have eaten the leaves.

What do cabbage, lettuce, and spinach have in common? They all have leaves that you may have eaten in a salad. When you eat a piece of lettuce, you are eating the food that the plant made and stored in its leaf.

▲ **Grazing cattle**

THINK ABOUT IT

List all of the plant parts you ate yesterday.

ACTIVITY

Comparing Leaves

Most leaves have the job of making food and storing it. Yet there are many different shapes and types of leaves. In this activity, you'll have the chance to observe leaf adaptations.

DO THIS

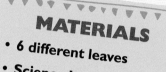

MATERIALS
- **6 different leaves**
- **Science Log data sheet**

1 Make a data table like the one shown. Your data table will need to be longer so you'll have room to draw in it.

2 Look at the leaves. Sort them into Group A and Group B. You may group the leaves any way you wish, but the leaves in each group should have some common features.

3 On your data table, draw a picture of each leaf from each group. Also write a short description of each leaf.

4 Record your reasons for grouping the leaves the way you did.

LEAF COMPARISONS	
Group A	**Group B**

THINK AND WRITE

1. How are the leaves in Group A the same as and different from each other? How are the leaves in Group B the same as and different from each other?

2. Compare the leaves in Group A with the leaves in Group B. How are the leaves in each group the same and different?

3. Share your results with others. Find out how they grouped their leaves.

4. **INTERPRETING DATA** In the activity, you collected data and recorded the information in a data table. When you think about the data and decide what it means, you are interpreting data. Now it is time to think about what you discovered. How will you interpret the data you have collected about the leaves?

Leaf Album

In the activity, you could have grouped your leaves in many different ways. Let's look at the characteristics of leaves.

Perhaps you grouped your leaves according to the shape of the leaf. The broad, flat part of the leaf is called the *blade*. It is in the blade that most photosynthesis occurs. Many leaves are broad and flat. Others are oval or heart-shaped, feather-shaped, or shaped like groups of short, thick needles.

Another way you might have grouped your leaves is by the types of edges of the blade. For example, the edges of rubber tree leaves are smooth. A white oak leaf has edges that look as if something has taken a bite out of it! Other leaves have edges that look like the blade of a saw. They have small notches, or teeth.

THINK ABOUT IT

Why do you think leaves have so many different shapes?

Leaves have a variety of shapes.

Fig tree leaf ▶

▲ **Eastern cottonwood leaf**

Blue ▶ **spruce sprig**

White mulberry leaf ▼

Rubber tree leaf ▼

Plants of Deciduous and Coniferous Forests

You may recall that two main types of forests grow in temperate zones. These are deciduous forests and coniferous forests. Deciduous forests have trees such as beech, oak, and hickory. Coniferous forests have trees like pine and fir. The plants in each forest must have adaptations that help them survive.

Leaves ▶ from an oak tree

Oak

Apple trees, oak trees, and grasses have **simple leaves,** leaves that have only one blade. The trees in deciduous forests have leaves that are flattened so that they can catch as much sunlight as possible. Why is it important for leaves to "catch" sunlight?

▲ Oak tree

Black Walnut

The leaves of some plants in deciduous forests have many blades that are joined together to form **compound leaves.** The little parts that make up compound leaves are called *leaflets.* The black walnut tree is one type of tree that has compound leaves.

▲ Black walnut tree

◀ Compound leaf from a black walnut tree

White Pine

Pines are evergreens that often grow in coniferous forests. Their leaves look like needles. Evergreens, such as white pine trees, keep their leaves throughout the winter. The narrow shape and waxy coating help protect the needles from drying out, or losing too much water.

▶ Eastern white pine needles

▲ Eastern white pine tree

Rhododendron

Not all evergreens are pines. Plants like the rhododendron (roh duh DEN druhn) are also considered evergreens because their leaves do not drop off in the fall. The leaves have a waxy upper surface. It helps them keep in moisture and protects them from cold temperatures.

▲ Rhododendron in bloom

▲ Waxy leaves of the rhododendron

Poison Ivy

Some plants contain poisons that make them harmful to eat. Poison ivy is one of the few plants that is harmful both to eat and to touch. The berries are poisonous, and the leaves have an oil that irritates skin and causes an itchy rash. Poison ivy has compound leaves made up of three leaflets.

THINK ABOUT IT

How are leaves adapted to their geographical location?

▲ Poison ivy

▲ Leaves of the poison ivy plant

Plants of Tropical Rain Forests

▼ **Split-leaved philodendron**

As you discovered in Section A, tropical rain forests are wet throughout the year. Plants in a rain forest must have adaptations that help water run off their leaves. If the leaves held water, mosses or other plants could grow on the leaves. This would cut down on the plant's ability to make food.

Philodendron

The leaves of the philodendron are thick and waxy. A "gutter" runs down the middle of the leaf. This gutter can funnel the water down to the tip of the leaf, where it drips off.

▲ **Water can run down the leaf's gutter and off the leaf**

Bromeliad

Bromeliads (broh MEE lee adz) often grow on the trunks of rain-forest trees. Bromeliads have long, sword-shaped leaves that may have sharp edges. This shape keeps water from collecting on the leaves. However, bromeliads often hold a lot of water in the base of their leaf clusters. Why do you think this is an advantage?

◄ **Water in the leaf cluster of a bromeliad**

▲ **Bromeliads growing on a tree limb**

THINK ABOUT IT

What different ways could you now group the leaves from the activity on E52?

Roots

You've just read about leaves, one of the main parts of a plant. If you've ever helped weed a garden or moved a plant from one container to another, you've seen another main part of plants—roots.

Plants need water and nutrients in order to grow. Roots take in water and minerals from the soil. Roots also hold plants in the soil so they stay in place and don't blow away. Many roots store food the plant makes so it can be used at a later time.

Roots can spread wide and deep. Many roots branch into smaller roots, the same way a tree's limbs branch into smaller limbs. The total length of the roots of some plants is amazing. The roots of one rye plant can be more than 600 kilometers (373 miles) long!

It's important for plants in every kind of environment to have roots that help them get water. In temperate areas, roots often cover a wide area and grow deep into the soil. The oak tree in the picture is 20 meters (66 feet) tall. In this picture, you can see the roots grow about as deep as the tree is tall. The tree's roots also extend out in a circle that is as large as the circle made by its branches.

▲ Oak tree

A mesquite bush grows in the desert. There the soil near the surface is nearly always dry. So mesquite roots grow unusually far down—30 meters (98 feet) to reach water in the soil that runs under the desert.

▲ **Mesquite bush in Death Valley, California**

The cactus has shallow roots that spread out in a wide area near the surface of the soil. It doesn't rain often in the desert, but when it does, these roots can soak up a lot of water. Between rains, the cactus stores this water in its thick stem.

THINK ABOUT IT

What might happen if the mesquite bush had only shallow roots?

▲ **Saguaro (suh GWAHR oh) cactus in desert**

Different Kinds of Roots

All roots do some of the same jobs. They bring water and nutrients from the soil into the plant. They anchor the plant. They also store food made by the plant. Still, not all roots look alike. Plants have a variety of roots.

▲ This carrot has a taproot system.

Taproots

A taproot system has one main root. It grows straight down deep into the soil. The taproot has smaller roots branching out from it. You are eating taproots when you eat carrots or beets.

▲ Grasses have a fibrous root system.

Fibrous Roots

A fibrous root system has many small branches. There is no main root. Many grasses have fibrous root systems.

▲ An orchid has an aerial root system.

Aerial Roots

Aerial roots start above the soil and grow downward. Many rain-forest plants have aerial roots. These plants include orchids. Aerial roots cling to tree branches and absorb water and nutrients from the tree or from the air.

THINK ABOUT IT

Why are different root systems necessary?

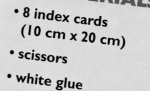

(A)(C)(T)(I)(V)(I)(T)(Y)

Tree Root Models

Now that you've had a chance to read about roots, you can make models of the above-ground part of the roots of two different types of trees. How might one kind of tree root be better than another in certain situations?

DO THIS

❶ Fold each index card in half lengthwise.

❷ Cut four of the cards as in diagram 1.

❸ Cut the other four cards as in diagram 2.

❹ Glue the cards together to form two models.

❺ Draw diagrams of the two models.

❻ Blow gently on each model. What happens?

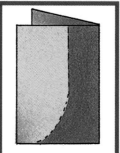

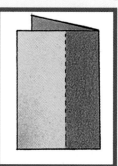

▲ **Diagram 1**   ▲ **Diagram 2**

THINK AND WRITE

1. How are the two tree-root models different?

2. Think carefully about the models. What kind of underground roots would each tree need to keep the wind from blowing it over?

Looking Back The bottoms, or bases, of many rain-forest trees spread into fan-shaped sections where they meet the ground. These bases prevent the trees from falling down during high winds.

ACTIVITY

How Stems Work

You have read that leaves make food and that roots take in water and nutrients. There's still another plant part that is important for plant survival. Try this activity to find out more.

DO THIS

❶ Fill the jar $\frac{3}{4}$ full of water. Add about 24 drops of food coloring and stir.

❷ Put the stem of the carnation in the water. Leave the jar of water in a warm place for 2 days.

❸ Observe the flower twice each day, once in the morning and once in the afternoon. Record any changes in the flower.

THINK AND WRITE

Write a paragraph to tell where the food coloring traveled in the flower. You can also make a drawing to help explain your answer.

Stems

Think about this: Where do plants get support to help hold them up? How do they get water and nutrients from the roots to the leaves? In the activity, you discovered that the third important plant part is called the *stem*.

Stems have tiny tubes that are like the highways of plants. Some of the tubes carry water and nutrients up into the plant from its roots. Other tubes take food from the leaves through the plant.

Some stems grow below the surface. These stems are called **tubers,** and they store the food that plants make. This stored food can be used later by the plant, or you might eat it. White potatoes, like the ones shown here, are one kind of tuber. Jerusalem artichokes are another kind of tuber.

QUICK CHECK

LESSON 1 REVIEW

❶ What are the main jobs of leaves, roots, and stems?

❷ How are the leaves of rain-forest plants adapted to their wet environment?

❸ In what way are the tubes in stems like highways?

2 MAKING NEW PLANTS

A flower can give you a lot of pleasure. You enjoy its shape, color, and smell. Did you ever grow a flower from a seed that you planted? What you really did was grow a plant. The flower was a part of that plant.

As a part of the plant, the flower has a job. That job is to make new plants. How do flowers do this? To begin to find out, look closely at the parts of a flower.

ACTIVITY

Looking at Flowers

DO THIS ✂

MATERIALS
- flower
- scissors
- hand lens
- Science Log data sheet

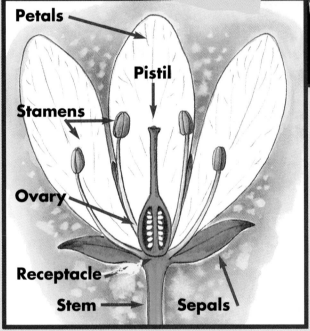

1. Look closely at the outer parts of your flower. Find these parts: stem, receptacle (top of stem where it is attached to the flower), sepals, petals. Use the diagram to locate the parts. Draw what you see.

2. Now look at the inner parts of the flower. You must first remove the sepals and petals. Find these parts: stamens, pistil, ovary (the bulging bottom part of the pistil).

3. Touch the tips of the stamens. Is there anything on your finger? What does it look like?

4 **CAUTION: Be careful
when you use scissors.**
Use scissors to cut open the
ovary. Use the hand lens to
observe the inside of the ovary.
What do you see inside?

THINK AND WRITE

Draw your flower. Compare it
with the diagram. Did you find
all of the parts in your flower?
Label the parts of your drawing.

From Flower to Seed

You've just read that the job of a flower is to make new plants. But, you might wonder, how does this happen? Read on to find out more.

Most plants grow from seeds that are formed in flowers. For example, a bee lands on a flower, such as a cherry blossom, and drinks the sweet liquid inside.

As the bee drinks, its body rubs against the flower's stamens. As you've seen, the **stamens** are covered with a yellowish powder. This powder is really pollen grains that were produced by the stamens. The pollen grains contain male sex cells.

The bee flies to another flower, and the pollen carried by the bee from the first cherry blossom lands on the pistil of another cherry blossom. The *pistil* is the female part of the flower that receives pollen.

▲ **Black cherry blossom**

▲ **Honeybee feeding on and pollinating cherry blossoms**

◄ **The petals of the cherry blossom have started to wilt, exposing the developing fruit at the center.**

The process of moving pollen from stamens to pistils is called **pollination** (pahl uh NAY shuhn). The pollen grain sends a long tube down into the ovary. Then a male sex cell moves down the tube and joins with a female sex cell in the *ovary*. After the female and male sex cells come together, a seed begins to grow.

As the seed grows, a fruit develops around it. When most people think of fruits, they think only of things like apples or peaches. However, fruits also include acorns, cucumbers, and tomatoes. A fruit is anything that has seeds.

▲ **Fruits from temperate regions**

▲ **Fully developed cherries from Emmett, Idaho**

Fruits from tropical regions ▶

THINK ABOUT IT

Draw a diagram that shows how flowers make new plants.

How Seeds Spread

When ripened cherries fall to the ground, their seeds may grow into new cherry trees. These trees may produce new flowers—and start the cycle of life all over again.

In order to grow, plants need space and sunlight. Most seeds will not grow in the shade of other plants. For this reason, seeds need to be scattered about where they will have a chance to grow. The seeds of different plants are spread in a variety of ways.

▲ A new cherry tree may grow from this cherry seed.

Wind carries many seeds. Maple seeds have "wings" that help them travel farther. Dandelion seeds drift far on feathery "parachutes."

Water carries the seeds of some plants, like the sea chamomile (KAM uh myl) and the coconut.

▲ Dandelion seed dispersal

▲ Silver maple leaves

▲ Coconut seeds are spread by the water.

E68

Some seeds have spines, hooks, or sticky substances. They help the seeds stick to animal fur—or to you. Eventually the seeds fall off, and they may begin to grow.

Animals such as birds eat fruits with seeds inside. Sometimes birds drop large seeds to the ground. They might swallow small seeds. These pass through the birds' bodies and reach the ground in the droppings of birds.

Some plants shoot their seeds into the air. For example, when the seeds of an impatiens (im PAY shee ehnz) are ripe, a touch causes the slender fruit capsule to split open. The seeds pop out and scatter.

▲ Seeds can even stick to you!

◀ Birds can help spread seeds.

▲ One touch to the slender fruit capsule of the impatiens will cause the seeds to burst out!

QUICK CHECK

LESSON 2 REVIEW

❶ What adaptations do seeds have to help them get to areas where they can grow?

❷ Explain why bees and other insects are important in pollination.

❸ Why is it unlikely that you would find a sprouting coconut in the desert?

3 PLANT DEFENSES AND PROTECTION

When you cross a street, you wait for a green light or a Walk sign, don't you? How do you protect your head when you ride a bike? You wear a helmet. What are some other ways you protect yourself? What are some ways other people help keep you safe?

Like you, other living things have ways to protect themselves from harm. Cats scratch. Dogs bite. Skunks squirt a bad-smelling liquid at predators.

In this lesson, you'll find out that plants also have defense adaptations for survival. You'll also discover the way one person helps protect plants in a national park.

How Plants Defend Themselves

As you may recall, animals need adaptations to protect themselves from predators. Plants need defense adaptations for the same reason. If you've ever grown a garden or helped out on a farm, perhaps you've seen the harm insects or other animals can do to plants.

▲ What adaptations does this kitten have to protect itself?

Cactus plants store water inside their thick stems. Sharp leaves, called *spines,* keep thirsty animals away.

The leaves of the nettle look harmless and tasty. But the stems below each leaf have sharp prickles. The prickles contain chemicals that irritate the skin of animals.

Holly leaves have a waxy coating that makes them very tough. They also have spines around their edges. Not many animals try to eat holly leaves.

Pairs of teasel leaves hold pools of water after a rainstorm. As insects try to climb the stems, either the water blocks their path, or they fall in and drown.

Passionflowers contain poisons that kill most creatures that try to eat them. Animals learn to stay away from such poisonous plants.

You've seen some of the ways plants, much like animals, defend themselves from predators. In many places, forests need protection from human activities, disease, or insects. Read on to find out more.

▲ Barrel cactus

◄ Stinging nettle

▲ Holly leaves

▲ Teasel leaves

▲ Passionflower

THINK ABOUT IT

Why do plants need protection?

Ron Nagata, Sr.
National Park Resource Manager

Sometimes plants have humans to protect them and see that they have good growing conditions. Read about Ron Nagata and his work.

When Ron Nagata was about 16, he took his first hike into the crater of Haleakala (hah lay ah kah LAH) volcano with his mom and brother. That was when Nagata made up his mind to become a park ranger.

Haleakala National Park in Hawai'i sits on top of Haleakala mountain, a volcano that no longer erupts. The park has many ecosystems. There are grassy fields, shrublands, and tropical rain forests. It is Nagata's job to protect all of the plants and animals in the park.

"The resource management staff helps protect natural resources so that people will always be able to enjoy them," says Nagata. At Haleakala, that means preserving the native plants and animals. *Native* means those plants and animals that are found naturally in a place.

▲ Ron Nagata

For example, the silversword is an unusual plant that is native to Hawai'i. The plant has long, narrow leaves covered with silver hairs. It lives for about 20 years. Nagata says that park rangers protect silverswords because Hawai'i is the only place on Earth where the plant grows.

E72

Nagata and his staff also help to protect the nene (NAY nay), a goose that is native to Hawai'i. Nenes were almost wiped out a few years ago. In the 1940s, there were only 50 left. Biologists saved the nene by catching some of the birds and letting their young grow up in protected areas. Then they let the grown-up birds go in places like the national park, where people could keep them safe.

People who work in national parks often have college degrees. However, having a degree is not enough. "In this job, you have to like the outdoors and hiking," says Nagata.

"I was born here in Hawai'i," Ron Nagata explains. "I started out leading hikes in the park. Now I'm running the resource management program here. I told my mother 30 years ago that I wanted to become a park ranger. I'm really proud of the fact that I did it."

▲ **The nene (NAY nay) goose**

QUICK CHECK

LESSON 3 REVIEW

1 You've read about ways some plants have adapted so animals won't destroy them. Write one reason these adaptations are important.

2 List three ways a forest worker helps forests. Tell why you would or would not like to be a forest worker.

✓ DOUBLE CHECK

SECTION C REVIEW

1. Roots, stems, and leaves are plant parts. Write about what each part does for a plant.

2. The colors as well as the odors of many flowers attract various kinds of insects. Why is this a useful adaptation?

I REFLECT

It's time to think about the ideas you have discovered during your investigations. Think, too, about your many accomplishments.

SUMMARIZE

Answer the following in your Science Log.

1. What **I Wonder** questions have you answered in your investigations? What new questions do you have?

2. What have you discovered about forests? How have your ideas changed?

3. Did any of your discoveries surprise you? Explain.

Layers of the Forest

A deciduous forest has four layers. At the top is the canopy. The canopy has tall trees. The understory is next. It has short trees. Then comes the shrub layer. It has bushes. The herb layer is on the bottom. It has grass. Coniferous forests and rain forests also have layers.

CONNECT IDEAS

1. How might plant growth change if the world's rainfall decreased? Explain your answer.

2. Many people think that trees in the rain forest should not be cut down. However, the people who cut down the trees to use for lumber or to clear the land for farming have different feelings. As you can see, there is more than one side to the situation. If you were going to help a friend understand something about the destruction of the rain forest, what would you say?

3. Explain why sand might not be good for growing all plants.

4. An orange tree grown outdoors produces flowers and juicy fruit. An orange tree grown indoors may produce flowers but will not produce fruit. Explain why this happens.

SCIENCE PORTFOLIO

1. Complete your Science Experiences Record.

2. Choose one or two samples of your best work from each section to include in your Science Portfolio.

3. Complete A Guide to My Science Portfolio to tell why you chose each sample.

I SHARE

Scientists share their discoveries and ideas and learn from one another. How can you share what you've learned?

Decide

▶ what you want to say.

▶ what the best way is to get your message across.

Share

▶ what you did and why.

▶ what worked and what didn't work.

▶ what conclusions you have drawn.

▶ what else you'd like to find out.

Find Out

▶ what your classmates liked about what you shared—and why.

▶ what questions your classmates have.

THE IMPORTANT PARTS OF A PLANT

Pistil

Petal

Stamen

Leaf

Stem

Root

I ACT

Science is more than discoveries—it is also what you do with those discoveries. How might you use what you have learned about forests?

▶ Perhaps there's a forest near where you live. Research the ecosystem of that forest. Find out if any endangered plant or animal species live in the forest. What can you do to help preserve them?

▶ Visit a nearby farm. Talk to a farmer about the soil in the area. How much humus is in the soil? Are fertilizers used to help make the crops grow? What problems, if any, does that cause?

▶ If you recycle paper, fewer trees may be cut down. Recycle paper at school and at home. Start a paper-recycling project in class if you don't have one already. Talk to teachers and students in other classes about having a recycling program for the whole school.

THE LANGUAGE OF SCIENCE

The language of science helps people communicate clearly when they talk about nature. Here are some vocabulary words you can use when you talk about forests with friends, family, and others.

bacteria — tiny organisms found nearly everywhere. They can be seen only with a microscope. Most bacteria are harmless or helpful. Bacteria in the soil break down humus into nutrients. **(E43)**

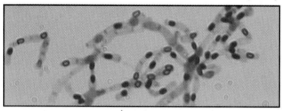

▲ This is what bacteria look like under a microscope.

blade — the broad, flat part of a leaf. Most photosynthesis occurs in the leaf blade. **(E54)**

chlorophyll — a green substance used by plants to make food. The food-making process is called *photosynthesis*. **(E18)**

community — all the plants, animals, and organisms that live together in an area. The living things in a community interact, or affect each other. A community is the living part of an ecosystem. **(E35)**

compound leaf — a leaf made up of many leaf blades. **(E55)**

▲ The black walnut leaf is a compound leaf.

coniferous forest — a forest that grows in cooler temperate regions in which most trees bear cones and have needlelike leaves all year. Many forests of mixed types have both coniferous and deciduous trees. **(E18)**

deciduous forest — a forest that grows in temperate regions in which most trees lose their leaves in the fall. Many forests of mixed types have both deciduous and coniferous trees. **(E18)**

These are the layers of the deciduous forest. Though the layers are not exactly the same, all forests have layers.

Canopy layer—the top layer of a forest, formed by the tallest trees.

Understory layer—the layer that is beneath the canopy and has shorter trees.

Shrub layer—the layer of short, woody plants beneath the understory.

Herb layer—the layer that is nearest the ground. Low-growing plants such as grass are in the herb layer.

fungi — living things that break down dead plants and animals for food. Unlike plants, fungi have no chlorophyll, so they cannot make their own food. **(E43)**

humus — a mixture of once-living bits of plant and animal matter and wastes from plants and animals. Soil that contains a large amount of humus is black, fertile, and rich in nutrients for growing plants. **(E43)**

nutrients — the materials that plants need in order to live and grow, such as calcium and nitrogen. Plants get nutrients from soil rich in humus. Fertilizer added to the soil also provides nutrients. **(E46)**

ovary — in a flower, the part in which female sex cells are formed. When the flower is pollinated, a tube to carry a male sex cell grows into the ovary. When male and female sex cells join, one or more seeds start to grow in the ovary. Then the ovary becomes a fruit. **(E67)**

ecosystem — the living organisms in a community and all the nonliving things they depend on. The community depends on nonliving things such as air, water, and soil. **(E35)**

food chain — a chain of living things that shows what animals eat and how all living things provide energy for others. **(E35)**

▲ A simple food chain

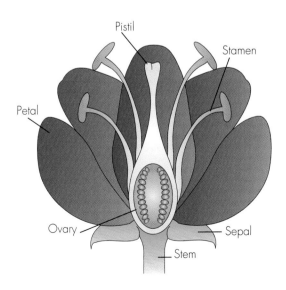

photosynthesis — the food-making process in the leaves and other green parts of plants. In photosynthesis, plants combine water and carbon dioxide in the presence of sunlight to make sugar. Oxygen is given off in the process. Chlorophyll in plants captures the sun's energy. **(E51)**

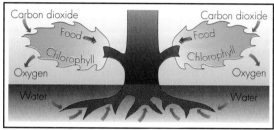

▲ Photosynthesis

pistil — the female part of a flower. It has a sticky top, a stalk, and an ovary at the bottom. Pollen grains land on the top and stick to it. A pollen grain that sprouts grows through the stalk and enters the ovary. **(E66)**

polar zone — a part of Earth that has long, very cold winters and short, cool summers. **(E16)**

pollination — the movement of pollen from the stamen, or male part of a flower, to the pistil, or female part of a flower. Pollination starts the reproductive process in flowering plants. **(E67)**

simple leaf — a leaf that has only one blade. **(E55)**

soil — a mixture of bits of rock material and remains of living things, or humus. **(E41)**

stamen — the flower part that produces pollen. **(E66)**

stem — the plant part that connects the roots with the leaves. **(E63)**

temperate zone — a part of Earth that has hot summers and cold winters. **(E16)**

topsoil — the top layer of soil that contains most of the humus found in soil. **(E47)**

tropical zone — a part of Earth that has long, hot summers and short, warm winters. **(E16)**

tuber — a plant stem that grows underground and contains stored food. A white potato is a tuber. **(E63)**

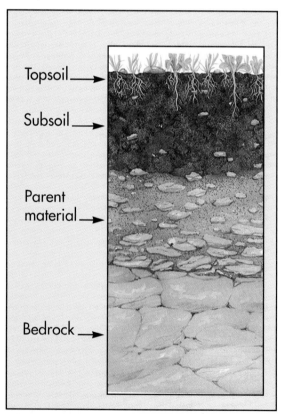

Topsoil

Subsoil

Parent material

Bedrock

▲ Soil profile

REFERENCE HANDBOOK

Safety in the Classroom

Doing activities in science can be fun, but you need to be sure you do them safely. It is up to you, your teacher, and your classmates to make your classroom a safe place for science activities.

Think about what causes most accidents in everyday life—being careless, not paying attention, and showing off. The same kinds of behavior cause accidents in the science classroom.

Here are some ways to make your classroom a safe place.

THINK AHEAD.
Study the steps of the activity so you know what to expect. If you have any questions about the steps, ask your teacher to explain. Be sure you understand any safety symbols that are shown in the activity.

WATCH YOUR EYES.
Wear safety goggles anytime you are directed to do so. If you should ever get any substance in your eyes, tell your teacher right away.

BE NEAT.
Keep your work area clean. If you have long hair, pull it back so it doesn't get in the way. If you have long sleeves, roll them or push them up to keep them away from your experiment.

OOPS!
If you should have an accident that causes a spill or breaks something, or if you get cut, tell your teacher right away.

YUCK!
Never eat or drink anything during a science activity unless you are told to do so by your teacher.

KEEP IT CLEAN.
Always clean up when you have finished your activity. Put everything away and wipe your work area. Last of all, wash your hands.

DON'T GET SHOCKED.
Sometimes you need to use electric appliances, such as lamps, in an activity. You always need to be careful around electricity. Be sure that electric cords are in a safe place where you can't trip over them. Don't ever pull a plug out of an outlet by pulling on the cord.

Safety Symbols

In some activities, you will see a symbol that stands for what you need to do to stay safe. Do what the symbol stands for.

CAUTION	This is a general symbol that tells you to be careful. Reading the steps of the activity will tell you exactly what you need to do to be safe.
	You will need to protect your eyes if you see this symbol. Put on safety goggles and leave them on for the entire activity.
	This symbol tells you that you will be using something sharp in the activity. Be careful not to cut or poke yourself or others.
	This symbol tells you something hot will be used in the activity. Be careful not to get burned or to cause someone else to get burned.
	This symbol tells you to put on an apron to protect your clothing.
	Don't touch! This symbol tells you that you will need to touch something that is hot. Use a thermal mitt to protect your hand.
	This symbol tells you that you will be using electric equipment. Use proper safety procedures.

Using a Hand Lens

A hand lens magnifies objects, or makes them look larger than they are.

▲ This object is not in focus.

Sometimes objects are too small for you to see easily without some help. You might want to see details that you cannot see with your eyes alone. When this happens, you can use a hand lens.

To use a hand lens, first place the object you want to look at on a flat surface, such as a table. Next, hold the hand lens over the object. At first, the object may appear blurry, like the object in **A.** Move the hand lens toward or away from the object until the object comes into sharp focus, as shown in **B.**

▲ This object is focused clearly.

Making a Water-Drop Lens

There may be times when you want to use a hand lens but there isn't one around. If that happens, you can make a water-drop lens to help you in the same way a hand lens does. A water-drop lens is best used to make flat objects, such as pieces of paper and leaves, seem larger.

MATERIALS
- sheet of acetate
- 2 rectangular rubber erasers
- water
- dropper

DO THIS

❶ Place the object to be magnified on a table between two identical erasers.

❷ Place a sheet of acetate on top of the erasers so that the sheet of acetate is about 1 cm above the object.

❸ Use the dropper to place one drop of water on the surface of the sheet over the object. Don't make the drop too large or it will make things look bent.

A water-drop lens can magnify objects. ▶

Caring For and Using a Microscope

A microscope, like a hand lens, magnifies objects. However, a microscope can increase the detail you see by increasing the number of times an object is magnified.

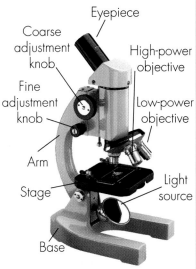

▲ **Light microscope**

CARING FOR A MICROSCOPE

- Always use two hands when you carry a microscope.
- Never touch any of the lenses of the microscope with your fingers.

USING A MICROSCOPE

1 Raise the eyepiece as far as you can using the coarse-adjustment knob. Place the slide you wish to view on the stage.

2 Always start by using the lowest power. The lowest-power lens is usually the shortest. Start with the lens in the lowest position it can go without touching the slide.

3 Look through the eyepiece and begin adjusting the eyepiece upward with the coarse-adjustment knob. When the slide is close to being in focus, use the fine-adjustment knob.

4 When you want to use the higher-power lens, first focus the slide under low power. Then, watching carefully to make sure that the lens will not hit the slide, turn the higher-power lens into place. Use only the fine-adjustment knob when looking through the higher-power lens.

Some of you may use a Brock microscope. This is a sturdy microscope that has only one lens.

1 Place the object to be viewed on the stage. Move the long tube, containing the lens, close to the stage.

2 Put your eye on the eyepiece, and begin raising the tube until the object comes into focus.

▲ **Brock microscope**

Using a Dropper

Use a dropper when you need to add small amounts of a liquid to another material.

A dropper has two main parts. One is a large empty part called a *bulb*. You hold the bulb and squeeze it to use the dropper. The other part of a dropper is long and narrow and is called a *tube*.

DO THIS

1. Use a clean dropper for each liquid you measure.

2. With the dropper out of the liquid, squeeze the bulb and keep it squeezed. Then dip the end of the tube into the liquid.

3. Release the pressure on the bulb. As you do so, you will see the liquid enter the tube.

4. Take the dropper from the liquid, and move it to the place you want to put the liquid. If you are putting the liquid into another liquid, do not let the dropper touch the surface of the second liquid.

5. Gently squeeze the bulb until one drop comes out of the tube. Repeat slowly until you have measured out the right number of drops.

▲ Using a dropper correctly

▲ Using a dropper incorrectly

Measuring Liquids

Use a beaker, a measuring cup, or a graduated cylinder to measure liquids accurately.

Containers for measuring liquids are made of clear or translucent materials so that you can see the liquid inside them. On the outside of each of these measuring tools, you will see lines and numbers that make up a scale. On most of the containers used by scientists, the scale is in milliliters (mL).

DO THIS

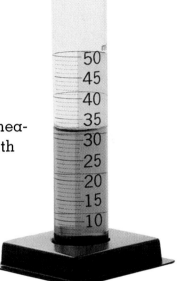

❶ Pour the liquid you want to measure into one of the measuring containers. Make sure your measuring container is on a flat, stable surface, with the measuring scale facing you.

❷ Look at the liquid through the container. Move so that your eyes are even with the surface of the liquid in the container.

▲ There are 32 mL of liquid in this graduated cylinder.

❸ To read the volume of the liquid, find the scale line that is even with the top of the liquid. In narrow containers, the surface of the liquid may look curved. Take your reading at the lowest point of the curve.

❹ Sometimes the surface of the liquid may not be exactly even with a line. In that case, you will need to estimate the volume of the liquid. Decide which line the liquid is closer to, and use that number.

▲ There are 27 mL of liquid in this beaker.

Using a Thermometer

Determine temperature readings of the air and most liquids by using a thermometer with a standard scale.

Most thermometers are thin tubes of glass that are filled with a red or silver liquid. As the temperature goes up, the liquid in the tube rises. As the temperature goes down, the liquid sinks. The tube is marked with lines and numbers that provide a temperature scale in degrees. Scientists use the Celsius scale to measure temperature. A temperature reading of 27 degrees Celsius is written 27°C.

DO THIS

1 Place the thermometer in the liquid whose temperature you want to record, but don't rest the bulb of the thermometer on the bottom or side of the container. If you are measuring the temperature of the air, make sure that the thermometer is not in direct sunlight or in line with a direct light source.

2 Move so that your eyes are even with the liquid in the thermometer.

3 If you are measuring a material that is not being heated or cooled, wait about two minutes for the reading to become stable. Find the scale line that meets the top of the liquid in the thermometer, and read the temperature.

4 If the material you are measuring is being heated or cooled, you will not be able to wait before taking your measurements. Measure as quickly as you can.

The temperature of this liquid is 27°C. ▶

Making a Thermometer

If you don't have a thermometer, you can make a simple one easily. The simple thermometer won't give you an exact temperature reading, but you can use it to tell if the temperature is going up or going down.

DO THIS

 Add colored water to the jar until it is nearly full.

❷ Place the straw in the jar. Finish filling the jar with water, but leave about 1 cm of space at the top.

❸ Lift the straw until 10 cm of it sticks up out of the jar. Use the clay to seal the mouth of the jar.

❹ Use the dropper to add colored water to the straw until the straw is at least half full.

❺ On the straw, mark the level of the water. "S" stands for *start*.

❻ To get an idea of how your thermometer works, place the jar in a bowl of ice. Wait several minutes, and then mark the new water level on the straw. This new water level should be marked C for *cold*.

❼ Take the jar out of the bowl of ice, and let it return to room temperature. Next, place the jar in a bowl of warm water. Wait several minutes, and then mark the new water level on the straw. This level can be labeled W for *warm*.

—W

—S

—C

▶ You can use a thermometer like this to decide if the temperature of a liquid or the air is going up or down.

Using a Balance

Use a balance to measure an object's mass. Mass is the amount of matter an object has.

Most balances look like the one shown. They have two pans. In one pan, you place the object you want to measure. In the other pan, you place standard masses. Standard masses are objects that have a known mass. Grams are the units used to measure mass for most scientific activities.

DO THIS

1 First, make certain the empty pans are balanced. They are in balance if the pointer is at the middle mark on the base. If the pointer is not at this mark, move the slider to the right or left. Your teacher will help if you cannot balance the pans.

◀ **These pans are balanced and ready to be used to find the mass of an object.**

2 Place the object you wish to measure in one pan. The pointer will move toward the pan without the object in it.

3 Add the standard masses to the other pan. As you add masses, you should see the pointer begin to move. When the pointer is at the middle mark again, the pans are balanced.

4 Add the numbers on the masses you used. The total is the mass of the object you measured.

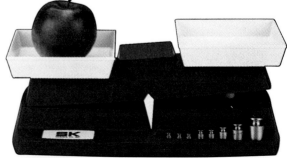

These pans are unbalanced. ▶

Making a Balance

If you do not have a balance, you can make one. A balance requires only a few simple materials. You can use nonstandard masses such as paper clips or nickels. This type of balance is best for measuring small masses.

DO THIS

1 If the ruler has holes in it, tie the string through the center hole. If it does not have holes, tie the string around the middle of the ruler.

2 Tape the other end of the string to a table. Allow the ruler to hang down from the side of the table. Adjust the ruler so that it is level.

3 Unbend the end of each paper clip slightly. Push these ends through the paper cups as shown. Attach each cup to the ruler by using the paper clips.

4 Adjust the cups until the ruler is level again.

MATERIALS
- 1 sturdy plastic or wooden ruler
- string
- transparent tape
- 2 paper cups
- 2 large paper clips

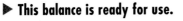

▶ **This balance is ready for use.**

Using a Spring Scale

A spring scale is a tool you use to measure the force of gravity on objects. You find the weight of the objects and use newtons as the unit of measurement for the force of gravity. You also use the spring scale and newtons to measure other forces.

A spring scale has two main parts. One part is a spring with a hook on the end. The hook is used to connect an object to the spring scale. The other part is a scale with numbers that tell you how many newtons of force are acting on the object.

DO THIS

With an Object at Rest

1 With the object resting on the table, hook the spring scale to it. Do not stretch the spring at this point.

2 Lift the scale and object with a smooth motion. Do not jerk them upward.

3 Wait until any motion in the spring comes to a stop. Then read the number of newtons from the scale.

With an Object in Motion

1 With the object resting on the table, hook the spring scale to it. Do not stretch the spring.

2 Pull the object smoothly across the table. Do not jerk the object. If you pull with a jerky motion, the spring scale will wiggle too much for you to get a good reading.

3 As you are pulling, read the number of newtons you are using to pull the object.

Making a Spring Scale

If you do not have a spring scale, you can make one by following the directions below.

MATERIALS
- heavy cardboard (10cm x 30cm)
- large rubber band
- stapler
- marker
- large paper clip
- paper strip (about 1 cm x 3 cm)
- 100-g masses (about 1 N each)

DO THIS

1 Staple one end of the rubber band (the part with the sharp curve) to the middle of one end of the cardboard so that the rubber band hangs down the length of the cardboard. Color the loose end of the rubber band with a marker to make it easy to see.

2 Bend the paper clip so that it is slightly open and forms a hook. Hang the paper clip by its unopened end from the rubber band.

3 Put the narrow paper strip across the rubber band, and staple the strip to the cardboard. The rubber band and hook must be able to move easily.

4 While holding the cardboard upright, hang one 100-g mass from the hook. Allow the mass to come to rest, and mark the position of the bottom of the rubber band on the cardboard. Label this position on the cardboard 1 N. Add another 100-g mass for a total of 200 g.

5 Continue to add masses and mark the cardboard. Each 100-g mass adds a force of about 1 N.

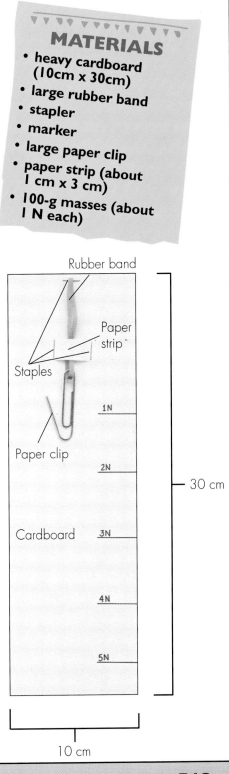

R13

Working Like a Scientist
Is Soup a Lowfat Food?

Mrs. Hazlet's fourth-grade class had learned about nutrition. They knew what they should eat and what they shouldn't. Fat was one of the things that they knew was not good for them in large amounts. Mrs. Hazlet had told them that they should not have more than about 75 grams of fat per day. She had the class form groups to find one kind of food that is low in fat. Margie, Anna, and Kevin were all in one group.

Anna said, "Where do we start?"

Margie said, "Let's start with soup. Soup shouldn't have much fat. It's mostly water."

Kevin said, "That sounds right. Maybe soup would be a good food to start with."

"Okay," Anna said. "What kind of soup? Do all soups have the same amount of fat?"

"That's a good question. I don't know the answer," Kevin said. "Do you?"

"No," Margie said.

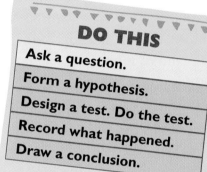

DO THIS

| Ask a question. |
| Form a hypothesis. |
| Design a test. Do the test. |
| Record what happened. |
| Draw a conclusion. |

Asking a question is the first part of any investigation. You must ask your question carefully so that you will be able to test it. Anna asked, "Do all soups have the same amount of fat?" That question can be answered scientifically. She did not ask, "Are all soups the same?" That question would be hard to answer scientifically.

The next step of any investigation is to think of one answer to your question. This possible answer to your question is called a hypothesis. When you think of the answer, you are *forming a hypothesis.* The question Anna asked was, "Do all soups have the same amount of fat?" There are just two possible answers to that question—yes or no. Read on to find out what Margie, Anna, and Kevin thought.

DO THIS

Ask a question.

Form a hypothesis.

Design a test. Do the test.

Record what happened.

Draw a conclusion.

Anna said, "I think that soups may have different amounts of fat. Some soups may have more and some may have less."

Kevin said, "Why do you think that?"

Anna said, "Some soups are like water. Some soups are more like milk and cream. Clam chowder is like milk."

Margie said, "*One* kind is. I've also had a kind that's like tomato soup, so it's more like water. But Anna may be right. I think I agree with her."

Kevin shrugged his shoulders. "Her idea sounds okay to me. But let's make sure we're all thinking the same thing. We think soups have different amounts of fat. Soups that are like water may have less fat. Soups that are more like milk may have more fat."

"Right," Anna said. "So how do we find out?"

"We investigate!" Kevin said.

After you ask a question and form a hypothesis, you must think of a way to test your answer. You must *design an experiment* to test whether your answer is correct.

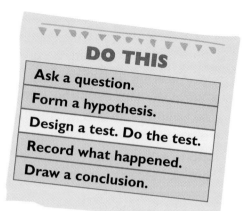

▼▼▼ ▼▼ ▼▼▼▼▼ ▼ ▼▼

DO THIS

| Ask a question. |
| Form a hypothesis. |
| Design a test. Do the test. |
| Record what happened. |
| Draw a conclusion. |

Margie said, "This should be easy to test. We can get the labels from a lot of different soup cans."

"Right," Anna said. "We'll get the labels and classify the soups into two groups, creamy soups and watery soups."

Kevin said, "Then we can read the labels and find out how much fat each kind of soup has."

"Yes, but we need to be sure to use the same amount of soup for each measurement," Anna said.

"The labels will tell us the size of one serving. We can just compare the ones that are the same," said Kevin.

"We need to get labels from a lot of different kinds of soups. And we need to know if the soups are creamy or watery," Margie said.

"That's easy," Anna said. "We'll ask the other people in the class to bring in soup labels and describe each soup to us so that we can classify it."

Nutrition Facts	Amount/serving	%DV*	Amount/serving	%DV*
Serv. Size 1 cup (240mL) condensed soup Servings About 1	**Total Fat** 5g	**4%**	**Total Carb.**18g	**3%**
	Sat. Fat 2g	**5%**	Fiber 0g	**0%**
Calories 140 Fat Cal. 50	**Cholest.** Less Than 10mg	**1%**	Sugars 0g	
*Percent Daily Values (DV) are based on a 2,000-calorie diet.	**Sodium** 1660mg	**35%**	**Protein** 6g	
	Vitamin A 35% • Vitamin C 0% • Calcium 0% • Iron 2%			

Margie, Anna, and Kevin designed a way to test their hypothesis. They also planned a way to collect the information. Another word for information is *data.* The next important step in their investigation was to find a way to *record the data.*

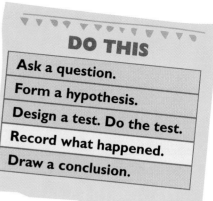

DO THIS

| Ask a question. |
| Form a hypothesis. |
| Design a test. Do the test. |
| Record what happened. |
| Draw a conclusion. |

Kevin, Margie, and Anna sat at a table with what seemed like hundreds of soup-can labels in front of them.

"Oh, no," Anna said. "What are we going to do? How can we make any sense out of all of this?"

Margie frowned. "It's really a mess. But what if we started by just separating the labels into groups? Then we could make a chart. We could label one column *Creamy Soups* and one *Watery Soups* and list the grams of fat in a serving of each kind of soup. Most of the labels list an eight-ounce serving, so we could use those and throw the rest away."

Kevin said, "Good idea. We could list each kind of soup and the number of grams of fat it has in the right column."

"Oh, I see," Anna said. "Then we can add up the total grams of fat in the soups when we get done with our test."

Margie agreed. But then she thought about something else. "There's one more thing we have to remember. We must have exactly the same number of creamy soups and watery soups. If we don't, it would not be a fair test."

Kevin, Anna, and Margie sorted their labels. You can see part of their data in this chart.

Data from Soup Labels		
Names of Soups	Fat in Creamy Soups/ Per 8 Ounces	Fat in Watery Soups/ Per 8 Ounces
Cream of Potato	3g	
Cream of Broccoli	5g	
Cream of Mushroom	7g	
Chicken Noodle		3g
Bean with Bacon		4g
Beef Noodle		4g

"But this chart is hard to read," Margie said.

"I know," Anna said. "Let's make a bar graph. We can have two bars to show the grams of fat in watery and creamy soups."

Kevin drew the bar graph you see here.

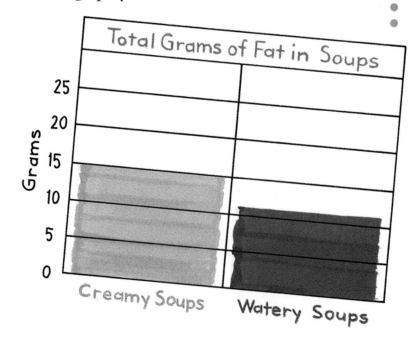

After you have collected the data, you need to see what it tells you about whether your answer to the question was correct or incorrect. You do this by seeing if the data supports your hypothesis and by *drawing a conclusion.*

DO THIS

| Ask a question. |
| Form a hypothesis. |
| Design a test. Do the test. |
| Record what happened. |
| Draw a conclusion. |

"Well," Anna said, "what do you think?"

"I don't know," Kevin said. "It seems to me that creamy soups and watery soups can have the same amount of fat."

"That's what it looks like to me," Margie said. "Look here," she said as she pointed to the bar graph. "These are nearly equal."

"They are," Anna said. "Are you surprised? I am."

"I am, too," Margie said. "Water doesn't have any fat, but some watery soups sure do."

"I think we've found out something important that we can share with the class," Kevin said. "Maybe a lot of people think the way we did!"

"You're right," Anna said. "Let's make a poster to show everyone what we found out."

If your first answer is not correct, you have not failed. Margie, Anna, and Kevin learned something surprising about soups. The data they collected didn't support their hypothesis that watery soups would have less fat than creamy soups. This often occurs with an investigation. When something happens that you don't expect, you can learn from it. You can use that information to start asking other questions. You may need to form a different hypothesis and design a new experiment. However, you are able to build on what you know.

R19

Note: Page numbers in italics indicate illustrations.

ACKNOWLEDGMENTS

For permission to reprint copyrighted material, grateful acknowledgment is made to the following sources:

Addison-Wesley Publishing Company, Inc.: From "Potatoes from the Andes to You" in *The Amazing Potato Book* by Paulette Bourgeois. Text © 1991 by Paulette Bourgeois.

Atheneum Publishers, an imprint of Macmillan Publishing Company: "Fossils" from *Something New Begins* by Lilian Moore. Text copyright © 1982 by Lilian Moore.

Children's Television Workshop, New York, NY: "Virtual Reality: Computers Create Lifelike Worlds You Can Step Into" by Brianna Politzer from *3-2-1 Contact* Magazine, May 1992. Text copyright 1992 by Children's Television Workshop.

Cobblehill Books, a division of Penguin Books USA Inc.: Cover photograph from *Sea Otter Rescue* by Roland Smith. Copyright © 1990 by Roland Smith.

Harcourt Brace & Company: Cover illustration from *The Great Kapok Tree* by Lynne Cherry. Copyright © 1990 by Lynne Cherry.

Highlights for Children, Inc., Columbus, OH: "The Peanut Patch" by Eileen Van Kirk from *Highlights for Children* Magazine, June 1992. Text copyright © 1992 by Highlights for Children, Inc.

Lerner Publications Company, Minneapolis, MN: From *The Great Barrier Reef: A Living Laboratory* (Retitled: "An Australian Mangrove Forest") by Rebecca L. Johnson. Text copyright © 1991 by Lerner Publications Company.

Little, Brown and Company: From "The Rainbow" in *One at a Time* by David McCord. Text copyright 1935 by David McCord.

Lothrop, Lee & Shepard Books, a division of William Morrow & Company, Inc.: Cover photograph from *Earth Alive!* by Sandra Markle. Photograph copyright © 1991 by Galen Rowell/Mountain Light Photography.

Macmillan Publishing Company, a Division of Macmillan, Inc.: Cover photograph by George Ancona from *Mom Can't See Me* by Sally Hobart Alexander. Photograph copyright © 1990 by George Ancona. Cover illustration by Jennifer Eachus from *In the Middle of the Night* by Kathy Henderson. Illustration copyright © 1992 by Jennifer Eachus. Cover illustration from *The Rock* by Peter Parnall. Copyright © 1991 by Peter Parnall.

Margaret K. McElderry Books, an imprint of Macmillan Publishing Company: Cover illustration by Ian Wallace from *The Name of the Tree* by Celia Barker Lottridge. Illustration copyright © 1989 by Ian Wallace.

National Geographic WORLD: From "Glaciers: Rivers of Ice" (Retitled: "Huge Rivers of Ice") in *National Geographic WORLD* Magazine, January 1990. Text copyright 1990 by National Geographic Society. Illustrations by Jaime Quintero and George Constantino. From "Leafing Leopards! Why Am I Green?" in *National Geographic WORLD* Magazine, June 1992. Text copyright 1992 by National Geographic Society.

Orchard Books, New York: Cover illustration from *The Life and Times of the Apple* by Charles Micucci. Copyright © 1992 by Charles Micucci.

Clarkson N. Potter, Inc., a member of the Crown Publishing Group: From *Our Changing World: The Forest* by David Bellamy. Text copyright © 1988 by Botanical Enterprises Publications Ltd.

G. P. Putnam's Sons: Cover illustration by David Shannon from *The Boy Who Lived with the Seals* by Rafe Martin. Illustration copyright © 1993 by David Shannon.

San Juan School District, Montezuma Creek Elementary School, Montezuma Creek, UT: "Canyons" by Andrew Jones from *Rising Voices*, selected by Arlene B. Hirschfelder and Beverly R. Singer. Published by Charles Scribner's Sons, an imprint of Macmillan Publishing Company.

Simon & Schuster Books for Young Readers, New York: Cover illustration from *A Tree in a Forest* by Jan Thornhill. © 1991 by Jan Thornhill.

Gareth Stevens Publishing, Milwaukee, WI: "Rainforest Medicines" from *Why Are the Rainforests Vanishing?* by Isaac Asimov. Text © 1992 by Nightfall, Inc. and Martin H. Greenberg.

Franklin Watts, Inc., New York: From *Spill! The Story of the Exxon Valdez* by Terry Carr. Text copyright © 1991 by Terry Carr. Map courtesy of Vantage Art, Inc.

PHOTO CREDITS:

To The Student: Page: iv Dennis Galante/Envision; v(t), NASA; v(b), Francois Gohier/Photo Researchers; vi(l), The Bettmann Archive; vi(r), Westlight; vii(l), Tom Till; vii(r), Sinclair Stammers/Photo Researchers; viii(l), Phil Degginger/Color Pic; viii(r), E.R. Degginger/Color Pic; x, The Stock Market; xi(t), Comstock; xi(b), Myrleen Ferguson/PhotoEdit; xii, Comstock; xiii, David Young-Wolff/PhotoEdit; xiv(l), Comstock; xiv(r), David Young-Wolff/PhotoEdit; xv(t), Richard Nowitz/Photo Researchers; xv(b), Annette Stahl; xvi(l), David Young-Wolff/PhotoEdit; xvi(r), Michael Newman/PhotoEdit.

Unit A: Harcourt Brace & Company Photographs: A4-A5, A6(t), A6 (b), A8, A9, A10-A11, A18, A21, A24, A25, A29, A36, A41(t), A41(b), A42(t), A42 (b), A43(t), A43(b), A49 (b), A50, A58, A66, A70(b), A74, A80(t), A80 (bl), A80(br), A81,A82 (r), A89(b), A92(t), A92(b), A93(t).

All Other Photographs: Unit A Divider: Manfred Gottschalk/Tom Stack & Assoc. A1, Manfred Gottschalk/Tom Stack & Assoc.; A2-A3 (bg), Willard Clay/FPG International; A3 (inset) William E. Ferguson; A7, Erick L. Heyer/Grant Heilman; A12 (bg), Obremski/The Image Bank; A12, (t), John Colwell/Grant Heilman; A12, (inset) Dennis Galante/Envision; A27 (t), Gerhard Gscheidle/Peter Arnold, Inc.; A27(b), MacDonald/Envision; A28, Grant Heilman; A32 (t), Manfred Gottschalk/Tom Stack & Associates; A32 (b), Marc & EvelyneBernheim/Woodfin Camp & Associates; A33 (l), Jean Higgins/Envision; A33 (t), Peter Menzel/Stock, Boston; A33 (b), M. Zur/Envision; A37 (l), Steven Mark/Envision; A37 (r), Rudy Muller/Envision; A38, (t), Guy Powers/Envision; A38 (c), Amy Reichman/Envision; A38 (b), Dennis Gallante/Envision; A39, Steven Mark Needham/Envision; A40 (t), Alan Pitcairn/Grant Heilman ; A40 (inset) Amy Reichman/Envision; A44 (l), Grant Heilman/Grant Heilman A44 (r), Grant Heilman/Grant Heilman ,A45 (t), Larry Lefever/Grant Heilman ; A45 (c), Thomas Kitchin/Tom Stack & Associates; A45 (bl), Tim Gibson/Envision; A45 (br), Grant Heilman/Grant Heilman ;A46 (t), Grant Heilman/Grant Heilman ;A46 (b), Grant Heilman ;A46 (tl), Robert Barclay/Grant Heilman ;A46 (br), Grant Heilman/Grant Heilman ; A47 (l), Don & Pat Valenti/Tom Stack & Associates;

A47 (r), Grant Heilman;A48 (t), Grant Heilman/Grant Heilman;A48, (b), Grant Heilman/Grant Heilman ;A49 (t), Wanda LaRock/Envision; A49 (c), Barry L. Runk/Grant Heilman ; A52-A53 (t), Timothy O'Keefe/Bruce Coleman Inc.; A55 (l), Barry L. Runk/Grant Heilman;A55 (r), Runk/Schoenberger/Grant Heilman ;A55 (c), Runk/Schoenberger/Grant Heilman ; A55 (inset) Roger & Joy Spurr/Bruce Coleman Inc.; A64 (bg), Comstock; A64 (t), Michael Ventura/Bruce Coleman Inc.; A64 (inset) E. R. Degginger/Color-Pic; A65 (l), Runk Schoenberger/Grant Heilman; A65 (r), Runk Schoenberger/Grant Heilman; A67(t), Grant Heilman/Grant Heilman ; A67 (c), Grant Heilman/Grant Heilman ; A67 (b), S.L. Craig Jr./Bruce Coleman; A68 (c), Amy Etra/Photo Edit; A68 (b), Amy Etra/Photo Edit; A68-A69 (t), Amy Etra/Photo Edit; A6 (t), The Image Bank; A69(b), Amy Etra/Photo Edit; A7(l), Amy Etra/PhotoEdit; A70(r), Amy Etra/Photo Edit; A7 (c), Viesti Associates, Inc.; A71, Roger Wilmhurst/Bruce Coleman, Inc.; A73(r), Keith Gunnar/Bruce Coleman Inc.; A73 (c), Wendell Metzen/Bruce Coleman Inc.; A75, Ana M. Venegas; A7 (b), Ana M. Venegas; A76-A77 (t), Ana M. Venegas; A78-A79 (t), Lisa Quinones//Black Star; A79(b), Lisa Quinones/Black Star; A82 (bg),Gary Cralle/The Image Bank; A82, (inset), James H. Carmichael/Bruce Coleman Inc.; A84 (t), George H. Harrison/Bruce Coleman; A84 (c), Martin Rogers/Woodfin Camp & Associates; A84 (b), Kevin Schafer/Peter Arnold, Inc.; A85(tl), Grant Heilman/Grant Heilman ; A85(tr), William E. Ferguson; A85 (bl), Wilfred G. Iltis/William E. Ferguson; A85, (br), Michael J. Balick/Peter Arnold, Inc.; A86 (t), Arthur N. Orans/Murial Orans; A86 (b), E. R. Degginger/Color-Pic; A86 (cr), Jane Grushow/Grant Heilman ; A86(cl), Kevin Schafer/Peter Arnold, Inc.; A88, National Portrait Gallery; A8 (t), The Bettmann Archive; A90-A91 (bg), Wendell D. Metzen/Bruce Coleman, Inc.; A91 (l), David Young-Wolff/Photo Edit; A91(r), Lawrence Migdale/Stock, Boston; A92-A93 (bg) Grant Heilman/Grant Heilman ; A9 (b), Lee Foster/Bruce Coleman Inc. ; A94, Larry Lefever/Grant Heilman ; A95 (t), Runk Schoenberger/Grant Heilman .

Unit B: Harcourt Brace & Company Photographs: B4-B5, B6 (b), B7, B8, B9, B10-B11, B13, B15, B22, B24, B27 (l), B2 (r), B29, B39, B46, B49, B50(r), B55, B67(r), B74, B78, B82-B83, B85, B86(l), B90(t), B90(b), B94 (b).

All Other Photographs: Unit B Divider: Jeffrey L. Rotman/Peter Arnold, Inc. B1, Carl Roessler/Bruce Coleman, Inc.; B2-B3(bg), Carl Roessler/Bruce Coleman, Inc.; B3 (inset) Bob & Ira Spring; B6 (c), Greg Ryan-Sally Beyer; B12 (t), Tom Tracy/The Stock Market; B12 (bg), Uniphoto; B23 (l), Carl Purcell/Photo Researchers, Inc.; B23(r), Brian Parker/Tom Stack & Associates; B25, Johnny Johnson/Earth Scenes; B26, Kaz Mori/The Image Bank; B28, Four by Five; B30-B3 (bg), Jeff Dunn/Stock, Boston; B32, Larry Lefever/Grant Heilman ; B32-B33(bg), Clyde H. Smith/Peter Arnold, Inc.; B33 (l), Jim Strawser/Grant Heilman ; B33 (r), Thomas Hovland/Grant Heilman ; B36, Y.F. Chan/Superstock; B37, Jack Fields/Photo Researchers; B38 (c), Jeff Gnass/The Stock Market; B38(bg), David R. White/The Stock File; B38(inset) Lucy Ash/Rainbow; B40(l), W&D McIntyre/Photo Researchers; B40(r), NASA; B40(t), Erwin and Peggy Bauer/Bruce Coleman, Inc.; B41 (t), Kenneth W. Fink/Bruce Coleman, Inc.; B41(b), Schafer & Hill/Peter Arnold, Inc.; B42, G. Petrov/Washington Stock Photo; B43, G. Petrov/Washington Stock Photo; B44(l), E.R. Degginger/Bruce Coleman, Inc.; B44 (r), Kjell B. Sandved/Photo Researchers; B45(r), Michael Pitts/Animals, Animals, Inc.; B45(bg), Joy Spurr/Bruce Coleman, Inc.; B47, Jeffrey L. Rotman/Peter Arnold, Inc.; B48(t), Fred Bavendan/Peter Arnold, Inc.; B48(b), John Stern/Animals, Animals; B50(l), Michael P. Dadomski/Photo Researchers; B51

(t), Tom Bean/The Stock Market; B51(c), Patrick Grace/Photo Researchers; B51(b), Francious Gohier/Photo Researchers; B52(t), Carleton Ray/Photo Researchers; B52(c), Bill Wood/Bruce Coleman, Inc.; B52(b), Comstock; B53 (l), Scott Johnson/Animals Animals; B53(r), Allan Powe/Bruce Coleman, Inc.; B54(l), Patti Murray/Earth Scenes; B54(r), Scott Camazine/Photo Researchers; B56, Fred Bruemmer/Peter Arnold, Inc.; B58, Oxford Scientific Films/Animals Animals; B59(t), William E. Ferguson; B59 (b), Hans Reinhard/Bruce Coleman, Inc.; B60, (t), Australian Institute of Marine Science; B60, (b), Australian Institute of Marine Science; B62 (t), Ted Horowitz/The Stock Market; B62(inset) Jeff Gnass/The Stock Market; B64, George Herben/Alaska Stock Images; B65, Steve Arbrust/Alaska Stock Images; B66, Dan McCoy/Rainbow; B67 (l), McCoy/Rainbow; B68-B69, (spread) Randy Brandon/Alaska Stock Images; B70(t), Tom Bean; B70, (b), Gamma Liaison; B72, Earl Cryer/Gamma Liason; B73, Anchorage Daily News/Gamma Liason; B76 (t), Tom Myers; B76(b), Michael Baytoff/Black Star; B76-B77, Jeff Schultz/Alaska Stock Images; B77, (inset) Natalie B. Forbes; B79, Vanessa Vick/Photo Researchers; B80, Tom Myers; B81, Alissa Crandall/Alaska Stock Images; B86 (r), M.H. Colmenares; B88-B89(spread) John Scowen/FPG International; B89(l), Melissa Hayes English/Photo Researchers; B89(r), Brian Parker/Tom Stack & Associates; B91 (t), Al Grillo/Alaska Stock Images; B91 (b), David Young-Wolff/PhotoEdit; B92, Dan McCoy/Rainbow; B93, Scott Camazine/Photo Researchers; B94(t), John S. Flannery/Bruce Coleman, Inc.

Unit C: Harcourt Brace & Company Photographs: C3 (br), C4-C5, C7 (tr), C8, C9, C10-C11, C13, C14, C16, C19, C21, C29, C30, (t), C30(b), C31, C32 (b)C34, C35, C36, C37(t), C37(b), C38, C40, C41, C42, C43(t), C43, C44(t), C44(b), C45 (t), C45 (c), C45(b), C46(r), C47, C50, C52, C53 (t), C53 (b), C57, C58, C59(t), C59(b), C60 (t), C68, C71 (r), C72(r), C77(r), C92 (t), C92(b), C93(b).

All Other Photographs: Unit C Divider: Mason Morfit/FPG; C1, FPG International; C2-C3(bg), FPG International; C6(t), FPG International; C6(c), The Bettmann Archive; C6(b), Al Assid/Stock Market, The; C7(c), Chuck O'Rear/Westlight; C7(b), Richard T. Nowitz; C7 (tl), The Granger Collection; C12(t), Mason Morfit/FPG International; C12(bg), Dan McCoy/Rainbow; C12, (inset) Gary Buss/FPG International; C18, David R. Frazier; C22-C23, (bg), Grant Faint/The Image Bank; C24, Paul Elsom/The Image Bank; C26(c), Smithsonian Institution; C26(b), The Granger Collection; C26(t), The Bettmann Archive; C27, The Bettmann Archive; C28-C29 (bg), Dan McCoy/Rainbow; C32(bg), Fukuhara/Westlight; C32(t), Chuck O'rear/Westlight; C33, W. Cody/Westlight; C34-C35(bg), Grant Faint/The Image Bank; C39(bg), Chuck O'Rear/Westlight; C46(bg), Comstock; C64(t), Bruce Forster/AllStock; C46, (inset), Michael Newman/PhotoEdit; C51, Richard Megna/Fundamental Photographs; C54(t), Susan Murray/Colorado Symphony; C54(b), Schlabowske/Time/Life Photo Lab; C55, Schlabowske/Time/Life Photo Lab; C60(b), Dr. Tony Brain/Science Photo Library/Photo Researchers; C62 (t), Stan Osolinski/Dembinsky Photo Association; C62(b), Franz Gorski/Animals-Animals; C63 (r), Peter Arnold, Inc.; C64 (l), The Granger Collection; C64 (r), The Granger Collection; C66-C67(bg), Larry Keenan Assoc./The Image Bank; C66(t), The Granger Collection; C66 (b), The Bettmann Archives; C67, The Image Works; C70 (l), Chuck O'Rear/Westlight; C70(r), Dan McCoy/Rainbow; C71(l), Frank Siteman/Photri Inc.; C72 (c), E. R. Degginger/Color-Pic; C76(t), The Bettmann Archives; C76(b), Stephen Simpson/FPG International; C80t), Tom Wilson/FPG International; C80(b), Robert E. Hager/FPG International; C80(cr), W.E.Roberts/Photoedit; C81(l), Eric Schnakenberg/FPG International; C83, Peter Menzel; C84, Peter Menzel; C85, Hank

Morgan/Rainbow; C87, Peter Menzel; C87, Peter Menzel; C88, Peter Menzel; C89, Peter Menzel;C90-C91, (bg), Alan Kearney/FPG; C91(l), Roy Morsch/Stock Market, The; C91 (r), Dan McCoy/Rainbow; C92-C93 (bg), Phillip M. Prosen/The Image Bank; C94(t), Montes De Oca/FPG International; C94(b), Fundamental Photographs; C95(l), E. R. Degginger/Color-Pic; C95 (r), Westlight; C96, Joe Baraban/The Stock Market.

Unit D: Harcourt Brace & Company Photographs: D4-D5, D6(t), D7(b), D8, D9, D10-D11, D19, D21, D24, D25(b), D31, D34, D43, D45 (all), D50, D53(l), D60, D61, D72, D73, D79, D82(l), D88, D92(t), D92(b), D93.

All Other Photographs: Unit D Divider: John Kieffer/Peter Arnold; D1, Tom Till; D2-D3(bg), Tom Till; D3(inset), Tom Till; D7(t), Gamma Liaison; D12(bg) Comstock; D12(t), Robert Falls/Bruce Coleman, Inc.; D12(b), E. R. Degginger/Color-Pic; D13t), Stephen Frisch/Stock, Boston; D13(b), Kevin Syms/David R. Frazier; D14(t), Tom Till; D14(b), William E. Ferguson; D15(l), E. R. Degginger/Color-Pic; D15(r), E. R. Degginger/Color-Pic; D18, Ferdinando Scianna/Magnum; D20(l), E. R. Degginger/Color-Pic; D20(r), E. R. Degginger/Color-Pic; D22(l), William E. Ferguson; D22(r), David R. Frazier; D23(tr), David. R. Frazier; D23 (bl), E. R. Degginger/Color-Pic; D23(bc), Art Resource; D23(br), E. R. Degginger/Color-Pic; D23(cr), E. R. Degginger/Color-Pic; D23 , Ron Kimball; D23, (tl), William E. Ferguson; D25(t), Eric A. Wessman/Stock, Boston; D26-D27(bg) Tom Till; D26(t), Tom Till; D26 (b), Tom Till; D27, Tom Till; D28 (t), Museum Of New Mexico; D28 (b), San Ildefonso polychrome, ca. 1922. Courtesy The Southwest Museum, Los Angeles ; D29 (t), Laboratory of Anthropology, Santa Fe.; D29(c), Laboratory of Anthropology, Santa Fe.; D29(b), Laboratory of Anthropology, Santa Fe.; D30 (bg) William E. Ferguson; D30 (t), John Kieffer/Peter Arnold, Inc.; D30(b), Tom Till; D32Ed Cooper Photography; D33t); Jim Steinberg/Photo Researchers; D33(b), The Image Works; D40, Nathen Benn/Stock, Boston; D40 (t), BPS/Terraphotographics; D41, (b)BPS/Terraphotographics; D42-D43(bg) Runk/Schoenberger/Grant Heilman; D44, BPS/Terraphotographics; D45b), Tom Till; D46(t), Tom Till; D46(c), Tom Till; D46(b), Joe Carrillo/Stock, Boston; D47 (t), Tom Till; D47(b), Tom Till; D48, Tom Till; D49(tr), Henry K. Kaiser/Leo de Wys Inc.; D49(bl), BPS/Terraphotographics; D49 (br), Dan Suzio/Photo Researchers; D49 (cl), Tom Till; D51 (l), Spencer Swanger/Tom Stack & Assoc.; D51 (r), Jack Fields/Photo Researchers; D51b), Ed Cooper Photography; D52(t), Greg Ryan & Sally Beyer; D52(b), Randall Hyman/Stock, Boston; D53 (r), David Wells/The Image Works; D54, Steve McCutcheon; D56(bg), William E. Ferguson; D56 (t), Bob Daemmrich/Stock, Boston; D56(inset) Tom Till; D58 (b), Peter Arnold/Peter Arnold, Inc.; D59 (t), Ken Lucas/BPS/Terraphotographics; D59(b), William E. Ferguson; D59 (c), J&L Weber/Peter Arnold, Inc.; D62 (t), William E. Ferguson; D62(b), Sinclair Stammers/Photo Researchers; D62, William E. Ferguson; D63 (t), B. Miller/BPS/Terraphotographics; D63(b), William E. Ferguson; D64(t), Francois Gohier/Photo Researchers; D64 (b), Tom McHugh/Nat. Museum of Nat. History; D65, William E. Ferguson; D66 (t), Saunders/BPS/Terraphotographics; D66(c), Itar-Tass/Sovoto; D66(b), Photo Researchers; D67(bg), William E. Ferguson; D70(l) William E. Ferguson; D70(r), William E. Ferguson; D71(l), Tom McHugh/National Museum of Natural History; D71((c), J&L Weber/Peter Arnold, Inc.; D71(r), PHoto Researchers; D76, (bg), Art Wolfe/AllStock; D76 (t), Stephen Frink/Waterhouse Stock Photo; D76(t), Terry Donnelly/Dembinsky Photo Assoc.; D76 (b), Gordon Wiltsie/Peter Arnold, Inc.; D77(b), Crandall/The Image Works; D78-D79 (bg), Art Wolfe/AllStock; D80(l), Tom Myers; D80 (r), Bill

Gallery/Stock, Boston, D81 (t), Billy Barnes; D81(b), Cary Wolinsky/Stock, Boston; D82(r), Martin Miller/Positive Image; D84(l), Ed Cooper Photography; D84 (r), Joseph Solem/Camera Hawaii; D85(t), J. Robert Stottlemyer/Biological Photo Service; D85 (c), W.L. McCoy/McCoy's Image Studio; D85(b), Bob & Ira Spring; D86(t), Julie Houck/Stock, Boston; D86(c), Jeff Foott/Tom Stack & Assoc.; D86(b), David Young-Wolf/PhotoEdit; D87, (l), Laurance B. Aiuppy; D87(r), Laurance B.Aiuppy; D90-D91(bg), Ruch Buzzelli/Tom Stack & Assoc.; D91 (l), Ken Lucas/Biological Photo Service; D91(r), Dembinski Photo Assoc.; D94, (inset) Breck P. Kent/Earth Scenes; D94, Franco Salmoiraghi/The Stock Market; D95, Art Wolfe/AllStock.

Unit E: Harcourt Brace & Company Photographs: E7, E8, E9, E10-E11, E14, E22, E23, E25, E26, E36, E39, E40, E44, E53, E57(tl), E61, E62, E65(b), E76 (t).

All Other Photographs: Unit E Divider: H. Mark Weidman; E1, Tom Till; E2-E3(bg), Tom Till; E3, (inset) Thomas R. Fletcher/Stock, Boston, E6, Murial Orans; E12(t), J. Lotter/Tom Stack & Assoc.; E12(inset) E. R. Degginger/Color-Pic; E12(border) FPG Internatinal; E13, H. Mark Weidman; E15(r), Coco McCoy/Rainbow; E15(r), Ira Spring; E18(t), Tom Stack & Assoc.; E18(b), John Gerlach/Tom Stack & Assoc.; E21 (t), H. Mark Weidman; E21 (c), William E. Ferguson; E21(b), Murial Orans; E21(bg), Brain Parker/Tom Stacks & Assoc.; E30, H. Mark Weidman; E38, (bg), Superstock; E38, (t), Ed Cooper PhotoraphE; E38, (inset) William E. Ferguson; E41 (l), Mark C. Burnett; E41 (r), Mark C. Burnett; E41 (b), Mark C. Burnett; E42, Charlie Ott Photography/Photo Reseachers; E43(c), William E. Ferguson Photography; E43(b), BPS/Terraphotographics; E47 (t), Rod Plank/Dembinsky Photo Association; E48, Stephen E. Cornelius/Photo Researchers; E50(bg), Uniphoto; E50(t), Uniphoto; E50, (inset) Aaron Haupt/David R. Frazier; E51, (t), Erich Geduldig/Naturbild/OKAPIA/Photo Researchers, Inc.; E51(b), David E. Frazier; E54 (c), E. R. Degginger/Color-Pic; E54(tl), E. R. Degginger/Color-Pic; E54(tr), Jerome Wexler/Photo Researchers; E54(bl), Phil Degginger/Color-Pic; E54(br), E. R. Degginger/Color-Pic; E55 (tl), Hermann Eisenbeiss/Photo Researchers; E55(tr), Michael P. Gadomski/Photo Researchers; E55 (bl), Murial Orans; E55(br), William E. Ferguson; E56(tl), Alvin E. Staffan/Photo Researchers; E56 (tr), E. R. Degginger/Color-Pic; E56 (bl), Aaron Haupt/David E. Frazier; E56 (br), M.L.Dembinsky, Jr. / Dembinsky Photo Assoc.; E56(cl), Kenneth Murray/Photo Researchers; E56(cr), William E. Ferguson; E57(tr), E. R. Degginger/Color-Pic; E57(bl), Gary Retherford/Photo Researchers; E57(br), Kjell B. Sandved/Photo Researchers; E59(l), Dale Nichols/Rich Franco Photography; E59(r), Terry Donnelly/Dembinsky Photo Assos.; E64-E65(t), G.V. Faint/The Image Bank; E66 (t), E. R. Degginger/Color-Pic; E66(b), Harry Rogers/Photo Researchers; E67(t), Bonnie Rauch/Photo Researchers; E67(c), David R. Frazier; E67(b), Leonide Principe/Photo Researchers; E68(t), E. R. Degginger/Color-Pic; E68 (c), E. R. Degginger/Color-Pic; E68 (b), Camera Hawaii; E69 (t), William E.Ferguson; E69 (c), Dwight Kuhn; E69(b), E. R. Degginger/Color-Pic; E70, Walter Chandoha,; E71(c), Ian J. Adams/ Dembinsky Photo Assoc.; E71 (c), William E. Ferguson; E71(tr), Willard Clay/Dembinsky Photo Assoc.; E71 (bl), Ken Brate/Photo Researchers Inc.,E71 (br), Scott Camazine/Photo Researchers Inc.,E72 (t), Ronald Nagata, Sr.; E72-E73(b), Ronald Nagata, Sr.; E74(inset) David R. Frazier; E74-75(bg), William M. Partington/Photo Researchers Inc.; E75(inset) Gary Braasch/Woodfin Camp & Assoc.; E76 (t),Tony Freeman/PhotoEdit; E77(t), Larry Lefever/Grant Heilman ; E77 (b), Hank Morgan/Photo Researchers Inc.; E78(l), Runk Schoenberger/Grant Heilman .